BARCELONA

By the same author

The Canary Islands after the Conquest
Before Columbus
The Spanish Armada

BARCELONA

A Thousand Years of the City's Past

BY

FELIPE FERNÁNDEZ-ARMESTO

SINCLAIR-STEVENSON

First published in Great Britain by
Sinclair-Stevenson Limited
7/8 Kendrick Mews
London sw7 3hg, England

British Library Cataloguing in Publication Data
A CIP catalogue record for this book is available from the British Library.
ISBN: 1-85619-046-3

Photoset by Rowland Phototypesetting Limited
Bury St Edmunds, Suffolk
Printed and bound in Great Britain by
Clays Limited, St Ives plc

Contents

Preface vii

Fatherland – The 'Ample Horizon' – The Cockpit of a European Conflict – 'Spain Has Arrived' – 'The City of Prodigies'

Illustrations

For the loan of and permission to reproduce pictures in this book, grateful acknowledgement is made to the following:

Institut Municipal d'Historia de Barcelona (IM) (Gardeners' Guild, Charles V 1535, Charles III 1731, Firing Inquisition 1820, Friars' massacre 1835, Death of General Bassa 1835, Barricades 1843, Tragic Week 1909, Palau Nacional 1929)

Lunwerg Editores, Barcelona (Pérez Puigjanè/Domingo) (Cathedral, Bridge of Sighs, Colonnades plaçà Reial, Columbus statue, Casa Milá, Parc Güell)

Arxiu Mas, Barcelona (AM) (Man and griffin, St George, Dalmau Virgin and *consellers*)

Architectural Association (AA) (Café Torino, Casa Batlló, Casa Milá)

Ancient Art and Architecture Collection (AAA) (Ajuntament, Casa Vicens)

George Wright (Cathedral cloister, Boqueria shop-sign)

Philadelphia Museum of Art/A.E. Gallatin Collection (PMA) ('Dog Barking at the Moon')

Robert Harding Picture Library (RH) (Sagrada Familia)

Allsport (Pascal Rondeau) (Olympic stadium)

Preface

Planning can create cities which are almost innocent of history. There must have been a time when Alexandria or Constantinople seemed rather like Brasilia or Milton Keynes. Considered from one point of view, Barcelona is that sort of place, called into existence rather than having 'just growed'. The Barcelona that can be seen today from a distance – from the air, say, or at the end of a geographer's or sociologist's gaze – is the creation or victim of nearly a century and a half of assiduous planning. The building of modern Barcelona has occupied a period of western history when urban planning has been at its most consciously 'scientific' and 'rational', largely indifferent to history and unwilling to accept from the past any lessons except those of what not to do. In 1854, her refashioning began under the influence of one of the first and greatest in the modern tradition of urban planners, Ildefons Cerdà, whose schemes were as free of historical allusions as was possible in that romantic and nostalgic period. Since then, the two most influential urban plans proposed for the further development of the city – those of Jaussely in 1905 and Le Corbusier and others in 1932 – were broadly in the same tradition, the first a mild reaction, the second an extreme intensification. Something like ninety per cent of the present metropolis has been built during the era of modern scientific planning.

This book is about the other ten per cent, with only a sidelong attempt made to attribute a past to the history-less city. Anyone who wants an account of planned Barcelona will find it abundantly supplied in the existing literature. In these pages, the planning era is seen as one more episode in a long history of accidents, which have haphazardly fashioned the stones of a very old city, over a very long period of time.

What I want to do is take readers into the fabric of old Barcelona – or take them round it, if they are already there – and characterise and, in patches, chronicle its past. I try to use the city as a document of its own history, using buildings and streets not just as illustrations or backdrops, but as the substance of the story and the evidence for the argument. 'Visual' or palpable evidence makes for 'impressionistic' history, but ought to be particularly appropriate in an attempt to describe the setting of a society which has leapt fairly rapidly from semi-literacy to tele-addiction. This is a book for travellers to

Barcelona, including those who make the journey without leaving their armchairs.

Some limitations which had better be confessed right away are among the results. First, I deal only with a small part of the huge agglomeration of which Barcelona today is the heart and, loosely used, the name. Only the parts I am interested in and know about – the old town, Montjuic, Barceloneta and the Eixample – feature in these pages, with glances at neighbouring but still, by today's standards, relatively old and central districts like Sants, Corts and Hostafrancs. The book is dominated by an area enclosed in the irregular hexagon of the Paral·lel, the Rondas and the Parc de la Ciutadella, which contains the great glory and paradox of Barcelona: a well-preserved pre-industrial city, rich in antiquities and medieval streets, in the middle of a modern conurbation. I know of nowhere else except Cairo which has anything comparable on a similar scale (and Cairo is a much younger city than Barcelona).

Secondly, I concentrate on roughly the thousand years to 1929, with only short excursions outside those chronological limits; the periods dealt with by summary justice – Roman, Visigothic, Moorish, Frankish, Republican, Francoist and democratic – seem rather a lot, when listed, but to write the history of Barcelona in very remote or very recent times would demand mastery of disciplines which are not my own. I believe, in any case, that the formative experience of the part of the city I am concerned with here did not begin before the tenth century; and, as a matter of fact, little has been added to its fabric – though much, admittedly, to its life – since the 1930s.

To cover even a mere millennium of history in a single short book can only be done by feats of comprehension and faults of omission. I have had to make ruthless judgements about what to assume and what to leave out. Nor can it be done interestingly, I suspect, within a conventional framework; and some readers may, I fear, react at first sight to the contents of this book as one does on first beholding an American menu. The logic of an approach which juggles the chronology and jumbles conventional categories is this: I divide the history of Barcelona into five relationships which have had a formative influence on broadly successive but overlapping phases of the city's past. I start with her landward environment because for more than her first thousand years Barcelona was an almost entirely landward-looking city. There is no convincing evidence that she had any sort of markedly maritime character until about the twelfth century; but the sea then rapidly became the dominant source of influence on her development, until the stagnation or decline of her commerce and of her seaborne 'empire' in the fifteenth century. Early-modern Barcelona, it seems to me, was dominated by her relationship with the Spanish monarchy; a chapter on Barcelona and the sea is therefore followed by another on Barcelona and Spain. I see nineteenth-century Barcelona as formed by her relationship with what I call the Catalan world – or 'Catalonia', in inverted commas, because I mean not the place of that name but 'Catalonia' as Catalanists conceived her, as a nation and a culture – rather than by the material changes, the industrial revolution and the history of conflict which occurred in the same period. The last chapter focuses – not, I admit, with anything like pedantic rigour – on Barcelona's relationship with Europe, because it seems to me that a role as a self-consciously 'European' community was espoused by the Barcelonese as an alternative to a 'Spanish' identity, with peculiar intensity in the present century.

Most city-histories are labours of love and this may be the first book about Barcelona to be written from an appreciable emotional distance. I am a devoted admirer of Barcelona's beauty and energy but I find that, like one of those tryingly beautiful and energetic women whom all men are able to identify among their acquaintances, she can excite passion only for short periods. Unlike most of her previous historians, I do not share her self-perception and am not taken in by her self-description. There is a lot about her I dislike. Like the fascinatingly lurid whores of the Raval, she can be brash, noisy, gaudy and unwholesome. Her vitality is often exciting, but always tiring. Her variety is rich, but not quite rich enough, to my taste, to be unstaled by custom. I am afraid that many of my friends in Barcelona will abhor this book, without noticing the sincere tribute that struggles for utterance, as I write, against my attempt at dispassionate criticism. In fairness to them, I should say that my interest in Barcelona has arisen out of a very long programme of study of Spanish history and historiography, and my sense of the 'Spanishness' of Barcelona, which is a strong theme in this book, would not necessarily be shared by someone approaching the subject from a different perspective. Still, most of my readers will come to Barcelona, like me, with an outsider's eye and a visitor's priorities; and I hope any Barcelonese who read it will be interested to see themselves as others see them.

In the text of a book about Barcelona there can be no good reason for using any language except Catalan for the names of Catalan people and Catalonian places and institutions. Technical terms are explained in the text when first mentioned. In notes and the bibliographical

essay, some Catalans' names appear in Castilian form when cited from
the title-pages of books in Castilian. Many books are available in both
languages and I have used and sometimes quoted from either version
indifferently, according to whichever I had to hand: this has caused
me some uneasy moments, as when I have quoted from a Castilian
translation of a Catalan book by Jaume Vicèns Vives, who hated to
express himself in Castilian; but I have found it the only practical
course. The medieval rulers of Barcelona are called by their Catalan
names (with other names commonly used in brackets or in a note) and
for the period after 1137, when the counts of Barcelona became kings
of Aragon, I have called them 'count-kings', following the preferred
usage of Catalan medievalists. From 1412, however, the city had
foreign rulers and the style of 'count' faded even from Catalan usage.
From the late fifteenth century onwards, I use the term 'king' and, for
kings' names, whatever language seems most appropriate. It would be
ludicrously affected in a book in English to disguise Ferdinand the
Catholic as 'Ferran II' or the Emperor Charles V as 'Carles I' or Philip
II as 'Felip I'. I call the inhabitants 'Barcelonese' because this usage
seems ineradicable in English, not because I approve of it: a form like
'Barcelonine' derived from Catalan, rather than Castilian, would be
preferable, if possible. I am sure most readers would have liked a
general map, but as these are distributed free of charge by the Spanish
Tourist Office, it would be pointless to add to the cost of the book by
including them.

Among the debts I have incurred, I ought particularly to mention
those to the late Edwin Ardener, Raymond Carr, Joan Gili, Clive
Griffin, Michael Hurst, Henry Kamen and Xavier Roig, who have all
contributed, in general or particular ways, to how I have come to think
about Barcelona. The errors which are bound to arise in any attempt
to deal with a big subject over a long period of its history are my sole
responsibility.

OXFORD
September 1990

I

'The Earth shall yield Rewards . . .':

Barcelona and Her Landward Environment

La mar no te l'han presa, ni el pla, ni la muntanya
qu s'alça a tes espatlles per fer-te de mantell.

(You're undespoiled by sea, or plain, or by the mountains
that rise behind your shoulders, a mantle for your back.)

– J. Verdaguer, 'A Barcelona'

Aunque es poco lo que el diablo me pone delante, es bueno y muy
bueno.

(Although what the Devil has laid before me is small in extent, it is
good and very good.)

– attributed to Don Juan José of
Austria, contemplating the plain of
Barcelona from the hill of Tibidabo, in
November 1668.

THE DOG IN THE NIGHT: THE PROBLEM OF BARCELONA'S HISTORY

Miró's painting of a dog barking at the moon is a 'problem' picture which challenges onlookers of every sort to ascribe their own 'meanings' to it. I have heard it discussed as a skit on Goya, an anti-fascist allegory and a metaphor of the *commedia dell'arte*. Readers of detective fiction may recognise it as a vision of a non-event: like Holmes's problem of the Dog that Barked in the Night, an image of the difficulty or absurdity of explaining something which never happened, the frustration of a natural consummation. The dilemma of Miró's dog, howling at an unattainable object, is like the plight of Barcelona's historians, condemned to try to explain a similar negative: why Barcelona, which has all the amenities of a metropolis and all the self-consciousness of a capital, never became either a sovereign city in the Middle Ages – when such a status was still attainable – or a seat of government in modern times. The first problem of Barcelona's history is a problem of what she is not: neither a Venice nor even a Lisbon. Her qualifications to become both were equally impressive at different, successive stages of her past.[1]

For instance, when a new viceroy of Catalonia was appointed in 1622, the congratulations of Barcelona were tendered by an ambassador, attended by two hundred carriages, in what was rumoured to be the most magnificent procession ever seen in the streets of Madrid. Twenty years earlier, the city's representative at court was honoured with so much pomp that 'even the leading nobles of this Court', he reported, 'say that the nuncio of his Holiness himself has never been given such a reception, nor the envoy of the Emperor or other princes, and the Castilians are all amazed and awestruck that an ambassador who is a vassal of the king should be received with so much honour'. From inside the Spanish monarchy, Barcelona affected the status of a foreign power and her representatives swaggered like the emissaries of a foreign potentate.[2]

This was more than play-acting: the leaders of Barcelona still inhabited the mental world of a Mediterranean city-state, a unit of organisation inherited from antiquity and typical of Mediterranean life during most of Barcelona's history. Even in early modern times, she belonged to a specialised world, in which sovereign city-states survived. Genoa – an old enemy – was one of Barcelona's main trading partners, Venice one of her oldest rivals. Her own independence could so easily have been more than an affectation. In the high Middle Ages, she possessed all the ingredients of potential statehood, along with the other great emporia of her part of the world, Pisa, Genoa and Marseilles. Yet of all those, Barcelona had the slightest experience of a statelike role, and remained furthest from fulfilling her potential as a *polis*.

Nearly a thousand years ago, when her expansion began, she might have become the Venice of the western Mediterranean; about five hundred years later, when that destiny was frustrated, she might have become the Lisbon of eastern Iberia. Instead, she became a provincial capital, which is what she is now: a big provincial capital and, by Mediterranean standards, the heart of a mighty conurbation – the biggest on the western Mediterranean seaboard; but still, to the conscious shame of most of her thinking citizens, only a provincial capital. She still claims, or some of her residents claim for her, a special cultural status, as 'head and hearth' – *cap i casal* – of Catalonia, or as a peculiarly 'European' city of Spain. And some Catalanists still cherish political ambitions on her behalf, as, for instance, the future capital of a Catalan state in a federal Europe or in a Spanish *Bund*. Yet these claims and ambitions are themselves, I believe, the results and symptoms of historic frustration. A problem of unfulfilled potential and a type of heroic failure are subjects of this book.

THE REACH OF THE HINTERLAND

Venice and Genoa are crowded out of their hinterlands – one by marsh and water, the other by mountains. Genoa's paltry 'Riviera' is easily dominated from the city but could never satisfy the imperial or commercial ambitions of the citizens. Venice eventually put down roots in the soil of the Po valley but her *terraferma* was conquered from offshore by a city that had grown rich by other means. Neither the Genoese nor the Venetians ever cultivated with their hinterlands the close links, commercial and political, which have always characterised Barcelona.

She used to have a little 'riviera' of her own: a broad but shallow coastal strip, now called the Pla de Barcelona, which is smothered by the outgrowth of the town today but which once served as a market-garden, at first to sustain and later to supplement the diet of the city. The explorer in Barcelona can still come across surprising survivals from this rural past in the suburbs. A *masia* – a farmhouse of the prosperous early-modern peasantry – survives in the plaça de Málaga, close to the central railway station; another – rather grand – occupies the corner of the Passeig Maragall with the carrer de Frederic Ramola. The Can Carabass, a splendid rural villa of the late eighteenth century, can be found in a patch of green between concrete and tarmac. The remains of the villages of Santa Eulàlia de Vilapicina and Sant Martí dels Provençals stand small among tower-blocks. Substantial *masias* still to be seen in the carrer de Piferrer and the carrer del Doctor Salvador Cardenal are monuments of the wealth of the seventeenth-century peasants of the *camp*. This was Barcelona's first hinterland, the expensive, productive farmland that surrounded the town.

The mutual dependence of Barcelona and the hinterland was like a long courtship, consummated only in the late nineteenth century, in the intimacy with which the city reached out and enclosed virtually all the countryside and the formerly rural communities, between the sea and the mountains, in a capacious embrace. Cotton factories played a role reminiscent of that of monasteries in the Middle Ages, carrying standards of urban civilisation into rural areas. The valleys of the Rivers Llobregat and Ter in the 1850s attracted cotton masters who wanted to take advantage of cheap labour and hydraulic power and escape the increasingly militant organised labour inside Barcelona. Meanwhile, the advantages of employment in the city set up a migration in reverse. A feature that characterised Barcelona from the eleventh century was that rural families owned urban property and vice versa. This was accentuated during the era of rapid growth and industrialisation by the bourgeois fashion for acquiring a rural retreat and by the intense family feelings that united the *hereu* (the 'heir' and family head-designate) back in the homestead with siblings and cousins who set out to try their hands at city life.

Now Barcelona and her immediate hinterland have blended indistinguishably. The threshold towns of Badalona, Sant Cugat del Vallés, Terrassa, Sabadell, Manresa and Mataró, fed with industry from Barcelona, drawing in population from the countryside, have grown outwards into the advancing city of the last hundred years. Beyond lies a huge area which is the parkland of the conurbation, where the Barcelonese go to spend their leisure in recreation or devotion: Montserrat, Sitges, Montseny, Núria, even the Costa Brava are now permanent or seasonal adjuncts of Barcelona.

The rest of Catalonia lies across mountains which are not always visible, through haze and pall, from inside the mesh of the streets. Two natural roads are cut through the mountains by the valleys of the Rivers Besós and Llobregat; before industrialisation, through these narrow arteries the life-blood of Catalonia – most of it in the form of wine and grape spirit – used to flow by way of trade into Barcelona to be pumped into the Mediterranean. Looked at from Catalonia, the city lies outside the mountains, like a heart that has somehow jumped out from behind its ribs. Access has always been difficult. The historic roads were few and hard. The main Roman road to Tarragona from Empúries went inland through Molins del Rei before easing its way back to the coast; from Molins, the way through Cervera took travellers to Lleida. Cardona and Ripoll were reached by hazardous tracks through Sabadell, Terrassa and Manresa, and Granollers and Vic respectively, following the Besós before climbing the mountains. In the twelfth century, a loaded mule took eight days of hard pounding to get to Tortosa through Tarragona, nineteen to Béziers through Girona. Until the late eighteenth century, when the Pont de Molins del Rei was rebuilt in stone, there were no thoroughly safe bridges, not even a road purpose-built for heavy traffic, on any of these approaches. Yet without easy access or adequate communications, Barcelona built up in the Middle Ages a relationship of political and economic interdependence with the country beyond the mountains.

Barcelona grew out of her hinterland; not, like Venice and Genoa, out of the sea. Since the late eighteenth century, at least, when Antoni de Capmany compiled a 'commercial history' of the city, tracing Barcelona's industrial and maritime vocation back to the remotest antiquity,[3] historians in the service of a bourgeois ideal have obscured the real nature of Barcelona's remote past. The hick town of Roman times became a medieval metropolis almost without drawing on the sea for anything except fish and local cabotage. Though the comparison would be shocking, even sickening to most Barcelonese (who remain convinced of their city's peculiar past and distinctive destiny) Barcelona's urban identity developed in the Middle Ages in the same way as that of many of Spain's inland centres of civilisation: as the market of a small region, the court of a small principality, the magnet of a numerous clergy and the preferred place of residence of an aristocracy flush with returns from rural investment and the profits of war. Commerce and manufacture followed; in Barcelona's case, a long time afterwards. The first building 'boom' revealed by the topography and archaeology of Barcelona happened in the late tenth century; the next, nearly a hundred years later, can be linked fairly directly with evidence of agrarian-based wealth and Moorish gold, earned by the threat or exercise of violence. Not until the twelfth century does evidence of Barcelona's commercial take-off into an era of large-scale, long-range trade begin to accumulate. This was a history more reminiscent of Burgos than Venice.

The last two hundred years have covered up the traces of Barcelona's courtly past. It is true that even the smelly, crumbling back streets of the old town still often have houses of a passé opulence, hidden by the shadows and the grime; but most of them are business fronts of the eighteenth and nineteenth centuries, monuments to the prosperity of makers and traders. The exceptions are the carrers dels Lledó and de Montcada, where rows of medieval palaces still convey the flavour of an ideal 'Spanish' city. The oldest examples are in the Lledó, and sadly decayed; the carrer de Montcada, however, houses the Museu de Picasso and is therefore heavily frequented by intellectual tourists and sympathetic developers. It was, perhaps, an example of late thirteenth- and early fourteenth-century town planning in origin, driven straight from the church of Santa Maria del Mar to the Capella de Marcús; it became the most fashionable address in late-medieval Barcelona. Isolated vestiges of what were once aristocratic quarters remain elsewhere – the lush but crumbling Casa dels Gualbes is in the carrer de Regomir, once the bed of a canal; the Palau Centelles defies the horrible modern townhall extension from across the plaça de Sant Miquel; the Paulau Fiveller of 1571 in the plaça de Sant Josep Oriol was built for a great patrician dynasty when the carrer dels Lledó became too shabby for its scions. On the whole, other great surviving buildings of today are palaces not of an urban aristocracy but of civic spirit, or of commercial prestige, or of an administrative bureaucracy, or of God. Five hundred years ago, the visitor would have found a different atmosphere, where the tone of grandeur was set by the private town-houses of patricians whose main interests lay in the land beyond the walls or, in many cases, in urban rents. The effect would have been more like that of Burgos or Valladolid – where, as in Barcelona, church and court were well represented – or even Cáceres or Avila. The motto of the Junta de Comerç – the body that regulated Barcelona's trade in the late eighteenth century – was *Terra dabit merces undaque divitias*, the earth shall yield rewards and the waves their wealth. It fairly expresses the order of events in Barcelona's history.

THE COMING OF THE COUNTS

Barcelona's potential for expansion was very limited before she became the seat of the rulers of Catalonia. The site of the city has so few natural attractions that only a 'regional' state could fully appreciate Barcelona. Before the rise of such a state, the occupying powers had allegiances diffused through vast lands or located in distant capitals. For the Romans, Visigoths, Moors and Franks, Barcelona could never have the importance she assumed for the rulers of a principality rooted in and confined to her own hinterland. Once she was in those rulers' power, the links that kept Barcelona anchored, as it were, to her landward environment were political as much as economic. Genoa often acquired temporary despots; the patricians of Venice in the high Middle Ages had to stay on their guard against the dynastic ambitions of some doges; but neither city ever had a king. Barcelona, on the other hand, was a courtly centre long before she became a trading centre of any significance.

Her first greatness was owed to the warrior-paladins who made her their home, and who came over the mountains from the agricultural heartland of the interior of Catalonia, the plain of Urgell. They acquired Barcelona by conquest in the late ninth century and formed the long-lived dynasty that came to be known as the House of Barcelona. They adopted the city as their most favoured place of residence; they endowed it with religious foundations which stimulated urban growth; they kept – and sometimes spent – their treasure there; and as the state they ruled developed, they concentrated in Barcelona such permanent institutions as they created. By the early tenth century Barcelona was already, in a sense, the 'capital' of a sovereign principality, which would come to be known as the principality of Catalonia, and the court of its rulers, to whom she gave the title of Counts of Barcelona. In about 911, Count Guifré II, son of the founder of the princely dynasty, chose a house of religion outside the walls of the city for his mausoleum. His neglected grave, marked by an inscription discovered among rubble in the monastery of Sant Pau del Camp, deserved better of the Barcelonese; it was comital patronage, of which Guifré's choice of burial-place was the first known act in a long tradition, that elevated their city from the status of a modest *ville carrefour* or frontier garrison.

Of the man acclaimed as 'founder' of the House of the Counts of Barcelona, even less trace survives in the modern city. Only the visitor brave enough to enter the dark alley of the carrer Amargos, under its straggling balcony-plants and dangling laundry, will find the painted ceramic plaque proclaiming – almost certainly wrongly – that this was the limit of the palace of Guifré the Hairy (d. 898), whose lifetime achievements were exceeded only by his posthumous renown. His is one of the oldest legends by which Catalan patriotism is nourished. By prowess and slaughter he united several counties of the Frankish empire's Spanish march – which gave him a specious claim to be the 'national' unifier of Catalonia. Though he was almost certainly the direct heir of his predecessor, the fact that he was for long the most clearly discerned progenitor of all subsequent Counts of Barcelona also gave him a mythical role as the founder of 'national' independence. A gem of the propaganda of the twelfth-century counts, the *Gesta Comitum Barcinonensium*, has him returning from exile to reclaim his birthright, recognised by his mother 'because he was hairy in certain unusual parts of the human body': the mother's skill in divining his identity from this fact was the more remarkable since she had not seen him since his childhood.[4] The biblical resonances of the hairy man's defrauded birthright were ambiguous, perhaps; but Guifré combined the rights of Esau with the merits of Jacob. According to an even later

legend, the d'or and gules bars of the arms of Barcelona were established when the King of the Franks drew fingers dipped in crusading
blood across the shining surface of Guifré's shield.[5]

The achievements of the real Guifré seem to belong to the context
of a struggle for supremacy in the Spanish marchlands between his
own family, that of Sunifred of Urgell, his father, and the longer-
established and more distinguished dynasty of Bernard of Septimania.
Bernard's father was St William of Toulouse and until the 830s or
perhaps 840s his family had an impressive record of service to the
Carolingian house. His own attitude to the House of Charlemagne was
equivocal. Succeeding to his duchy in 801 at the age of seventeen, he
displayed adolescent truculence in resisting Carolingian nominees to
ecclesiastical benefices. Ten years later, however, he was at court as
custodian of the young heir to the throne, the future Charles the Bald,
whom, perhaps, he guarded too closely. He was suspected of an
amorous intrigue with the empress and banished to the March, where
his military failures exposed him to the insinuations of his enemies
and the vengeance of his prince.

Conflicts at court brought Bernard's death and execution in 844.
The struggle to possess his inheritance dominated the politics of the
march for the next thirty years. Between 870 and 878 Guifré and his
brothers systematically conquered almost all the Frankish counties
south of the Pyrenees, expelling Bernard's descendants and other
interlopers who were intruded from the Frankish kingdom in the
course of the quarrels. This was not, however, an anti-Frankish
triumph. Guifré's legitimacy derived from a title of Carolingian origin
which he always used and never exceeded; he continued to date
documents by the regnal years of his Frankish suzerains; his heirs
continued to apply to the heirs of Charlemagne for their formal
confirmation in office and, often, for confirmation of their charters
and ecclesiastical foundations.[6]

Yet the 'regional' nature of Guifré's triumph was unmistakable. A
dynasty rooted in the region had definitively ousted 'foreign' rivals,
and from now onwards the warrior-aristocracy of the mountains was
led by counts that shared its own limited horizons. The county of
Barcelona acquired pre-eminent rank early, perhaps during the lifetime
of Guifré; after his death, the title of Count or Marquess of Barcelona
was always reserved for the senior member of the dynasty. And though
the Pyrenees were never thought of as a frontier, and the political
world of the Catalan counties continued to embrace Aragon, Aquitaine,
Languedoc and Provence, the main objectives and the consistent thrust

of expansion were, for a time, concentrated south of the mountains. Guifré himself seems to have been responsible for conquests in the area of Ausona and Ripoll; according to a pious recollection of his son, he acquired Montserrat, Catalonia's holy mountain, and perhaps reached the plain of Tarragona. Even the most modest southward advances were conspicuous after a long period of stagnation. Though the chronicle tradition extols conquests, state-building was rather a matter of colonising underpopulated areas with trustworthy vassals and with religious communities capable of exploiting the land productively. Such constructive endeavours are the subjects of all the documents that survive from Guifré's time. His donations to and foundations of churches cover the entire period of his activity: Santa Maria de Formiguera, 873; Santa Maria de la Grassa, jointly with his brothers, 878; Sant Joan de Ripoll, where the count's sister was abbess, 885; Sant Joan de les Abadesses, 887; Santa Maria de Ripoll, consecrated in 888 and then endowed with a further charter, issued by Guifré and his brothers, in 871; Sant Pere de Ripoll, 890. As well as these grants to what were or became the great religious houses of Old Catalonia, Guifré 'restored' the bishoprics of Ausona and Vic. Clerical adulation for donors was usually expressed in highly coloured language; yet the terms in which a synod at Barcelona recalled Guifré's generosity a few years later particularly captures the churches' sense of obligation to him: 'After many years had passed, the Lord, moved with pity for that land [Ausona], made arise the most noble prince Guifré and his brothers, who, filling men of diverse provenance and lineage with pious love, managed to return the famous church, with its dependencies, to its former state.' Here, and in the recollected facts recorded in later charters, are hints of Guifré's success in attracting population to the lands of the march. Only one of his charters to new settlers has survived: that of Cardona, paraphrased in a later document – but there were probably others, and in much of his territory the religious communities he patronised were his surrogates. In Ripoll, above all, which he adopted to be his mausoleum, his memory was celebrated. A legend like Guifré's could only be secured by lavish generosity towards the custodians of the historical record.[7]

Guifré seems more remarkable for his loyalty to the Carolingian dynasty than for his exercise of effective independence in his counties. The Catalanist legend has obscured the real historical problem, which is that of identifying the roots of deference to the Frankish house among the warlords of the marcher lands, at a time when centrifugal forces were tearing the Frankish empire apart. Nor does Guifré's division of his inheritance among his sons suggest he had any strong vision of a 'unified' future for the Catalan lands. He did, however, leave three legacies which profoundly modified the future of Catalonia: the prominence of the county of Barcelona; the survival of an enduring dynasty; and the legend itself, which was a more powerful stimulant to the growth and survival of Catalanist sentiment in modern times than any real achievement of a Dark Age strong man could ever have been.

THE SEA OF OYSTERS

What did the early counts want Barcelona for? Historians' usual answers are: as an avenue to the sea, or as a frontier stronghold. Neither answer is really satisfactory. To understand how little Barcelona had to offer, a critical look at her earlier history is necessary; Barcelonese historians have generally been reluctant to take it. A great deal was formerly at stake, in the internal politics of Spain, in the search for a great Roman or even pre-Roman past for Barcelona. It was a point of honour for Catalan historians in the last century, and for much of this, to insist on the 'continuity' of Catalan history, and therefore of settlement in Barcelona, back to the origins of an autochthonous nation. Theories verging on the silly – of Barcelona as a pre-Roman 'capital' for instance, or of two 'Iberian' cities on the site of modern Barcelona – have been part of the result. A chestnut recently rescued from neglected embers is that of Barcelona as a 'Phoenician' foundation, which relies on a joke of Ausonius, unsupported by archaeological evidence. 'Punic Barcelona pains me,' wrote Ausonius to a friend, much as a modern visitor might decry the consumerism of the place – without meaning to imply that it was literally a Phoenician city. 'Punic' was an epithet charged with derogatory commercial connotations, like 'American' in some circles today.[8]

The entire Pla de Barcelona – not just the great hill of Montjuic, but the surrounding plain as well – was densely settled in pre-Roman times: so much archaeological bric-à-brac, so widely dispersed, has turned up in the last fifty years that the fact is incontrovertible; but none of the evidence suggests a strictly urban culture, except for two small groups of pre-Roman coins: the first bears the name 'Laiescen' – which may have nothing to do with Barcelona, despite the seductive similarity of the name with the Roman name for the local inhabitants, the Laietani, which has led many scholars into rash assumptions. The second is inscribed 'Barkeno' and can be dated with confidence to the third century BC. To refuse to recognise a prefiguration of the name of Barcelona in this might be excessively scrupulous. But if there is a pre-Roman city in present-day Barcelona, it seems, from received archaeological wisdom which a mere historian is unqualified to challenge, that it must have been located on nearby Montjuic and not on Mont Tàber, which became the heart and citadel of Barcelona from Roman times. Roman Barcelona was built on 'virgin' soil.[9]

When a Roman colony was founded on Mont Tàber, probably shortly before the reign of Augustus, Montjuic was inherited from previous eras of settlement as a ritual centre. Finds from there include an impressive 'aedile's seat', set ceremonially in the midst of the remains of some form of stone embrasure, with an inscription – dated on rather hazardous calligraphic grounds – of early in the second half of the first century BC. The centre of settlement, however, was henceforth transferred to where its remains can still be seen, between and beneath the stones of the medieval city.

It is all too easy to imagine Roman Barcelona as a much bigger and more opulent place than it really was: an imaginary walk around the ruins – which any reader who goes to Barcelona or lives there can undertake in reality – seems to demonstrate an impressive level of civilisation, on a grand scale. Such a perambulation might begin among the graves that line the Roman street that lies under the plaça de la Vila de Madrid; even the evidently humble dead who were buried here in the late second or early third centuries had in most cases substantial stone sarcophagi or urns for their ashes.[10] From the graveyard one can pick up what may have been a Roman approach to the city in the carrer dels Arcs by following the carrer de Canuda. This route reveals the towers of the fourth-century city gates, abutted by what may be the remains of an aqueduct; the sight is awesome: the towers are extremely substantial, hardly out of scale with their medieval super-structures or the medieval and eighteenth-century buildings which surround them; only the cathedral, behind and a little to the north, dwarfs them, and it was built nearly a thousand years later.

The initial impression is reinforced by the excitement of discovering, in the middle of a conurbation of nearly three and a half million people, a set of Roman walls which can not only be detected in the street plan but also be seen above ground in patches and stretches – a long stretch in the north-west corner, from the west gate to beyond the north gate, and picturesque patches in, for instance, the plaça dels Trapiners and the carrer del Call, where a Roman tower can be visited inside a draper's shop. A similar survival, sustaining a later structure, is the temple, some columns of which hold up the fine medieval palace where the Centre d'Excursionistes is now housed; only two of the original columns survive intact, and the charm of the setting has been diluted by a restoration which, in the interests of making the columns visible in their entirety, has robbed them of their function in the medieval building: but their nearly ten metres of height (and corresponding corpulence) conjure up a temple of important dimensions and, no doubt, considerable cost.

Further north an astonishing complex of Roman floors and foundations can be viewed underneath the palaces of the medieval count-kings and early-modern royal lieutenants, which adjoin just inside the north wall of the old city. The area used to be thought to enclose the Forum – which must really have been higher and more central, in the plaça de Sant Jaume, where the civic centre is still located. It does contain what may have been an important public space, arrayed with the pedestals of seven statues. Most of it, however, seems to have belonged to two areas with contrasting functions: nearer the centre of the town, towards the south, an area of prosperous houses, one of which has a bath, and workshops; and at the extremity, in a late development built after the fourth-century walls, a small, probably Christian graveyard and an early Christian basilica of three naves.[11] In the foundations of the counts' palace, re-used Roman masonry, some of it bearing inscriptions, is exposed. The public baths, decorated with mosaics of Neptune, have been covered up in the plaça de Sant Miquel, once beautiful, now disfigured by the ugly townhall annexe; but their origins are well documented in an inscription commemorating their patron, the praetor Lucius Minicius Natalis. He had served in Africa, Pannonia and Rome itself under Hadrian and Trajan; his son served in Britain and was born in Barcelona. The baths they endowed had 'porticoes and a duct for the water'. This cosmopolitan family, who brought to Barcelona experience of a vast swathe of the Roman world, must have seemed sophisticates in this provincial city where they erected what was, after the temple, the most lavish civic monument of the time.[12]

Roman Barcelona is so exciting and so accessible as to be a danger to susceptible imaginations. In reality it was, as Pomponius Mela reported, a 'small town' of ten or twelve hectares, dwarfed in the region by Tarragona and Empùries; doubly provincial: 'small' not only by imperial standards but also those of the province. The towers that are so striking from a distance were built up by successive late antique and early medieval improvements; their original height may have been barely a third of what it is now. Scholars' attempts to discover or invent an amphitheatre for Roman Barcelona have, so far, been unsuccessful and unconvincing respectively. It had the status of a *colonia*, but only some of the amenities.

An idea of the tone of life in late Roman Barcelona comes through sermons written by, or attributed to, St Pacianus, the bishop of the city in the late fourth century. In his *Cervus* he excoriated the abiding pagan custom of donning beast's head-masks and a gold-trimmed toga to exchange gifts on New Year's Day. His *Paraenesis* conjures up a picture of the basilica in his day, thronged with penitents. The weepers on the threshold, fasting in filthy clothes, begged for admission on their knees, kissing the hands of the poor, prostrating themselves before priests, imploring the intercession of deaconesses. More privileged were those penanced only to attend in the narthex along with the catechumens – those adults applying for baptism and under instruction – where they could listen to Mass but not take any direct part. The *prostrati* could worship in the nave, but only in penitent garb. In the last stage of penance, the confessant could do everything except present the gifts at the altar and receive communion. The impression is of a close-knit community in which the hierarchy of wealth is challenged by the hierarchy of penance, and in which the rich man is a beggar at heaven's gate. St Pacianus's flock kept him so busy that he could not reply to a letter within forty days – partly, no doubt, because of his battle against pagan morals, but partly, presumably, because the Christians of Barcelona were a growing community, commanding an enviable status.[13]

It was also 'a pleasant place' with 'rich people'; the correspondence of Ausonius with Paulinus of Nola and the poetry of Avienus (from where these characterisations are taken) may conceal an irony, or reflect a tradition, but seem compatible with the archaeological evidence. The wealth came not from trade but from agriculture and fishing: the 'sea rich in oysters' commended by Ausonius, the products of the Pla.[14] These were presumably the attributes that made Barcelona esteemed in the period from the fifth century to the seventh or, at least, chosen by Jordanes, Orosius and St Isidore (writers of the narrative sources of the period) as a suitable place in which to locate important events. Historians have talked unhappily – through almost the entire tradition – of a Visigothic 'capital'. This is anachronistic and exaggerated, but under Visigothic rule Barcelona did establish a conspicuous reputation and underwent some modest growth. According to Jordanes, pity for the plight of the inhabitants of Hispania, smarting under the blows of less Romanised barbarians, moved the Romanophile Visigothic chief Athaulf to seize Barcelona 'with his most select men', leaving 'those who were less adept in arms' to occupy the interior.[15] The reason for this discrimination is left unclear, nor was it necessarily Athaulf, rather than Jordanes, who applied it; but it suggests that Barcelona was thought particularly desirable, or particularly defensible, or both. Perhaps, as it was Visigothic practice to make the army a charge on conquered or 'allied' territory, Barcelona drew the 'best men' because it commanded the richest land. Narrators of the next century of Gothic history continue to associate Barcelona with the chronicle of power: Orosius has Athaulf assassinated nearby;[16] Isidore additionally has Amalaric flee to the city before being murdered in his turn.[17]

This period was accompanied by some modifications of the urban space for which 'growth' may not be too strong a word. Between the fourth and sixth centuries the 'interval' between the building line and the ramparts was filled with new constructions: this seems to have represented a 'privatisation' of what had been public space. In the same period, some streets were narrowed by the extension of existing buildings: the street outside the temple portico was halved in width. In the mid-fifth century, a basilica with an adjoining baptistery was built, presumably to accommodate the heretical rites of the Visigoths; and a dwelling of noble dimensions appeared on part of the site of the present palace.[18] To assume any continuity of function for the palace area would be rash, but the written sources, with their catalogue of royal assassinations, do suggest that Barcelona was sporadically a courtly centre.

Did the stunted grandeur of Visigothic Barcelona survive the eighth-century conquests by the Moors and the Franks? The assumption that Barcelona has an inherent quality of greatness, which was somehow always there, encourages the application of what I think is a legendary model of her early medieval history: a 'pattern' seems to be detectable, of successive devastations and revivals, from which the supposed splendours of the Roman city re-emerge with phoenix-like resilience, while barbarian invaders temporarily suppress, but never permanently divert, her history. Historical patterns usually exist only in the eye of the beholder. The image of long-sustained indomitability has a suspiciously heroic ring. The underlying assumptions about the importance of Roman Barcelona and the destructiveness of barbarian invasions are probably false. Although I had better admit at once that, later in this book, I intend to offer a way of characterising Barcelona's subsequent history which has some similarities to the legend of her early medieval resilience, the period from the fourth century to the tenth appears more convincingly as one of patternless, rather faltering progress, untouched by the diviner's fire. Apart from the evidence that some Visigothic kings had a special fondness for the city, the provenance of the rulers seems to have made little difference.

In general, in the area between the lower Ebro and the Pyrenees in the eighth century, local chieftaincies seem to have been relatively strong, while affiliations to the larger states that competed for allegiance were relatively weak. The trend begun before the Visigothic monarchy was overthrown in the second decade of the century; continued during the near-century of Moorish domination that followed, and was not entirely extinguished by the Frankish conquest of the late and early ninth centuries. The only evidence that Barcelona had any special status in the region occurs in an Arabic chronicle tradition of the 770s, when attempts were being made in the name of the then ruler of the Muslim world, the 'Abbāsid Caliph at Baghdad, to enforce obedience, or at least to claim allegiance, in Moorish Spain. The 'Abbāsid appointee, 'Abd ar-Rahmān ibn Habīb, seems to have treated the submission of Barcelona as a matter of priority; the defiance he issued to the city's ruler, Sulaymān ibn Yaqzān al-Arabī, was rejected; he then marched against the upstart, to defeat near Valencia. This was typical of the history of threats to local power-centres from ambitious states which were consolidating and extending their power. North-east Spain lay between two such states: the emirate of Cordoba in the south and the empire of Charlemagne in the north. In the last quarter of the eighth century, local rulers were able to play them off against one another.[19] But a monster's jaws make a hazardous refuge, and Frankish victory, definitive in Barcelona by 801, led to the substitution of Moorish chiefs by Frankish counts. Under the new regime 'central' power was far more effective than under the Moors; the counts were genuinely the clients of the monarchy, to whom they owed their appointment and on whom they relied for support. On the other hand, they exercised the effective discretion always available to marcher-lords in distant frontier garrisons. Marchlands in the early Middle Ages were always potential states, natural arenas of the strongman who was capable of rapid, independent decisions and organised defence. The world from which Guifré the Hairy emerged in the ninth century had that in common with the kingdom of Castile founded by Fernando I in the eleventh century and the Portugal created by Afonso Henriques in the twelfth. From the perspective of Urgell, the conquest of Barcelona needed no special justification; even a modest town was important by regional standards, especially if 'packaged' between a productive plain and a sea of oysters.

THE RULE OF THE HINTERLAND

The triumph of Guifré and his successors was the result of a conquest of Barcelona from beyond the Catalonian mountains. If the Barcelonese ever forgot the fact, the castle of the Lords of Montcada, loyal vassals of the counts, was there to remind them, documented from 1029, dominating the Besós valley and controlling the city's water supply. The relationship of the Montcada with Barcelona demonstrated not only the political dominance of the hinterland but also the economic interdependence which followed. A dual way of life developed, both urban and rural, in what was still – to use an English term – a 'country town'. While the counts used the Montcada castle as part of a strategy of control, the family was joining the social world of the citizenry; at the time the castle is first documented, the castellan's brother was Archdeacon of Barcelona, and his son succeeded him when he died. The office continued to be held by members of his family till 1095.[20] The *Usatges de Barcelona* – a law code with a commercial flavour – is traditionally attributed to the reign of Count Ramon Berenguer I, but is really of a hundred years later, cunningly predated to give it enhanced prestige: it includes, however, a few genuinely eleventh-century ordinances which, regulating knightly ritual violence, convey a hint of the genuine tone of life in the city at a time of aristocratic preponderance.[21]

The métier of this élite was war, rewarded and supplemented by land. Barcelona's wealth in the late tenth and eleventh centuries came precisely from war and farming. The first known 'boom' – the earliest recorded phase of urban growth and embellishment – happened in the late tenth century. Historians have assumed that this must have been the result of an increase of commercially generated wealth; but there is no evidence to support that conjecture and it is at least as likely that the presence of the knights, the court and the growing colony of clergy and religious were the sources of stimulation. The growth of the cathedral chapter is the first clue to general growth: there were six canonries in 974, eight between 987 and 995 and seventeen by 1005. In 1009 the canons petitioned the bishop to release them land on which to build more accommodation for themselves – a sign of changing social habits but also a result of the pressure of expanded numbers in restricted space. A new canons' refectory seems to have been begun in about 1000. This pullulation of prebends would have been impossible without considerable investment by the counts in the cathedral chapter. The canons were growing in sophistication as well as in numbers: retiring to houses of their own, acquiring – in the case of Archdeacon Llobet in 1004 – a reputation for erudition and building up libraries worthy, in at least one instance, of attracting a reader as famous for his learning as the future pope, Gerbert of Aurillac. The canons were not the only people building. The alms house of the Pia Almoyna – its later premises still stand to the north-west of the cathedral – was founded in 1009. In 989 one of the burghs outside the walls, the *viles noves*, had a market of its own. The *vila nova* of Mercadal rose outside the main gate; that of Sant Pere around the monastery of Sant Pere de les Puelles, founded in 945, with the further *vila nova* of Els Arcs to its west. There was more growth towards the sea, between the modern via Layetana and carrer de Plateria, and, on the east, a small settlement under the walls of Santa Maria del Pi. In 985 Barcelona was a target of sufficient prestige to attract a raid by al-Mansur, the wide-preying vizir of Cordoba, who maintained his ascendancy at home by invincibility abroad.[22]

This raid – by vulgar repute 'the day Barcelona died'[23] – in one sense brought the city to life; it is the first event in Barcelona's history that can be reconstructed from documents, rather than chronicles. More than a hundred surviving documents refer to it directly or by implication. It was a psychological trauma; in language which may be influenced by a poetic tradition of laments for lost cities, every record evokes a horror-struck image of wanton destruction. But how much material damage was really done? Many of the surviving documents are records of endowments to religious foundations allegedly ruined by the raid. No one familiar with Spanish history in this period trusts such conventional asseverations, which are designed to enhance the glory of the new benefactors. Victimisation by a scourge of God was always an occasion for penitential self-indulgence, which tended to project an exaggerated impression of the penitent's sufferings. Hyperbole of every sort came easily in an age which attached no great value to emotional restraint. What might be lost in a raid by al-Mansur could be made up in an acquired treasure of martyr's bones, which not only hallowed the reputation of a place but also out-performed most other commodities as truck. In assessing the number of victims, it was therefore a form of pious excess which made the clergy err on the high

side. Thus, for example, if we can believe that the flames lit by the
raiders in the convent of Sant Pere de les Puelles 'utterly consumed'
the nuns, the martyrdoms reported in the monastery of Sant Cugat
were grossly exaggerated; according to twelve lists of the inmates
surviving from the period 975–1001, no more than four can have died
or disappeared in 985. Barcelona fell to al-Mansur on 6 July. The first
of the surviving post-raid documents is dated 15 August. Normal life,
with its bureaucratic routines, was quickly re-established. The counts
may have emerged strengthened from the experience: their vassals
rallied to their defence from all over Catalonia. When a new dynasty
came to power in the Frankish kingdom in 987, its suzerainty was
unacknowledged.[24]

Moorish hegemony did not long survive al-Mansur's death in 1002.
Its weakness was exposed when internal conflicts were unleashed
among the Moors by his younger son's inexpert putsch in 1008. Within
two years, a raid on Cordoba by a large expedition of Catalans, led by
their count, dramatically illustrated how the roles of victim and prey
had been reversed. Contemporaries hailed it as a turning-point which
'gave tranquillity to the Christians. And they went out and travelled
around the marchlands wherever they wished and they rebuilt many
fortifications and castles which had formerly been destroyed by the
power of the infidels.'[25] This was a sanguine assessment: the Catalan
raiders were mercenaries, called in to al-Andalus by one of the contend-
ing parties in the domestic squabbles of the decaying empire; the raid
was most important, perhaps, for its effect on Christian morale.
Meanwhile, the Cordoban state was enfeebled by seraglio-politics at
the centre, eroded by usurpations at the edges. In the 1030s it dissolved
among small, competing successor-states. Barcelona had an opportunity to profit from the disunity of al-Andalus, not so much by
expansion as by extortion, picking up plunder and creaming 'protection'. An illumination in Barcelona's twelfth-century *Liber Feudorum*
shows Count Ramon Berenguer I counting out coins from a lapful of
gold into his hand. His wife, Almodis, sits beside him, encouragingly
nudging him with her palms on his back. Count Ramon Bernat of
Béziers holds his free hand in a gesture of feudal dependence, while
Ramon Berenguer hands over the price of the counties of Carcassonne
and Razès. This was a well-remembered image. The sort of expansion
which his ancestors could contemplate only by conquest, Ramon
Berenguer could undertake by purchase. Late-eleventh-century Barcelona enjoyed a bonanza on the proceeds of booty, tribute, ransom,
payola and the wages of mercenaries, paid in Moorish gold. In the

1040s thirty-nine per cent of surviving recorded transactions in Catalonia were made in gold; by the 1070s the figure had risen to seventy-
seven per cent. In Barcelona proper, it was as high as ninety-five per
cent – a figure never again to be attained in the city's history. In the
same period the price of wine in the market place of Barcelona doubled.
It may be that Barcelona was particularly well favoured with bullion,
even by the standards of her Christian neighbours. In the last twenty
years of the tenth century, for instance, the coinage of Barcelona
almost disappeared from Catalan trade – to judge from the few surviving records – to be displaced by that of Valencia. It was probably a
case of the worse driving out the better money. Even the Valencia of
El Cid had less Moorish gold to mint than Barcelona.[26]

Other indicators suggest a correspondingly active economy. In 1058
a major 'public spending project' was recorded: a cathedral in the
Romanesque style made newly fashionable in neighbouring lands by
the patronage of the dynasty of Sancho the Great of Navarre. In 1060
a fastidious Moor was prepared to acknowledge that Barcelona was a
'great town'. From 1070, a lively market in land for building houses
is attested by numerous surviving conveyances which particularly
enriched the main urban landowners: the count, viscount and cathedral
chapter. The property boom was such that in 1082 Bonavita the Jew
sold for a large sum of five *solidi* a strip of land near Santa Maria del
Mar wide enough only for a wall. In 1079 Ramon Berenguer II and
his brother and co-ruler Berenguer Ramon conducted a hearth-count,
perhaps in order to facilitate the division of the fruits of their joint
inheritance; the surviving portion shows the range of trades practised
in the city, with textiles already occupying a prominent place, along
with the crafts that supplied the court's knightly residents – those of
leatherworkers and saddlers, armourers and purveyors of the parapher-
nalia of chivalry.

The varied economic opportunities of this period of expansion or
growth are demonstrated by the career of the family founded by Bernat
Udalard and his wife Persedia. They were first recorded in 1078, when
they bought an old house by the count's palace, ostensibly for a
dwelling. In fact they equipped it with workshops and a bakery, which
they conveyed to their daughter and son-in-law in 1095; they also
handed over three coffers, including one of Lombard and one of
Moorish manufacture. They borrowed capital from their son-in-law
with which to open more shops in a space beneath the ramparts; not
only did the son-in-law inherit these when they died in 1098, but also
accumulated more property in his own right, buying sites within the

walls from the count for a hundred silver *solidi* in 1097. Throughout
the last quarter of the eleventh century, rising stocks of wine and grain
in the city are suggested by the terms of surviving wills. This growth,
the extension of traditional activities, was the starting-point of the
expansion – diversification into new, long-range commercial activities
– in the next century.[27]

Urban growth, however, was still linked to rural wealth, and commercial fortunes were still founded on the productivity of the hinterland. The very origins of Barcelona as a great commercial centre can
be sensed in this period in the records of the activities of Ricart
Guillem, who, in the course of fifty years in the late eleventh and early
twelfth centuries, built up a fortune not only from selling wine but
also actually producing it on a growing domain of his own, which
extended ever further into the hinterland. Doubling as a moneylender,
he ended as a castellan as well as a citizen, a vassal of the Montcada
and Cabrera lineages, acquiring castles and seigneurial rights by purchase or holding them from his lords. While merchants bought into
the countryside, rural aristocrats nibbled into the city, sometimes
maintaining houses there, often colonising its churches and religious
communities with their relations. During the lifetime of Ricart Guillem, the archdeaconate of Barcelona was virtually a perquisite of cadets
of the Montcada family.[28] The career of a *bourgeois gentilhomme*
like Guillem might be mirrored, a little later, by aristocrats who
took to commerce. En Nunyo Sanç, in the early thirteenth century,
who like the king prided himself on owing his honour directly to God,
was one of the greatest shipping magnates of his day. The
divisions which geography tried to wedge between Barcelona and her
hinterland were transcended by community of interests and exchanges of personnel.

THE ROMANESQUE CITY

The period of transition, in which Barcelona was transformed from a
'country town' to a long-range emporium by a form of commercial
revolution, has left disappointingly little trace in the fabric of the
modern city. High-medieval prosperity meant that most of Romanesque Barcelona was pulled down and rebuilt later. For a flavour of
what Catalonia was like in the twelfth century, the visitor to Barcelona
has to go to the Museu de l'Art de Catalunya on Montjuic, where the
collection of wall-paintings transferred from rural churches shows the

high quality that Catalan money could buy, the search for classical and Byzantine models in which the artists engaged. The wolf of Sant Joan de Boi bares predatory teeth as he starts round in a classical pose; the seraphim of the apse with their feathery, eyed wings recall Byzantine mosaics. The Master of the Pantocrator of Sant Climent de Taüll was admired as much in his own day as in ours to judge from the expensive blue pigment he could afford to mix with an apparently lavish hand. In the streets, the explorer can get a sense of what the city has lost by matching the map to the documents that record the expansion of the twelfth century; in 1160, for instance, Ramon Berenguer IV granted a rabbi permission to build a new public bath just outside the city wall, where today the carrer dels Banys Nous curls in the spectral shadow of lost ramparts. Or else the surviving remains, too insignificant to attract high-medieval developers, can be picked out on a spiralling route which reveals more survivals as it gets further from the centre.

Sant Pau del Camp and Sant Pere de les Puelles were themselves redevelopments – twelfth-century rebuildings of tenth-century foundations. In Sant Pau, consecrated in 1117 as part of a monastic dependency of the great house of Sant Cugat del Vallès, capitals of Visigothic workmanship reappeared; this cannibalisation of old materials suggests an edifice of lowly status, and construction on the cheap. In Sant Pere, only part of the interior, heavily restored, survives from the building consecrated in 1147, but it includes a dome resting on pendentives and some impressive capitals of thick teguminous foliage. The Capella de Marcús and that of Sant Llàtzer are near-contemporaries. The first, now nestling in the crook of the arm of a huge modern building on the carrer dels Carders, was founded in 1166 as part of a house of repose for travellers and pilgrims by a rich merchant, Bernat Marcús. Of the Capella de Marcús only the nave remains and of Sant Llàtzer only the apse, utterly derelict but scheduled for restoration, while the rest of the structure has been appropriated for the dwellings and small businesses of this traditionally poor part of the town. It was part of a foundation for lepers established by Bishop Guillem de Torroja, who died in 1171.

These hospitals – that of the travellers and that of the lepers – flanked the late twelfth-century city. Evidence that building was in progress at the time in the centre can be seen on either side of the cathedral: to the north, the traces of older window-awnings imbedded in the thirteenth- and fourteenth-century fabric of the royal palace and in the outer wall of the Pia Almoyna; to the south, the cloister gallery

of the bishop's palace and the façade of the enigmatic little Capella de
Santa Llúcia. The documented building-history of this chapel gives it
a mid-thirteenth century date; but the chapel opened in 1258 by
Bishop Arnau de Gurb, who is buried in a Gothic tomb within, must
have been an adaptation of an older building. It looks shy and retiring
now, overawed by the adjoining cathedral, despoiled of most of its
wall-paintings and even of the cults of all the holy virgins to whom it
was originally dedicated, save St Lucy; but the decayed capitals of the
Annunciation and Visitation at the door suggest the hand of a lively
master.

The Communal Framework

Barcelona's relationship with her hinterland – economic dependence,
political subjection – was reflected in the government of the counts
and their clients. Anchored on a lee shore, straining to get out to sea
and exploit the opportunities of long-range commerce, Barcelona in
the twelfth-century seemed bound to a dynasty with a landward gaze.

In 1108 a family tragedy permanently altered Barcelona's institutions
of government. 'By God's terrible judgement and permission,' as
monks of Sant Cugat explained it, 'as a consequence of our sins, a
huge host of Moabites and other pagans, enemies of the name of
Christ, invaded parts of our fatherland.'[29] The reference was to a raid
by a force from Moorish Spain, recently reunited by the Almoravids,
a movement of frenzied chiliastic ascetics whose name – *al-murābitūn*,
or 'garrison folk' – signified ascetic withdrawal as well as holy warfare.
For most of the valley of the Penedés, the result of the raid was serious,
but reversible, the loss of a year's vines. For the family of the viscounts
of Barcelona, the effect was permanent; the only heir was carried off
into captivity. The luckless prisoner was still using the title of viscount
as late as 1139, when he was serving the Almoravids as captain of their
paid Christian militia, but he died in battle in 1142, fighting on his
captors' behalf, and his son, though continuing to attempt to manage
from afar the family's property in Catalonia, seems never to have
claimed the viscount's dignity. The office disappeared from
Barcelona.[30]

The power of the viscount, ruling the city as the count's permanent
and hereditary deputy, might have been replaced by a form of self-
government through some communal institution. This was the sort of
transformation which occurred frequently in twelfth-century northern

Italy, where many towns, nuclei of emerging city-states, were hardly much more 'developed' as urban communities than Barcelona.

The sort of organisation from which communal rule might have emerged was not unknown in Catalonia. A superior rank of citizens, known as the *boni homines* or *probi homines*, was recognised in Barcelona from the tenth century; they appear in an inscription from Sant Pau del Camp, entrusted with verifying the celebration of endowed masses, and they figure in many judgements, sales and wills as the 'godfathers' of the community, witnesses whose signatures had a peculiarly authenticating effect on the documents they attested. Early twelfth-century Cardona – presumably then a lesser place than Barcelona – had a charter granted by the viscount and abbot to a *communa* of heads of families, who were bound together by oath to protect each other against all adversaries, save the viscount and abbot themselves. It is hard to believe that Barcelona had no similar charter.[31] But the informal role of the *boni homines* never ripened into anything like a consulate; the commune, if there was one, never challenged the supremacy of an external lord. The administration of the city seems to have depended entirely on the counts, represented first by a viscount lodged in the Castell Vell, by the west gate of the city, later by a vicar and bailiff. The absence of any evidence of stirrings of civic feeling before the thirteenth century shows the immaturity – one might say, the underdevelopment – of Barcelona at a time when the towns which would later be despised as the abodes of bumpkins, like Cervera, Vic and Lleida, were electing consuls and challenging their bishops' monopoly of lordship, in a manner reminiscent of the birth of so many autonomous Italian communes.

The first recorded formal institution for sharing government with the citizens was granted by Jaume I in 1249; an assembly of resident heads of households could elect a committee of citizens of the highest rank, to be known as the *paers* to advise the count-king's officials. At a time when the city was growing rapidly, right of access to such an assembly must have been impossible to define and dangerous to regulate. In 1258, the count-king instituted a new system, with an executive council of twenty, chosen by two hundred electors who were to be representative of various estates and professions. Two years later, the size of the executive council was reduced to six, and between 1265 and 1274 a further trimming and adjustment of the structure produced the system that was to prevail as long as Barcelonese municipal 'liberty' lasted – until the Bourbon conquest of 1714. Five *consellers* would form the executive, chosen from – and initially by – the Consell dels

Cent Jurats, a representative assembly, nominally one-hundred strong.
After a generation of tentative experiment, the new system appears to
have satisfied the count-kings. Rival interests seemed to be held in
balance and popular unrest in check. The funnelling of communal
responsibilities into ever fewer hands suggests that the period of
instability had also been a period of social tension. From the last
quarter of the century, however, Jaume's successors had sufficient
confidence in the city regime to devolve power progressively to the
consellers and Consell. War was the motor that drove the engine of
municipal power; the count-kings traded the powers of vicars and
bailiffs for subsidies, ships and men.

The Violent Polity

An image of Barcelona, crushed to fit the ideal model of urban order
as conceived in the late fourteenth century, is preserved in a diagram
of 1389, in which the city is represented as a circle, divided into four
equal quarters radiating from a square 'stone of the corn square' in the
centre. Directions for finding the boundaries between the quarters are
enclosed in rectangular strips that intersect at the corn square at right
angles, in the manner of main streets.[32] The same model underlay the
description of an ideally planned city given, at about the same time,
by Francesc de Eiximenis, the Franciscan scholar who may have
formulated his ideas on urban planning during his time as a teacher
in Barcelona in 1381–3. He envisaged the perfect city as a circle of
walls, punctuated by four equidistant gates, from which straight streets
would lead to a plaza in the exact centre.[33] This pattern of perfect,
rational shapes, based on the relationship of the square to the circle
and on the supposed harmonies of mathematical exactitude, was an
aesthetic construction, intended to work because it was beautiful and
judged to be practical because it was a reflection of the cosmic order
created by God.

For much of the fourteenth century the government of the city
seems to have been regulated with something like the 'harmony'
idealised by Eiximenis. A wide range of trades and vocations was
always represented in the Consell de Cent and on the committee of
electors of the *consellers*. The ruling patriciate, without risk to its own
power, could associate the lower estates in some of the most solemn
acts of government. The Consell for 1334, for instance, was composed
of sixty-four patricians, three members 'learned in the law' and thirty-

eight representatives of various guilds (for the canonical number of one hundred members was never taken literally): eight of these were tailors, four cloth-makers and the notaries, spice-vendors, cobblers and harness-makers supplied three each; two each came from the ranks of the linen-makers, silversmiths, coopers, dyers and furriers, and the two cloth-workers' guilds supplied three between them. Every year on St Andrew's Day the Consell would be summoned to make the election of the *consellers*, by a complex procedure designed to entrench oligarchic control. The Consell appointed two leading citizens who chose ten others to join them in an electoral college, twelve-strong. These customarily included representatives of the lower estate: in 1301, for instance, a furrier, a tanner and a painter took part. The twelve withdrew in conclave emerging with the names of the five *consellers* for the following year, who then took their oath of office on the Book of Privileges of the city, in the presence of their predecessors and of the representative of the count-king. They swore to keep their deliberations secret, to give good council to the comital officials and to uphold justice and the liberties of Barcelona.[34]

Social harmony characterised the municipal institutions while little power was at stake. The encroachments of the Consell and *consellers* on the powers of the count-kings' officials gradually made competition for office fiercer, and the oligarchs less willing to trade condescension for deference. Little is known about the social problems of medieval Barcelona. The rapid exclusion of popular representation from the municipal institutions created by Jaume I suggests that the menace of popular unrest was already being felt in the boom-town of the third quarter of the thirteenth century. No unrest was serious enough to be recorded until 1285, when a low-born charismatic messiah called Berenguer d'Oller led a rising in the streets. Medieval cities often threw up such characters: 'natural' orators with a style based on mendicant sermons, an apocalyptic turn of phrase and a demagogue's ear for the grievances of the mob. Berenguer's passion for social justice may have been rooted in the doctrine of apostolic poverty, embodied and extolled by Franciscan preachers, or in the heresy of dominion by grace, which denied lordship and property rights to owners who were in a state of sin. Like many such successful rabble-rousers, surprised by their own power, he was a prey to pride and susceptible to self-aggrandisement. During his few weeks of power, d'Oller, with the assistance of 'assessors' who took over the government of the city, did not maltreat or even fully displace the proper authorities, but exercised a form of vigilance over them.

According to the testimony of opponents, they impeded the execution of the count-king's commands; but these rebels, as was commonly the case with popular movements in the medieval west, seem
to have been in awe of a monarch hedged by divinity. When Pere II
arrived on 24 March their power was voluntarily surrendered to him,
even though he appeared with only a small escort. D'Oller went to
kiss his hand but Pere denied him on the grounds that 'one king should
not kiss another'. He went meekly to his trial, less meekly to his
hanging, dragged through the streets. The rebels' programme has been
lost in the obscurity of an unreliable historical tradition. The official
version was that d'Oller intended to massacre the Jews, the clerks and
the rich, and hand the city over to the King of France. This is scarcely
credible but may preserve some echo of genuine sources of antagonism:
anti-semitism, anti-clericalism and class hatred. The chronicler's analysis tends to confirm the popular nature of the revolt, but it seems at
least that there were respectable elements out to exploit discontent; of
the thirty main conspirators punished six were probably *ciutadans
honrats* – citizens of the highest rank, with privileged access to the
institutions of government – or merchants, and one was a notary.[35]

Two years before the uprising of d'Oller, protests were heard in the
Corts against the municipal regime in Barcelona on the grounds that
justice was ignored, favouritism practised, and the food supply ill
managed. D'Oller's revolt has to be understood against that background. If it did represent a popular bid for a share of power in the
city, its suppression was effective. Riots and disorders were common in
the fourteenth century, but were directed against social and economic
targets, not political objectives. The insurgents of 1334 attacked the
houses of the grain monopolists; those of 1348 and 1391 victimised
the Jews. Not for a hundred years after d'Oller's rising was there any
continuous demand for the reform of municipal institutions on more
popular lines, until the crisis of 1391, which could be resolved only
by the admission of popular representatives to the deliberations of the
Consell de Cent.

These riots and rebellions erupted occasionally against a background
of habitual violence. The irrational little open spaces of the old
city, into which today extemporised playgrounds are crammed, were
medieval battlegrounds of gang warfare. Not even hallowed ground was
exempt. On 14 January 1348, for instance, the bishop's representative
purged the bloodstained cemetery of the church of St Baudilius by
aspersions and recital of the Miserere and other prayers;[36] this was
probably not an unaccustomed ritual. Whether or not popular unrest

on the grand scale of 1285, 1334 and 1391 was manipulated by factions of the well-to-do, it seems that routine rowdyism was practised or fomented by nobles and respectable citizens with an apparent stake in stability. One of the most unintelligible aspects of life in medieval cities was the acceptability of levels of violence which *pro rata* resembled those found today, say, in Medellín or downtown Manila.

In the absence of adequate judicial means of relieving tension between discordant neighbours and rival factions, gang warfare may have been socially functional, confining hostilities to predictable, ritual forms. The struggle to find judicial alternatives was led, perhaps, by the bishops rather than the count-kings, who were accused in the mid-fourteenth century of granting too many gages to undesirable roughnecks; presumably these hoodlums were retained by nobles and patricians or other rich citizens, since such gages were normally granted for services or cash. The practice was cited, for instance, in the reign of Alfons III, as a reason why surgeons, whose business might require them to go out at night, should be licensed to bear arms.[37] Shortly afterwards, episcopal efforts to replace strife with peace were recorded in the case of the factional feud between the partisans of two rival patrician families, those of the Pradell and Vilar. They swore to refer their differences to arbitration and to refrain from causing each other harm.

The case illustrated a further problem, however. Almost a quarter of the participants in this warfare of gangs were entitled to clerical immunity, although most belonged only to the lowest orders of the clerical estate. One of them even had to be absolved for his part in a homicide. In this respect, the case was typical; the tonsure, like the royal gage, was a refuge for hooligans. In January 1346, for instance, a minor cleric called Jacobus Roselli chopped off an adversary's hand; and there was a whole brood of tonsured clerks, the Panyols family, who seem to have made a career of thuggery. Though the bishop was anxious to provide factional hostilities with non-violent means of redress, he was obliged to protect these unworthy clerks from secular justice.[38]

Licensed by the crown, effectively protected by the bishop, street violence was ineradicable. It was contained only by the absence of any permanent class antagonisms and by the limitations of the power at stake. Though the count-kings retreated from the arena of city politics, the autonomy of Barcelona was still shadowed by their proximity, by the patronage they wielded, the jurisdiction they retained, and the source of 'graces' and 'mercies' they commanded. Had sovereignty

been up for grabs in Barcelona, its history might have been as turbulent
as that of Genoa. The brief periods when sovereignty was at stake, in
the rebellions of 1462 and 1640, were, as we shall see, bloody and
catastrophic.

THE CIVIC COCKPIT

The high-medieval shift of power from counts to *consellers* could not
easily be reversed. By the mid-1380s, however, Pere III (Pedro IV of
Aragon, r. 1336–87, who was called the Ceremonious from his regulation of the offices and rites of court and state, notwithstanding
his unceremonious treatment of enemies) was looking for ways of
increasing his influence over appointments, and his resources of patronage, through jobbery in the city. In 1386 he licensed citizens excluded
from office to meet and comment in public on 'the order which ought
to be had in certain matters touching the good and profit of the city
and of the common weal thereof'.[39] This was to institutionalise partisan
politics; a party of disappointed office-seekers, self-defined as 'certain
men of great affection towards the good estate of the said city and the
royal dignity' was now able to campaign against the faction in power.
There is no reason to suppose that the struggle was animated by
any ideological conflict or any clash of classes. The party of the
establishment, which would come to be known as the 'Biga', and the
'Busca' of the excluded were essentially factions of the élite, formed
by family and business ties, by personal and inherited friendships and
enmities. But because the establishment was an oligarchy, the Busca
included, or allied with, aspirants to office from outside the charmed
circle. This gave the reformers' programme a popular flavour and
enabled them, in hard times, to fill the streets in their cause.

The reformist programme was adumbrated in Pere III's decree.
First, the consellers were to include, in equal numbers, representatives
of three estates: those of the *ciutadans honrats* or city patriciate, the
merchants and the *menestrals*. The meaning of the last two categories
in the terminology of the time is open to dispute, but probably covered
independent traders and workers at every social and economic level.
Secondly, while the election of *consellers* was to remain the prerogative
of the Consell, the system which had evolved (by which admission to
the Consell was controlled in turn by the incumbent *consellers*) was
to be abolished in favour of a new electoral body on which the 'consuls'
of the merchants and artisans were to serve. To ensure a wider

distribution of offices, outgoing office-holders were to be ineligible for
re-election for at least two years; their salaries were to be 'moderate'
and monitored by the Consell; at the end of their terms of office, their
accounts were to be audited promptly. Each office was to be shared
equally among the three estates on a rota basis. This was not the
manifesto of a potential revolution but of a party of 'outs' who were
satisfied with every aspect of the system except their share in its profits.

Pere III died the year after the publication of the reformist programme. His successors, alarmed, perhaps by the bloodshed in the
streets during the pogrom of 1391, were unwilling to adventure
the loyalty of the city in the reformist cause. In 1436 and 1437, when
the names of Busca and Biga may first have become current, populist
agitation was decisively suppressed with the support of the count-king's
representative. Over the next decade, however, the attitude of the
comital authorities changed. Fear of social unrest at home at a time of
war abroad may have played a part; so might the personal sympathies
of the new governor of Barcelona, Galceran de Requesens. The count-
king Alfons IV (Alfonso V of Aragon, known, with little good and no
specific reason, as the Magnanimous, r. 1416–58) may have picked up
absolutist habits in his kingdom of Naples and conceived of a popular
alliance with which to discipline an unmanageable aristocratic estate.
Certainly, in the 1450s, the count-king's agents encouraged popular
movements, both in the towns – in favour of more access to offices –
and in the countryside – in favour of the emancipation of serfs.

The name 'Biga' probably signifies a large beam used in the construction of a building, the Busca a splinter, or piece of tinder or fragment
of kindling. The names, intended as a play on Our Lord's advice to
remove the beam in your own eye before attending to the mote in
your brother's, evoke the nature of the parties: the solidity of the
establishment, the incendiary menace of the challenge. In 1450
the Busca proclaimed a rival governing institution for Barcelona, the
'Syndicate' – or perhaps 'synod' is a better translation in this context
of the term 'sindicat' – 'of the Three Estates and People of Barcelona'.
The language in which the conflict was expressed is captured in the
debates of the Consell de Cent and particularly in a speech by a
merchant-member, Ramon Guerau, made in November 1453. He
justified the pretensions of the syndicate not on the grounds of ideology,
nor of the merits of the programme of 1386, nor even primarily because
of the inefficiency of the prevailing regime, but on the basis of two
vague emotional appeals: first, to the 'privileges and liberties of the
city' – though he admitted that he did not know exactly what these

were – and secondly to 'the will of God'. 'This city of ours is grieving,' he claimed, 'because those to whom the principal offices have come down have not regarded our ancient customs and privileges and liberties but rather have sought to place wilfulness over reason and profit above liberty.' The role of the syndicate was 'to inquire into, examine, demand and defend the rights and usages of the people'. God had 'inspired, invigorated and enflamed the people's estate . . . for God in His glory perceives their just intentions and therefore has opened their hearts to understanding; and so, committed to the safety of the people [la salut pública], they are resolved gloriously to give their lives in that cause'. The invocations of 'liberty' and 'public safety' are bound to excite a modern ear; but it was the tone, not the substance, of the Busca's polemics that was revolutionary, and 'God' and 'privileges' were traditional sources of legitimation of revolt.[40]

Still, the syndics' policies seem to have exceeded the programme of 1386. When with the governor's help they succeeded in reforming the electoral system and obtained a majority first in the Consell and then, in March 1455, among the consellers, they forced through economic reforms which suggest that important policy differences may have underlain the factional conflicts. Measures of protection for the shipping and textile industries served the interests of active merchants who may have been under-represented in the old regime. More suggestive still is the effort of the Busca, once in power, to devalue the coinage. The traditional reluctance of the city authorities to debase Barcelona's money probably originated in civic pride and suspicion of bad coin; its effect, however, had been to favour rentiers and landlords over those involved in manufacture and active trade. Most western currencies had been savagely debased in the mid- to late fourteenth century, when the Barcelonese croat had been left out of line with the once equivalent Aragonese florin, which, by the end of the century, was worth seventy-five per cent of its former value. As a result, the croat was forced out of circulation; Barcelonese products were overpriced in relation to their competitors and those on fixed incomes benefited at the expense of the creators of new wealth.

The Busca was a frail coalition, shattered by the impact of power. The unifying effects of a long period of 'opposition' were dispelled almost as soon as some members achieved office. The bouleversement of 1455 did not substitute 'democracy' for oligarchy; the élite was enlarged, but the new élite affected the habits and largely adopted the interest, of the old. The institutions of government were permanently affected; the consellers now always included one merchant, and a representative or two of *artistes* and *menestrals* – that is, the higher and lower trades respectively. The distinction between *artistes* and *menestrals* was invidious but indefinable. A handful of trades attracted special deference and were given enhanced status; their members formed 'colleges' (*collegis*) rather than the mere guilds and confraternities formed by followers of less prestigious vocations, and enjoyed a collective form of address, proper to the aristocracy, as '*collegis magnífics*'. Initially, this status was confined to notaries, surgeons, pharmacists and druggists (who were dealers in every kind of exotic product of small bulk and high value). Printers and booksellers were admitted in 1553, painters between 1682 and 1786, jobbers and couriers of the exchange in 1707, and silversmiths, long after the abolition of the political privileges of the *artistes*, in 1732. All the other crafts in the city belonged to the *menstralia* and had no more than one place among the *consellers* between them.[41]

This division of the trades and professions might have been calculated to give stability to the political system. The *artistes* purveyed goods and services of high value and were dependent on the custom and patronage of the rich; the representatives of the patrician and merchant estates could therefore generally count on the support of the *conseller* from those professions. Even the *menestrals* were all masters or self-employed men, who were well placed to influence the disenfranchised majority but who did not always share its interests. In the diary of the scribe of the Diputació, Jaume Safont, the admission of 'contemptible folk' to the ranks of the *consellers* threatened an 'earthquake . . . One might as well put billy-goats in the place as men of vile condition.'[42]. In practice, however, the newcomers adopted the outlook of those whose power they shared. In the next decade, when Barcelona rose in rebellion against the count-king, it was in the interests of the patricians and of their aristocratic allies from outside the city.

One reform not effected in 1455 was the *insaculació*, or lottery of office, which was spreading rapidly among Catalonian towns and institutions in the fifteenth century as a means of ensuring a fair distribution of power. In Barcelona, the election of the *consellers* remained in the hands of a committee of the Consell until 1493. The significance – if any – of this late introduction of the lottery is much disputed among historians. Traditionally, Catalan writers have represented it as an example of the royal will imposed on the city in contravention of sanctified 'custom'; but as it was such a common method of election, of such long standing elsewhere in the Crown of Aragon, the theory has lost favour with scholars. The introduction of an element of hazard might have served to diffuse the acerbity of elections: indeed, no introduction of the lottery system ever seems to have taken place without this virtue being urged on its behalf; there is no evidence, however, that elections in Barcelona at the time were particularly conflictive – certainly not in comparison with those of the time of the lottery's greatest popularity in other contexts, in the mid-fifteenth century. A measure which had once been seen as a limitation on the power of patrician-oligarchs may by now have favoured the old regime.

The reform was introduced as part of a 'package' of measures designed to restore some of the power of the patriciate: the Consell – still called the 'Council of One Hundred' – was enlarged to a strength of 144, among whom the patricians were to be best represented, with forty-eight places against thirty-two for each of the other estates; among the *consellers*, the *artistes* and *menestrals* were henceforth to share a single place, which each estate would supply in alternate years. In itself, the introduction of the lottery of office made little difference, merely shifting the intrigue and corruption to the selection of names to go into the sorting-urn. After nearly forty years in which electoral power had been shared among the estates, the lottery may marginally have favoured the plutocrats who could afford to manipulate a complex system of nominating candidates. Certainly, the old guard was satisfied. 'Please God,' wrote the chronicler Joan Carbonell, 'government will, little by little, be restored to proper hands, and all the said three estates of merchants, *artistes* and *menestrals* be expelled from it.'[43] If matters never actually reached that point, it may be because oligarchy was no longer under threat.

The terms of the struggle of Busca and Biga suggest that the Barcelonese patricians saw themselves as 'natural' rulers, empowered by some inherent superiority. This aristocratic self-perception seems to have grown in the late middle ages and sixteenth century. It may have been allied to a real change in the economic basis of the wealth of the élite; some historians have spoken of the transformation of the oligarchy from merchants to rentiers, although in reality finance, commerce and investment in land seem to have been allied activities. The nature of nobility was much discussed by the moral philosophers of the Renaissance – whether its essence consisted in virtue or riches or the exercise of arms. One of the patricians of Barcelona, Gabriel Turell, expressed his fellow citizens' claim to all three types, in 1476. 'Among these *ciutadans honrats* of Barcelona there are honourable men, rich and living in honourable estate, with horse and arms, splendidly attired and attended.' They were accorded the honours due to 'gentility' in all other cities. They had great possessions, large and well furnished houses, treasure and 'objects of magnificence'. 'Who,' Turell concluded, 'deserves more honour than these? For they are in charge of the government of the city, founded on the common weal, and they possess virtue. These men are not just citizens but very knights in their manner of life.'[44] They intermarried with the military aristocracy of the hinterland and, like their Venetian contemporaries, bought *terraferma* estates of their own, so that the distinction between urban patriciate and rural nobility became blurred. Despite the departure of the royal court after 1416, Barcelona remained a magnet for Catalan noblemen and a milieu as aristocratic, in the late fifteenth and sixteenth centuries, as almost any Castilian city. Among the aristocratic colonists, Enric, Count of Empúries, built in 1491 a house 'of a richness that could never conceivably be surpassed'. In 1498 the offices of the city were opened to knights and in 1510 to the nobility generally. The lower orders were not expelled from government, as Joan Carbonell had gloatingly foreseen, but swamped.

THE RISE OF THE BOURGEOISIE?

In 1392, the *consellers* installed a clock in the cathedral tower, with two men whose duty it was to bang a big bell every hour on the hour. Thus, they inferred, the residents of the city 'would be reminded to perform their contractual obligations'. This sort of device was becoming common in late fourteenth-century cities, but its resonant novelty must have had a startling impact on the citizens of Barcelona. The image of this hourly, unremitting summons to duty ringing out above their heads and in their ears suggests a city dominated by bourgeois values, a world in which the stroke of the clock determines the rhythms of life, as surely as the changing seasons in the countryside.[45] A historian summoned by these bells might be tempted to see the conflicts of the late Middle Ages as the result of the assertion of a claim to power by the rising bourgeoisie who now controlled the city's means of wealth and who, perhaps, as they imposed their values, claimed the means to enforce them.

This sort of analysis is defied by the profile of the bourgeoisie and the configurations of the conflicts. The only 'bourgeois mentality' detectable in the sources is one which aspires to share aristocratic virtues; the only 'capitalist' way of life is one modelled on the noble household. The gangs who fought in the streets and the parties who contested power in the Consell de Cent seem to have been factions – wide-ranging affinities divided not so much by class antagonism as by the divergent claims of kinship, clientage and competition for status, office and reward.

Like other medieval cities, Barcelona was a 'vertical structure' of society, in which the common bonds of citizenship, and the common interests they created, transcended divisions of class and even, in the confrontation of threats from outside, of faction. The walls, which divided the citizenry from the outside world and enclosed them in a shared space, were the symbols of a common identity. This does not mean that particular zones inside the walls had no special character of their own, nor that profound internal divisions were non-existent. The Jews' quarter was exempt from the privileges of citizenship and was well defined by boundaries of its own, though not all the Jews lived in it; but after the pogrom of 1391 prudent or enforced conversions first attenuated then obliterated the Jewish enclave. Other quarters were marked off by their amenities or the dictates of fashion, sometimes supplemented by more explicit controls. In about 1400, for instance, the plaça de Santa Ana was favoured by rich and noble residents: a knight's house there, with a garden, cost 650 lliures – nearly four times as much as the most expensive merchant's house in the old ghetto. As beggars followed fashion, the authorities banned 'prostitutes, shouters, the lame, the handless, the blind and many others who have disgusting diseases or lack parts of their hands, feet or legs.'[46] In other parts of the city the cost of housing varied from under twenty-four lliures to nearly 200. Nor did the walls create the unity of an ideal *polis*, where all the citizens knew one another. Barcelona at its height, with perhaps 40,000 inhabitants, was too populous for that. The public nature of medieval parish life, in which every major decision had to be solemnised or atoned for in the sight of one's neighbours, and in which news was undifferentiated from gossip, was peculiarly intense in medieval Barcelona, where there were only a few highly crowded parishes. Despite this – perhaps because of it – the city was full of seekers-after-privacy: rich men, who paid premiums for gardens and withdrawing-chambers, poor men like Pere Burgues, who in a case of 1405 claimed not to know his immediate neighbour because 'he does not interfere with anybody but only looks after himself'.[47]

The over-arching sense of community survived such grudging indifference and bitter hostilities because the privileges of citizenship were a common heritage that had to be maintained and a common interest

in the twelfth century, she became dependent on food supplies which Catalonia alone was never fertile enough to provide. The surplus grain of the hinterland was bought up on annual buying trips made by agents of the city at harvest time through the plain of Urgell, the bishopric of Vic and Roussillon. But by the early thirteenth century the buyers were regularly looking further afield – inland to the Ribera del Duero and, increasingly, to sources of seaborne supply. Improved maritime communications made grain from abroad cheap in comparison with hinterland prices, inflated by overland transport costs. The price of corn in the Barcelona market justified thirteenth-century businesses in shipping it from Sicily and North Africa. Although domestic production remained indispensable, the primary suppliers came to be found overseas. Barcelona leaned seaward, towards a destiny like Venice's or Genoa's.

II

'... And the Waves their Wealth':

Barcelona and the Sea

Oh! detura't un punt! Mira el mar, Barcelona,
com té faixa de blau fins al baix horitzó
els poblets blanquejant tot al llarg de la costa,
qu se'n van plens de sol vorejant la blavor.
I tu fuges del mar?

(Oh, Barcelona, stop a moment: take a look
At how the sea spreads blue towards the low horizon.
Look at the little towns, sun-bleached, along the coast,
That, gorged with sun, go out to sail along the blue.
And you want to flee from the sea?)

Joan Maragall, 'Oda Nova a Barcelona'

La vida de la galera
es molt llarga de contar:
Tres mesos he anat per aigua
sense mai terra trobar

(Life in a galley's
a tiresome task.
I've still not found land
in three months under sail.)

Fourteenth-century shanty

THE KEYS OF VOLITION

At the water's edge, above the harbour of Barcelona, raised aloft
on a gilded dome, the statue of Columbus commemorates his
links with the city where he gave, to his favourite patroness,
'the keys of my volition'. For a long time, he was a sorry figure,
besmirched and corroded by the grimy air, spattered with guano, his
face eroded to a clownlike mask.[1] Clever restoration has put that right,

but he still seems uneasily out of place, recalling the era in which he was placed here for the universal exhibition of 1888, when now-discredited theories of his Catalan origins were current. He faces away from Castile, his adopted homeland, which Catalans long blamed – some do so still – for having cheated them of the New World's rewards. And he is pointing, not westwards, towards his great discoveries, but in the opposite direction, out over the Mediterranean. Yet there is no mistake. The Mediterranean was the sea in which Columbus's mariner's vocation was formed; to the last years of his life he could recall the sailing directions from Cadiz via Barcelona and Genoa to Naples. It was also Barcelona's own sea, from which the city drew its life for much of its history, and on which most of its mariners pursued their way.

Catalans – perhaps including some Barcelonese – were early dabblers in the Atlantic. In common with other Mediterranean mariners in the early Middle Ages, they seem to have been deterred from Atlantic ventures by the strong adverse current that runs between the Pillars of Hercules. By the early thirteenth century, however, the commercial opportunities were sufficiently telling, and the available shipping sufficiently robust, to tempt Catalans to northern waters, to England and Flanders. Except in crossing the Bay of Biscay, shipping on that route never seems to have ventured far out into the open sea. In the fourteenth century, subjects of the House of Barcelona, especially from Majorca, made frequent sailings as merchants and missionaries to the islands of the African Atlantic and some of these voyages were insured in Barcelona. But it proved a relatively unrewarding route and by the end of the century seems to have been abandoned to the more handily placed Castilians and Portuguese. Had they persevered, the Catalans might have dominated the Atlantic sea lanes and beaten Castile to the discovery of America. The opportunity was fleeting, however; as it was, the first successful direct venture to the New World from Barcelona was not launched until 1749, partly because Catalans were formally excluded from Castile's oceanic possessions and had to conduct their trade with America through Castilian ports. No Catalan shipping was recorded in the Atlantic islands between 1366 and 1503.[2] By the time Catalan maritime enterprise turned back from its first Atlantic dabblings, Barcelona was already the centre of a seaborne empire of barely manageable proportions within the Mediterranean.

This impressive achievement was launched from a remarkably deficient base. For Barcelona does not have a good natural harbour. Its port was still inadequate – shallow, incommodious, unsafe – after the

building of the famous mole, 'very strong and stately', in the seventeenth century.[3] Experienced pilots were needed to cross the treacherous sand-bar. The entrance channel had only seventeen feet of bottom
and inside the harbour the average draught was only twenty-two feet.
For most of the history of Barcelona as a great sea port, shipping had
to anchor offshore and ferry the goods to and from the beach. In 1415
and 1423, the count-kings who made their entry to Barcelona by sea,
Ferdinand of Antequera (Ferran I in Catalan, Fernando I of Aragon,
r. 1412–16) and Alfons IV (Alfonso V of Aragon, r. 1416–58) had to
be welcomed along wooden jetties specially built over the beach to
receive them.[4] Even in the time of Antoni de Capmany, who wrote
in celebration of Barcelona's maritime history in the late eighteenth
century, the beaching of goods from an offshore anchorage was normal
practice, despite many prolongations of the mole, because of the
damage done by silting from the mouth of the Besós. The silt periodically closed the harbour mouth or made the entrance channel unavig-
ably shallow. Even in the early nineteenth century, ships could find
themselves shut in for a month or two at a time, or were obliged to
stand out beyond the bar and embark their goods from boats.[5]

Yet for at least five centuries, Barcelona managed to be a centre of
long-range commerce without building an artificial harbour. Roman
Barcelona probably handled little more than local, coastbound trade.
Before the first century BC. there may have been a settlement and
harbour to the south of Montjuic. In or shortly before the reign of
Augustus, when the heart of modern Barcelona on Mont Tàber was
settled with a Roman colony, a modest quay seems to have been
constructed at the foot of the hill, where a precipitate stream formerly
debouched into the sea. The Barcelona of those days was just a small
halt on the road from Tarragona to Empùries. When the trade of
Barcelona began to be well documented – or well represented in
surviving documents – in the eleventh century, it seems to have
been served by a facility known as the *portus* of Montjuic; this has
traditionally been assumed to have been a port to the south of the
present city, some distance from the modern centre, away from the
shoals created by the silts of the river mouths. *Portus* might mean a
market rather than a 'sea port'; and the slopes of Montjuic seem to
have been a sort of 'suburb' of Barcelona, where dwellings and 'towers'
were built from the early tenth century onwards. The area where ships
were beached could have stretched from the modern centre south
towards the mouth of the Llobregat.[6]

In 1060, although Barcelona was already a 'great town', according to the fastidious al-Bakri, the Barcelonese were still applying to Moorish ports to hire their galleys. By 1080 the counts possessed a fleet of their own, though it may not have been based in Barcelona; in that year the sons of Ramon Berenguer I (1024–76) agreed to keep in being the ships left by their father at his death, to divide any profits they yielded – presumably from war rather than trade – and to continue to build up the fleet. In 1094, Barcelona had a lighthouse – a different one, perhaps, from that recorded on Montjuic in 963 – which guided into port the Pisan fleet of 1113, bound for the conquest of Majorca. Two charters of Ramon Berenguer III (r. 1082–1131) mention what sounds like substantial seaborne trade. In 1104 he granted to the monastery of Sant Adrià de Besós a tenth of dues paid on 'all goods that come in on any ship in all my honour'; in the following year four Jews were granted a monopoly of the shipping home of ransomed Moorish slaves from Ramon Berenguer's dominions. That some, at least, of this sort of trade was going through Barcelona is suggested not only by the lighthouse but also by the terms of privileges Ramon Berenguer granted to the merchants of Pisa and Genoa when he visited those cities in 1116 and remitted the tax of one-fifth of the value of goods disembarked from galleys at Barcelona. Despite the deficiencies of her harbour, Barcelona was the point of departure of a fleet big enough to attempt the conquest of Majorca – 500 vessels strong, according to the doubtlessly exaggerated report of the poet who celebrated this expedition.[7]

What most inhibited Barcelona's long-range trade in the eleventh and twelfth centuries was probably the hostility of the inhabitants of the islands that barred her routes to the east and south. Though poorly placed for overland trade, Barcelona ought to have been a privileged point of access to the western Mediterranean sea lanes of the age of sail. A fast coastal current led almost all the way to Ibiza. The prevailing winds in summer took shipping quickly to the more easterly Balearics and, from there, swept on towards the great ports of the Maghrib. To get to the central and eastern Mediterranean was not so easy. The strong westerly currents were a help to shipping brave enough to follow the treacherous North African coast. Most seamen, however, preferred the slower but safer island-hopping route through the Balearics, Sardinia and Sicily. This was the start of an arduous haul. In the sixteenth century it could take twice as long to cross the Mediterranean from end to end as to cross the entire Atlantic Ocean from the Canaries to the Antilles.[8] In the early period of Barcelona's commercial expansion, the galley-dominated high Middle Ages, the technical limitations of shipping imposed modest ambitions on the carriers of commerce. Galleys were labour-intensive, dependent on ranks of thirsty oarsmen. A week's supply of fresh water was as much as most ships could carry. When the islands of the western Mediterranean were in unfriendly hands, the Barcelonese were trapped by the anti-clockwise flow of the coastal currents. In the thirteenth century, however, Barcelona's commercial power was transformed by the growth of her exclusively sail-powered commercial fleet and – even more – by the extension of the political control of her royal masters, the count-kings of the House of Barcelona, over the entire strategic springboard of the western Mediterranean: the island bases, and the Maghribi ports.

The favour of her counts, which had been so important in the early days of her growth, was still vital in nurturing Barcelona's bid for commercial ascendancy. In 1227, Jaume I granted her shippers preference rights in handling goods in and out of port, and in 1231 exemption from all dues in the Balearics, in 1268 foreign shippers in Barcelona were banned from handling goods other than their own. In the same year the Barcelonese were entitled to instal consuls to look after their shipping in foreign ports. Ten years earlier, Barcelona was appointed to mint the silver cash of exceptional purity which long anchored the Catalonian economy to the concept of sound money. The count-king announced that this right was given to the Barcelonese on behalf of his other subjects as well as themselves. These charters are bench-marks of Barcelona's rise during the making of the Catalans' empire: partly evidence, partly explanation of Barcelonese preponderance.[9]

'THE BEST DEED FOR A HUNDRED YEARS'

The expedition that began Barcelona's Mediterranean empire is recorded by an exceptionally privileged witness. The count-king Jaume I (Jaime I of Aragon, r. 1213–76) has left us that rare thing – the autobiography of a medieval king, reasonably authentic, reflecting royal inspiration and probably, in large part, royal composition. At the very least, it captures the self-image which the king wished to project and resounds with the chivalry which was, it seems, Jaume's only source of abiding and deeply espoused values. When he described his conquest of Majorca, the arguments which moved him to undertake it and the experience of crossing the sea to carry it out, the king revealed that he saw maritime war as a means of chivalric adventure *par excellence*, as if romance could be sensed among the rats and hard-tack of shipboard life, and the waves ridden like jennets. There was 'more honour' in conquering a single kingdom 'in the midst of the sea, where God has been pleased to put it' than three on dry land. The voyage was lingeringly and lovingly described: the numbers of ships, the sailing order of the fleet, the location of the guiding lanterns, the waiting for a wind, the cries of the watches exchanged when the ships made contact, the changes of breeze, the shortenings of sail, the heaving of the sea in a storm and the resolution and faith in God it called forth. No moment matched the moment of making sail. 'And it seemed a fine sight for those who stayed on shore, and for us, for all the sea seemed white with sails, so great a fleet it was.'[10]

Jaume's enthusiasm for seafaring was already shared by many of his Catalan subjects. Now it infected the warriors of his realm and helped to inspire a series of seaborne conquests. 'The best thing man has done for a hundred years past,' the king later wrote, 'God willed that I should do when I took Majorca.' Jaume probably meant that it was the best by the standards of chivalry, the deed of most daring and renown. It was an achievement of great importance, too, for the political future of the House of Barcelona, which began to create a network of island dominions, first in the western and central Mediterranean, later – with less success – in the Atlantic. By the end of the thirteenth century, the chronicler, Bernat Desclot, could claim with pardonable exaggeration that no fish could go swimming without the King of Aragon's leave.[11] The inception of the empire was more than just a Barcelonese enterprise. But as Barcelona became commercially dominant in the territories of the King of Aragon, it became a Barcelonese empire and, ultimately, a Barcelonese burden.

Despite the sea's appeal for Jaume and, increasingly, for members of the Aragonese nobility, landlubbers could not engage in seaborne exploits unaided. The merchants and masters of Catalonia and Provence were called on to provide shipping and expertise – just as, in the neighbouring realm of Castile, the merchants of Burgos subscribed to the conquest of maritime Lower Andalusia. Pere Martell, citizen of Barcelona, seems to have been responsible for organising logistic support for the conquest of Majorca. It is clear, however, that more than commercial motives were involved. In the circle of the king, where the idea of the expedition seems to have arisen, other impulses – chivalric, dynastic and political – were stronger. The house of Barcelona had an acute sense of dynasty. Atavistic appeals to common ancestry were often capable of ending clannish conflicts; if a particular policy could be represented in council as ancestral, that was always a useful and sometimes a compelling argument for its espousal. The memory of Count Ramon Berenguer III's expedition of 1114 had been kept vivid by the 'epic' version of the *Liber Maiolichinus*, just as the memory of the conquest of Valencia was to be sustained and revived by the diffusion and versification of the story of El Cid. At intervals throughout the twelfth century, further attempts to organise a conquest were made: first, new efforts in alliance with Genoa and Pisa by Ramon Berenguer III and Ramon Berenguer IV, later with Sicily by Alfons II. In 1204, the Pope authorised the creation of a see in Majorca when its conquest should have been accomplished.

The count-king Jaume, susceptible as he was to the nostalgia of lineage, also had more urgent political reasons to take his magnates abroad. The minority with which his reign began aroused rivalries for the regency and invited aristocratic usurpations of authority. Only in 1217, after ten years of almost continuous civil war, did Jaume make good his claims to have attained his majority. He was nineteen years old, heir to a depleted patrimony, legatee of troubled times. The cause behind which he might most easily have united his realm was the conquest of Valencia, a Muslim land abutting Catalonia to the south. But even if successful – and Jaume, who had tested Valencia's defences, had reason to think it would fail – such an enterprise could only fatten aristocratic domains of already indecent corpulence. Jaume's cause was better served by peace with Valencia, secured by the payment of tributes directly to himself. He preserved the peace with – or at least deferred the war against – Valencia, even at the risk of another magnate uprising.

To judge from the versions of debates in council preserved in Jaume's chronicle, Majorca proved an acceptable alternative partly because of its traditional appeal and partly because the king was lavish with promises of rewards. The relationship of the king to his Aragonese and Catalan nobles was never one of control. At its best, it was an *entente*. The debates unfolded with successive renewals of the pledges of feudal loyalty, by erstwhile rebels, under strict conditions. Entirely representative was the declaration of En Nunyo Sanç, Lord of Roussillon and Cerdagne, who would make the biggest contribution to the conquest and claim the largest reward. He reminded the count-king of the equivalence of their lineages, which they both owed equally to God. He acknowledged himself to be a vassal and to hold his lands by grant of the count-king's father, but he implied that part of his patrimony was attributable to divine election, rather than royal investiture. The Count of Empùries, who spoke after him in council, made this point explicitly on his own behalf and that of his kinsman, Guillem de Montcada: God had 'made them' and they held lands not only of the count-king but also 'of their own allod'. Indeed, all the dominions accumulated by the House of Barcelona were and would be circumscribed by a fudged line between sovereignty and suzerainty. En Nunyo Sanç went on to confirm his peace with the count-king and terms of his tenure of his lordships. He conceded to the crown, as of his own free will, the right to levy the pasture tax, the *bovatge*, in his dominions. He promised to aid the conquest with horse, foot and ships, including a hundred of his household knights. Next came the explicit condition: 'And you will give them part of the land and the movable wealth,' before the affirmation, 'And I have to serve you in that land, since God gives it to us to conquer.' Jaume's response was embodied in a charter issued at the representative assembly or Corts of Barcelona in 1228, before the expedition sailed, addressed to all the nobility: 'We shall give just portions to you and yours, according to the numbers of knights and men-at-arms whom you take with you.' The decision to attempt the conquest of Majorca was a good example of how contractual kingship worked.[12]

As well as contingents from this 'feudal' world of give-and-take, the conquest was the work of militias, mercenaries and ships from the 'bourgeois' world of the cities of Catalonia and Provence. These worlds were more thoroughly interpenetrated than is commonly supposed. Trade and land were distinct sources of wealth, but substantial amounts of both were often in the same hands and there was no 'class antagonism', but rather common interest, between them. The count-king Jaume's *Book of Deeds* gives the impression that the idea of the conquest originated in commercial circles in Barcelona and Tarragona. He describes the great banquet at Tarragona in November or December 1228, when Pere Martell entertained the count-king 'and the greater part of the nobles of Catalonia'. The question of Majorca is represented as arising by accident, but Martell was well prepared for it, explaining to the magnates the whereabouts of the Balearics, as if with an early map spread before him.[13]

In fact, the decision had been made by then. The preparation of a fleet against Majorca is mentioned in the count-king's 'contract of concubinage' with Countess Aurembiaix of Urgell of October 1228 – a document vital to the king's interest, in which he secured the reversion to the crown of the biggest territorial principality in his realms. This is not to say either that the Tarragona banquet was a fiction or that the conquest of Majorca was without commercial allure. Jaume regularly liked to discuss business after dinner: it was a typical social ritual of the Catalonia of his day. The account books of the city of Majorca after its conquest show that banquets to honour great events or stimulate appetites for civic transactions were a major source of expense, like the 'business lunch' today. It was characteristic, too, that a nautical technician and merchant like Pere Martell could act as host to the count-king and sit down with 'the greater nobles' without social embarrassment. An illustration of the event in an early manuscript of the chronicle shows the count-king at a table of his own, but no 'social distance' intervenes between the other diners. Some nobles, like En Nunyo Sanç, had coastal jurisdictions and ships of their own. Many merchants, especially from Barcelona, had investments in land.

Barcelona, alone or even in combination with the other great Catalan port of Tarragona, could not launch enough ships to conquer Majorca. The shortfall was made up by aristocratic shipowners and by the Crown of Aragon's subject-ports and allies beyond the Pyrenees, at Collioure, Perpignan, Narbonne, Montpellier and Marseilles. The Marseillais contribution – though the city was not beholden to the Crown of Aragon – may have been equal to or greater than that of Barcelona. The shipping for Jaume's expedition was in a sense a joint effort of the Catalan and Provençal worlds. It is tempting to see the cities of this region playing collectively in the conquest of Majorca the same role as the Venetians in the Fourth Crusade, ferrying respectively Aragonese warlords and Frankish 'pilgrims' for a share in the spoils . But none of them was a city-state in quite the same sense as Venice, and no sovereign territory was granted to them in the Balearics. The territorial rewards were modest plots for individual participants, as was promised by Jaume I to the men of Barcelona and Tarragona: 'May you have lands allotted to you, held from us and our successors and in fealty to us according to the customs of Barcelona' – meaning, perhaps, without intervention of intermediate lordship or else with the guarantee of heritability in the female line – 'and the portions which you will have there you will be able to sell and alienate, saving our fealty and lordship.'[14]

The strictly commercial rewards which therefore justified such widespread adhesion to the king's enterprise must have been considerable. Nothing is known of Majorca's trade before the conquest, except that the island was a notorious hotbed of piracy. Though a rather rough-and-ready form of exchange, piracy should probably not be too sharply distinguished from trade in this period. Most seafarers and most ships slipped in and out of both vocations without specialisation. Jaume made the depredations of the corsairs the *casus belli*, but it is reasonable to suppose that the merchants in his fleet aimed not only to suppress the pirates because they were pirates but also to supplant them in their more legitimate lines of business. Though many new products seem to have been introduced to Majorca by the conquerors, the island's role a staging post of the western Mediterranean seems to have been well established for generations, perhaps for centuries, before Jaume's conquest. The entrenched position of Moorish traders, and their privileged partners from Genoa and Pisa in the early thirteenth century, adequately explains the jealous anxiety of the merchants of Barcelona to break into the cartel, by force if necessary, on equal or preferential terms.

Crusading rhetoric justified the expedition and papal indulgences helped to launch it. Can religious motives be distinguished in the background of the conquest? The distinctively spiritual motives of the Holy Land crusaders who were spurred by the redemptive virtues of pilgrimage are not explicitly attested by any source for the conquest of Majorca. It remains possible that in a more general sense the conquest was seen as salutary because divinely ordained, even perhaps sanctified by the unfaith of the enemy. Pious avowals, beyond conventional invocations of Providence or assurances of godliness of purpose, are rare in Jaume's *Book of Deeds*. Usually it is interlocutors – bishops, for the most part – who are made to convey the more profound or more eloquent appeals to religion, which may be the work of a clerical interpolator or amanuensis. The conquest of Majorca, however, did inspire passages of exceptional fervour in the king's own mouth. When adverse winds made some of his company desire to abandon the voyage, Jaume answered them, by his own account, 'We are going on this voyage out of faith in God, and against those who do not believe in Him, and we are going against them for two purposes, either to convert or destroy them, or so that they may return that kingdom to the faith of Our Lord, and since we are going in His name, we confide in Him to guide us'. Votive effusions in time of peril are a long tradition of Mediterranean sailors, and it may be that this passage in the chronicle faithfully records a moment of uncharacteristic spiritual transport on Jaume's part. Sea storms, which recall Christ's stilling of the waters and the shipwreck of St Paul, easily induce moods of exaltation. More than merely just, Jaume represented the conflict almost as hallowed: first, by Moorish blood spilled in sacrifice; and, further or alternatively, by baptismal water splashed on infidel survivors. Yet even here the emphasis was on the legitimation rather than the sanctification of conquest; Jaume went on to justify his war in terms of traditional just war theory, waged for the recovery of usurped lands. This is the usual context of pious allusions in western Mediterranean texts. The numinous east, where Christ trod and relics seemed to swarm, was more productive of purely spiritual motives.[15]

So the conquest was launched for material gains, the presumed priorities of the Barcelonese. Yet this first foray in Mediterranean imperialism had some adverse effects for Barcelona. Access to a port at the heart of the trade routes on which her prosperity depended was an invaluable asset; but Barcelona's other gains were few. Her men were granted 226 houses in the city of Majorca – the same number as Lleida, fewer than Marseilles and Tarragona, though Barcelonese beneficiaries got a few more houses, granted indirectly via aristocratic donors. From the conquest of Ibiza and Formentera, effected by aristocratic initiative in 1235, Barcelona got even less by way of direct benefits. And it soon became apparent that Majorca would not be just a useful staging post for Barcelonese trade, but a dangerous commercial and industrial rival. The island became a centre of re-export for the entire Arago-Catalan world. The iron of Bayonne and Castile – the latter usually shipped from Seville – figs of Murcia and Alcudia, Ibizan salt, Sevillian oil and 'Greek wine' – perhaps Calabrian rather than strictly Greek – were, with slaves, the commodities brought in the largest quantities to Majorca, en route for elsewhere. The Aragonese dominions and north Africa predominate among the destinations represented in surviving shipping contracts. Between 1321 and 1340, for instance, forty-eight to fifty-nine per cent of sailings for ports outside the kingdom of Majorca were bound for Catalonia and twenty to twenty-eight per cent for Valencia. North Africa came a good third, with over 2,800 sailing licences surviving from the fourteenth century.[16]

Majorca was dependent on trade, but that is not to say that she was incapable of fostering new industries after the conquest. Commerce bred shipbuilding, especially after one of the Jewish cemeteries was turned into a shipyard by Sanç I (r. 1311–24). An appeal to the crown over conditions of employment of carpenters engaged in the building of six cogs in 1340 shows the scale of activity attained at a single moment. Some of the materials and skills of the shipwrights may also have been deployed in the remarkable armaments industry; in and around the 1380s, for instance, Pere de Vilalonga shipped literally thousands of crossbows to Flanders and England. The greatest industrial success of post-conquest Majorca was textiles, the most important product of the medieval industrial revolution, which fostered commerce whenever it was produced. Majorcan cloth was probably already coveted in the late thirteenth century; its production is documented from 1303. Its origins are obscure. Italian influence had been postulated to account for it, and Italians were generally the technicians and financiers of new colonial enterprise in late medieval Mediterranean islands; but the first evidence of Italian involvement in the Majorcan cloth industry is of Florentine operatives at work in the late fourteenth century. The industry may well have come, in the first place, with the majority of colonists, from Catalonia, probably from Barcelona itself. All these industrial activities were a direct challenge to the basic industries of Barcelona. And between 1276 and 1343, when Majorca was – with brief interruptions – an independent kingdom, the Barcelonese could not even count on a privileged place in the island's commerce.[17]

The range of new commercial and industrial activity, the prodigious economic growth of the century after the conquest, made Majorca a land of medieval *Wirtschaftswunder*, comparable with Madeira in the next century with its new products and 'nodal' trade, criss-crossing through the port on its way between distant producers and consumers. The chronicle of Jaume I eloquently expressed the potential of Majorca: it was the finest land, with the most beautiful city in the world; it was the king's favourite conquest, 'of most esteem than the kingdom of Leon'. In the eyes of Ramon Muntaner, writing in about 1325, the king's confidence seemed to be fulfilled. Muntaner was, of all the Catalan chroniclers, the most indiscriminate in his praise and the most ready with superlatives; but his encomium of Majorca rings true. It was 'a goodly isle, and an honoured one'. The count-king had 'made great grants to all his men, and good graces. And he peopled the said city and isle by means of more exemptions and privileges than any other city in the world; wherefore it has become one of the good cities of the world, noble and of greater wealth than any, and all peopled with Catalans, all of honoured provenance and good worth, whence have descended heirs who have become the most businesslike and best endowed people [*la plus convinent gent e mills nodrida*] of any city there may be in the world.' This concentration on the 'city', in despite of the rest of the island, is revealing. When outsiders thought of Majorca, they thought only of its staging post, just as today they think only of the tourist complex, on the same coast, centred on the same city. Muntaner also accurately perceived the conditions that enabled Majorca's economy to thrive; the economic freedom and low taxation that accompanied a sustained effort to draw settlers to the island. It became the priority of the Barcelonese élite to replicate those conditions in their own city.[18]

In the generation after Muntaner's encomium, Majorca's economic miracle seems to have run out of steam. Between 1329 and 1343 the population of the city fell dramatically from 5,256 hearths to 4,124. The loss of feudal 'independence' in 1343, when the island was re-absorbed under the direct rule of the King of Aragon, may have helped to bring the pioneering period to an end, to remove a source of incentives and to make Majorca a less stimulating place to live in and operate from. Yet if expansion was halted, prosperity continued, and if dynamism subsided, complacency prevailed. The *Manual de reebudes e de dades* – the municipal accounts of 1349 – captures the epicene contentment of the city fathers in the very year of plague. Theirs was a world of status linked to consumption, measured in costly feasts and ostentatious displays of loyalty to the mainland dynasty. At least seventy-six craftsmen and decorators were employed – some Moors, some Greeks, a few specifically slaves – to adorn the city chambers for the banquets. Two 'painters of altarpieces and battle flags' decorated hangings to celebrate the obsequies of the mainland queen. And the large sums spent on defence against the pretensions of the extruded island dynasty included the pay of eleven surgeon-bargers to serve the fleet. A society so abundantly supplied with quacks and craftsmen must have wallowed in surplus wealth.[19]

Barcelona had discovered what it was like to have a thankless daughter. Yet Majorca was only the first of a series of islands of the western and central Mediterranean, conquered by the House of Barcelona at long intervals over a period of about a hundred years. In the same period a string of Catalan – and largely Barcelonese – merchant colonies were established in north African ports under a loose royal protectorate. Barcelona's involvement in and influence on the establishment of this empire grew progressively, and her attitude was more directly exploitative than had been the case in Majorca. Ultimately, the more committed policy may have been the less remunerative. Barcelona's investment in overseas expansion came to exceed the return. Though never able to control Majorca she was able to share in the island's prosperity and develop trades of her own as a result. Majorca's era of prosperity, despite the competition in some fields, was also an age of expansion and prosperity for Barcelona. In the subsequent phase, of conscious imperialism, Barcelona overreached the limit of her resources and began to totter from the inevitable effects of immoderate greatness.

SICILIAN VESPERS, IMPERIAL SUNDOWN

The next burst of aggression from the House of Barcelona came in the 1280s and 1290s, some two generations after the first conquests, when Minorca and Sicily, with Malta and Gozo, were conquered, and a title to Sardinia and Corsica acquired. At about the same time, Minorca's client status was reasserted from the mainland by force of arms. No serious effort was ever mounted against Corsica; Malta and Gozo were not long retained; but in the 1320s an aggressive imperial policy reduced Sardinia to precarious obedience. Meanwhile, vassals of members of the House of Barcelona made conquests even further east, in Jarbāh and Qarqanāh and Greece. The impression of a growing island empire, reaching out towards the east – perhaps to the Holy Land, perhaps the spice trade, perhaps both – was reinforced by Aragonese propaganda. The count-king Jaume II, writing to the Pope in 1311, justified the growth of Aragonese *Hausmacht* in terms calculated to appeal to the crusading fervour of the Council of Vienne. Aragonese conquests, he claimed, were so that 'the Christian army, in proceeding towards the east by way of the sea, might always have islands of Christians to cling to'.[20]

Perhaps this was not altogether disingenuous; the House of Barcelona did toy from time to time with grand crusading schemes, and Catalan trade reached Alexandria and Constantinople. But as a guide to the nature and motives of Arago-Catalan expansion, the king's words are unreliable. The easterly vassal-states were only, at best, nominally 'Catalan' in chararacter and tenuously linked by juridical ties with the other dominions of the House of Barcelona. The Grecian dominions, for instance, were conquered by a *macédoine* of mercenaries of various provenances, whose lingua franca was Catalan, who called themselves the 'university' or company of Catalans, and who included a strong, genuinely Catalan contingent. But other nationalities predominated and the company's allegiance to the House of Barcelona was weak. The free-lances' acknowledgement, for most of the period of their survival, of the suzerainty of the heirs of the Sicilian throne (which by then also belonged to the House of Barcelona), was calculated to maximise their effective independence. After 1380, the territorial principalities they founded, the duchies of Athens and Neopatria, depended directly on the overlordship of the king of mainland Aragon; but that was a desperate throw, at a time of irresistible Turkish threat. Kings of Spain preserved the picturesque titles of 'Dukes of Athens and Neopatria'; memories of the company's exploits were preserved by the popularity of the chronicle of Ramon Muntaner, who devoted an enormous amount of space to an episode in which he had been a participant and which, he believed, illustrated Catalan prowess. Subsequent generations of Catalan nationalist historians were happy to follow Muntaner's lead. The existence of the Catalan duchies may marginally have increased the security of Barcelonese vessels returning on commercial voyages from the Levant. Otherwise, their part in the history of Catalan expansion was negligible.

Of the well-integrated Arago-Catalan world, the most easterly part, from the 1280s, was Sicily. Its conquest is usually seen as a chivalresque example of the dynastic self-aggrandisement of the House of Barcelona. At a more profound, and less conspicuous, level, it was a commercial venture by Barcelonese merchants. The count-king Pere II (Pedro III of Aragon, r. 1275–85) was married to the last Hohenstaufen claimant to the Sicilian throne, Constanza, daughter of Manfred of Sicily. But the Hohenstaufen were debarred from the Sicilian succession by apparently immutable papal decree. The solution to their dynastic crisis apparently most favoured by the Sicilian nobility – a republic under papal tutelage – was equally distasteful to successive popes, who had imposed Charles of Anjou as king. When the Sicilians rebelled against Charles, on 31 March 1382, alleging the licentiousness of his French soldiery as proof of his tyranny, Pere was already preparing – ostensibly for an invasion of Tunis – one of the largest armies the count-kings had ever taken outside their realms.

Whether the immediate circumstances that took him to Sicily were adventitious or contrived, Pere had probably been contemplating intervention in the island for some time past. His court was the normal place of refuge for Sicilian exiles. Giovanni di Procida, the old minister of the Hohenstaufen, who was alleged to have taken the glove of Manfred's 'martyred' heir, Conradin, as a pledge of vengeance, was there; so was Manfred's sister, the former Latin Empress of Byzantium; among the Sicilian and Neapolitan nobles surrounding Pere were two who were to be among his most effective military and naval commanders, Ruggiero di Loria and Corrado Lanza. Over them presided the claimant to the throne herself, Queen Constanza, who enjoyed the most privileged position of access to the king, waging 'war in her heart', as Muntaner said.

Pere had better reasons for invading Sicily than dynastic ambition or clannish revenge. The trading empire of Barcelona in the western Mediterranean could be almost sealed, at its western end, by the possession of Sicily; access to the eastern Mediterranean by Barcelona's Genoese, Pisan and Marseillais competitors could be overawed. Shipping between the two seas had to travel either through the Sicilian channel, which was relatively easy to navigate but equally easy to patrol and control, or through the notorious Straits of Messina, where Scylla and Charybdis lurked and where, according to Ibn Jubair writing in the twelfth century, 'the sea bursts through like a dam and boils like a cauldron'.[21] One of the main objectives of the island-empire of the House of Barcelona was probably to protect Barcelonese access to the lucrative trades of Barbary, which terminated in Maghribi ports: just as the Balearics screened their routes in the west, so Sicily in the east was the staging post for traders approaching North Africa from Naples, Amalfi and Venice.

If Sicily's strategic position made it peculiarly desirable to the House of Barcelona, its special value as one of the great granaries of the Mediterranean world gave it a special place in the commercial strategies of some Barcelonese merchants. Barcelona knew all too well the value of grain. Every year the agents of the city went out at harvest time to tour the plain of Urgell, and Vic, knowing that they were in a seller's market; normally they could not secure enough supplies within Catalonia proper and had to go farther afield to buy, to Roussillon, Valencia and Sardinia, sometimes to North Africa and Sicily itself. The common people of the city seemed to have regarded the corn supply as the *consellers'* main responsibility; suspicions of inefficiency or corruption in the regulation of the corn market was the commonest cause of disorder in the streets of medieval Barcelona. The great merchant houses of Perelada and Fiveller, who helped to finance the conquest of Sicily, appear to have had a more ambitious project in mind than merely securing supply. Together with the count-king himself, who seems to have been commercially enterprising as well as chivalrously adventurous, they had been trading in grain on such a scale as to suggest that they aimed at a dominating interest, perhaps near control. The common aspiration of merchant communities in the premercantile age was to become a 'staple' – that is, a monopolistic centre of distribution of some valuable commodity. This was usually possible only with goods of high value, small bulk and limited provenance; thus Venice became a staple for oriental spices, Genoa for alum and mastic. It may not have seemed impossible, however, for

Barcelona in the late thirteenth and early fourteenth centuries to aspire
to be something like a staple in the western Mediterranean for the
most elemental and universal product of medieval trade. With the
seizure of Sicily, the main granary and centre of production, such an
ambition must have come very close to real fulfilment. In the event,
Catalan merchants never got more than preferential terms of access to
the Sicilian grain-market: but that alone was enough to justify the
enthusiasm with which – as we learn from Muntaner – the Catalans
received the Sicilian embassy that came to invite Pere to invade.

Sicily was too big and too populous to be profoundly 'Catalanised'
by the conquest. Except for its kings and a few élite families, introduced
into fiefs carved from the royal demesne or wrested from earlier
generations of foreigners, most of Sicily remained an island *sui generis*,
untouched by personnel or institutions from Spain. Even the intruded
Aragonese aristocrats rapidly became Sicilianised and intermarried
with native families. Syracuse, Agosta and Catania acquired big
colonies of Barcelonese merchants, and the maritime customary law
of Barcelona was adopted there. Catania was one of the many places
outside Catalonia where Muntaner claimed one could learn both to
esteem Catalan virtues and to speak the Catalan language. Regulations
for these communities made by fifteenth-century kings showed that
they, too, tended to blend into the indigenous background as a result
of local marriages. The island was normally ruled, until 1409, by a
cadet line of the House of Barcelona; though the fraternal loyalties
which loosely bound the Aragon-Catalan 'empire' worked, on the
whole, surprisingly well, this meant that there were some passages of
friction which were prejudicial to the privileged position of Catalan
merchants in Sicily. And though profits were made from the Sicilian
connection, some Catalan resources had also to be sacrificed periodically, to defend the island from Angevin irredentism and to wage war
on the Italian mainland for the recovery of the 'second Sicily' in Apulia
and Calabria, traditionally united to the Sicilian crown. Despite these
limitations, however, Sicily was a vital part of the outworks of Barcelona's medieval trade – supplying grain, defending the gateway to the
Catalan 'lake' of the western Mediterranean – 'the head and protectress
of all the Catalans'.[22]

If Sicily illustrates the gentleness with which Catalan imperialism
could touch its victims, the next conquests revealed its most savage
face. The Sicilians had no difficulty in commanding Catalan respect.
The policy of the kings was more aggressive, the attitude of the
conquerors more contemptuous and the programme of colonisation

more radical in Minorca and Sardinia, and in both islands, in different ways, the endeavour failed. At the time of the conquests of Majorca and Ibiza, Minorca was left undisturbed, save for nominal client status and token tribute, as a Moorish vassal state; this was a common solution within the Iberian peninsula for Moorish states which could not be practically or profitably absorbed by Christian kingdoms. In the 1280s, however, Minorca assumed a new importance on the way to Sardinia and Sicily. It was an island of invitation to Barcelona's commercial rivals, the Pisans and Genoese, as well as an embarrassment to the Aragonese kings' crusading propaganda. It offered an opportunity for the young count-king Alfons II to demonstrate his mettle. Its conquest in 1287 was the most brutal in the history of the Aragonese monarchy. The great bulk of the population was rounded up and sold into slavery, temporarily glutting the markets of Ibiza, Valencia and Barcelona. Minorca was not an attractive island to settlers: without the mineral resources of Ibiza, it was too small to support any life that was not laborious, precarious and poor; the dispersal of the native labour force and the break in the continuity of agricultural exploitation made the prospects even bleaker. The demographic holocaust could not be made good. A century after the conquest, the wreckage remained. In 1370, houses abandoned by the Moors and never reoccupied were in a state of collapse. Shortage of the means of life was chronic; every corn-bearing ship that stopped at Minorca was obliged to offer its cargo for sale. Nor were the means of civilisation in greater abundance. In 1358, a lieutenant-governor of the island was killed by a blow on the head from a candlestick in a brawl at the high altar of the island's main church. Such was the tenor of life in this showpiece-centre of Aragonese imperialism.[23]

Barcelona's fate became inseparably entangled with that of the last Arago-Catalan island conquest. Aragonese rulers long coveted Sardinia. A constant anxiety of members of the House of Barcelona was their own conviction of the paucity of the patrimony. Pere III complained that neither he nor any of his ancestors possessed treasure. Catalan poverty and avarice were mocked by Dante and were proverbially notorious. From the political consequences of poverty – the overweening truculence of noble leagues of 'unions' in Aragon and Catalonia, the threat of oligarchy – kings sought to escape, whenever their strength permitted, either by conquering lands with which to boost their resources of patronage or by stimulating commerce in order to generate alternative sources of wealth. All their conquests must be understood against this background, and none more so than Sardinia, which was an exceptionally large island – the world's largest, according to the mistaken authority of Herodotus – and which was endowed with peculiar commercial attractions. It was a land which, thanks to the wheatlands of Trexenta and Gippi, normally produced a surplus of grain for export. Martin V, appealing to the Barcelonese to continue the struggle in Sardinia nearly a hundred years after the conquest was begun, preyed on the citizens' anxiety about their food supply by reminding them of Sardinia's yield of wheat. Sardinia also produced commercial quantities of two products – silver and salt, about which Aragonese official sources were strangely silent in the period leading up to the conquest. It lay, moreover, athwart important trade routes and was fringed with communities of Genoese and Pisan merchants, staging posts on the way to the Maghrib. Pope Clement VI thought Genoese commerce could not survive without access to Sardinia. After the subjugation of the emporium of Majorca and the granary of Sicily, the acquisition of the staging posts of Sardinia could almost be seen as a logical next step in the evolving protomercantilism of the Crown of Aragon. The western Mediterranean might even have become a Barcelonese gulf in the same way as the Adriatic had become 'the gulf of the Venetians'. Basic commodities of the western Mediterranean might have become subject to Catalan domination, if not control, as those of the eastern Mediterranean almost passed under the control of Venice. At the very least, it would be appropriate to see the military and naval strength of the kings of Aragon reinforcing the claims of 'excluded' merchant communities of the Tyrrhenian Sea, and especially that of Barcelona, to break into an area of established Genoese and Pisan preponderance; hence the main contributions to the conquering host came from trading cities – Barcelona, above all, Valencia, Tortosa, Tarragona.

Alfons III's vision of Sardinia, however, encompassed more than merely commercial exploitation. The displacement of Pisa's entrenched merchant quarters and the substitution of Catalans around the coast might have been practicable within the limited resources of Alfons's monarchy. To challenge the Genoese as well, and thereby drive them into an alliance with Pisa, was foolhardy. To attempt a wholesale takeover of Sardinia's wild and intractable interior and turn it, like Majorca, into an overseas extension of Catalonia was a fantasy induced by the traditional land-hunger of an impoverished dynasty. Beyond the luxurious, bourgeois toeholds of the foreign merchants, Sardinia was a savage land. There were only two sources of authority in the interior: the predatory sway of a few great families, of foreign

– generally Genoese – origins or affiliations, who exploited large tracts of land and exacted tribute or imposed jurisdiction in villages on or around their domains; and the intense, local loyalties of a society that was still tribal in its configurations. Indeed, the Catalans regarded the Sards as semi-bestial barbarians, whom they had no compunction in enslaving and whose Christianity they declined to acknowledge. The only formal institutions which spanned the whole island were the four 'Judiciates', divided between the Pisans and monopolising power that made the island élite, and especially the most powerful of them, the House of the Judges of Arborea, cooperate for a time with the Catalans. But the realisation that they had exchanged a present nuisance for a putative master soon induced a series of rebellions, not quelled for a century, which bled Catalan energies and wasted Barcelonese wealth. Sardinia was the 'Spanish ulcer' of the House of Barcelona or, even more appositely, Aragon's Ireland. Alfons's health was said to have been undermined by the Sardinian air, polluted, as the wars of conquest and resistance dragged on, by the exposed corpses of so many victims.[24] The Barcelonese merchants who were the paymasters of the war would come to sympathise with Petrarch's Syphax, who wished he had 'forever left that evil island to the pestilential wind and sea'.[25]

The militant hand of Arago-Catalan imperialism was revealed early. Sassari (Sásser in Catalan), for instance, was one of Alfons III's first attempts at creating a comprehensively Catalan colony. The native Sards were peremptorily and informally dispossessed by their con-querors in 1329. The king immediately set about the rationalisation and formalisation of this takeover by means of a *compartiment* or division of spoils. Between 1330 and 1333, 166 fees, comprising proprietorship of land, rights of jurisdiction and the obligations of knight-service were distributed, at least on paper, with 1,393 smaller plots of which only the use-right was granted away. Of the beneficiaries whose provenance is recorded, almost half were Catalans, most of them from Barcelona, nearly a third Valencians, over ten per cent Roussillonese and nearly five per cent Majorcans. Though the terms of the distribution, with the accent on knights' fees, were feudal, the breakdown of the settlers by designation reflects the commercial priorities of the conquest. Of those specified, 163 were merchants and their grants were on average worth double the mean. A large number of valuable grants made in 1330 went to members of a consortium who proposed to establish a silver foundry. The only other substantial categories were artisans (155), peasants (thirty-four), members of the liberal professions (thirty) and public officials, chiefly notaries (twenty-nine).[26]

The policy of 'Catalanisation' was pursued and extended with extraordinary tenacity. To some extent, like the Norman Conquest of England, it was conceived as a sort of tenurial revolution, to be achieved by introducing the language of feudalism into a society that in the past had barely known it. Fees were granted *iuxta morem Italiae*: the recipient had to reside in his fief (so that the beneficiaries were aristocratic cadets rather than great mainland lords), render a portion of its produce to the king in war, maintain fortifications and provide knight's-service. Fiefs were heritable in the main line but not alienable without royal leave; the lord's rights of jurisdiction were generally limited to civil cases. To the kings of Aragon, accustomed to remote overlordship of great fiefs that were virtual territorial principalities, in which royal rights were ill defined and reluctantly admitted, this system must have represented – had it worked in practice – a vast accession of power. By 1335, thirty-eight great fiefs had been created for Iberian nobles, and the native chiefs and *judices* had been turned into feudatories. But the latter were not easy to buy off. The Doria, in the north, were in almost continuous rebellion. The Arborea, driven by the insistent imperialism of Alfons's successor, the splenetic and combative Pere III, rebelled in the early 1350s and never returned to wholehearted allegiance. At Pere's court, elaborate plans were drawn up for the dispossession of the native aristocracy and the wholesale deportation of the commonalty as slaves. Sardinia would become a feudal Utopia, paying for itself. The holding of the first intended victim, the Donoratico family, would yield enough revenue for fifty knights; two years later, the Pisans could be eliminated, then the Doria and the Arborea. These plans were never implemented but Sards were shipped off, enslaved in thousands, especially between about 1370 and the end of the last revolt in 1442. Abused for the replenishment of depopulated Minorca, they made that island ungovernable. Most had to be repatriated as the price of peace.[27]

The only lasting colonial achievement to emerge from this febrile royal programme was the settlement by Pere III of the port of Alghero (Alguer in Catalan) which remained defiantly Catalan-speaking until the present day. Even this success was procured with difficulty. Many beneficiaries renounced their grants rather than take them up. Absentees had to be punished. Widows and bachelors were compelled to marry. For a while, in the late Middle Ages, Alghero, Sassari and Cagliari (the last gradually and bitterly extracted from Pisan grasp) were a sort of Catalan pale, beleaguered enclaves surrounded by a frequently hostile and largely indomitable world.

It is not clear that it was ever the conquerors' policy to exclude foreign merchants from Sardinia altogether. On balance, it seems more likely that they would have been satisfied with restricting or eliminating rival merchant quarters and encumbering foreign trade with prejudicial tariffs. But they never got the chance. Every rebellion forced concessions to Genoa or Pisa. The Catalans were paying heavily for what was, in effect, a commercial and political condominium.

Most of the crippling cost seems to have been borne by the merchants of Barcelona, who, for the sake of commercial footholds on the coast, were prepared to finance the acquisition of an empire. At first they did so with something like enthusiasm. In the reign of Alfons III only the clergy opposed the war. When the city voted 10,000 lliures 'for the defence of Sardinia', the clergy refused to pay their share and excommunicated the *consellers* for demanding it. In 1333, the notorious rabble-rousing preacher, Fray Bernat Puig, exhorted his flock to pray for the king to win victories 'against infidels but not against Christians'. A moment of alarm occurred in 1334: despite the fact that the *consellers* had urged the king to act energetically to finish off Sardinian resistance, they seem to have delayed payment of the 30,000 sous collected in Barcelona by order of the Corts for horsemen and bowmen for the Sardinian expedition; and when the four ships thus supplied did at last sail, they were seized by Genoese on their way to the island. Still, Barcelona's record of contributions to the Sardinian war was generally impressive. In 1335–6, as well as sending contingents and supplies paid for directly by the city, Barcelona supplied the count-king with 4,000 lliures cash for Sardinia.[28]

By the early fifteenth century, the disillusionment of Barcelona was complete and in the Corts of 1408–9 the merchants called for withdrawal from the Sardinian imbroglio. The modified victory – at least, the lasting peace – won by the Catalans in the next generation came too late. The Sardinian adventure contributed to the exhaustion of Catalonia's powers of expansion and to the diminished commercial prominence of Barcelona in the fifteenth century. In 1972, amid much rhetorical Catalan nostalgia, Alghero was officially twinned with Tarragona; the return ceremony on the Spanish mainland had to wait until after the death of General Franco so that the Catalan language could be freely used and Catalan nationalism freely indulged. It was the last feeble echo of a great imperial effort of the Middle Ages.[29]

Maghribi Protectorate, Barbary Trade

It has often been said that the island-conquests of the House of
Barcelona stretched eastwards, like stepping stones across the Mediterranean, towards the lands of saints and spices. Yet they also strew the
way south, towards the Maghrib, the land of gold. However alluringly
the islands may have pointed to Jerusalem, they also constituted a sort
of system of outworks of the Maghribi coast – a defensive line, drawn
across the sea, guarding routes of access to north-west Africa and
threatening to envelop it. Potential bases for a mainland conquest,
they were also, perhaps more importantly, strategic *points d'appui* of
economic warfare, for they lay across the African trade routes of other
trading states.

The nature and extent of the count-kings' commitment to political
involvement in the Maghrib are not easy to define. It is normally
assumed, for instance, that the most impressive armada, that launched
by Pere II against Collo (Alcoll in Catalan) in the emirate of Tunis in
1282 was merely a feint for the conquest of Sicily. Pere may have been
an opportunist, happy to strike at more than one target as the occasion
arose. But the very intensity of his propaganda, while it may disguise
his real intentions, testifies to the strength of Catalan feeling about the
Maghrib. The chronicle ascribed to 'Bernat Desclot' was written,
probably within a few years of the event, by a royal household official
who helped to prepare the expedition. His account can be taken
to represent the 'official' version: the count-king's desire to seize
Constantine (Barbary's great inland market) 'and subdue all Africa'
was genuine, and espoused for the honour of God and the sake of all
Christendom; if the Pope lent him aid he would stay in Africa, and
the barons professed themselves ready to send for their wives and
children. The next chronicle in the Catalan tradition is that of Ramon
Muntaner, an 'artless', impassioned and chivalrous writer who fought
in many of the campaigns he commemorates; with him the facts grow
more distorted and the propaganda more shrill. Muntaner's presence
in Sicily is not attested before 1300 and he seems to have played no
part in the conquest. He muddles the chronology and conflates the
count-king's achievements: Pere is another Alexander, who exceeds
Roland, Oliver, Tristan, Lancelot and numerous other heroes of
romance. The Saracens skulk and hide from him; the entire coast is
subdued. Muntaner's strength of feeling is more intense than that of
the chronicle of directly royal inspiration. The lost glory of the potential
conquest of Africa afflicts him deeply. His bitterness against the Pope

is more acute than his predecessor's. However unrealistic the ambition, and however faint of heart the kings, African conquest was a powerful image in the mental world of Catalan knights of the late thirteenth and early fourteenth centuries. The lions that strutted in the Aragonese royal menagerie implied unrealised hopes of exotic dominion, like the giraffes of the court of the Ming.[30]

Whether or not Africa was genuinely Pere's objective when he landed there in 1282, some form of protectorate, albeit not of formal mandate, in the Maghrib does seem fairly consistently to have been sought by the count-kings in the late thirteenth and fourteenth centuries. The history of the quest can be traced in a series of treaties between the count-kings and north African rulers, especially those of Tunis, in the century after St Louis's Tunis crusade. Sicilian merchants had been protected by agreed conventions in al-Mahdīya since the late eleventh century. Commercial treaties had been common since the early twelfth century between the Almoravid emirs and their successors on the one hand and the merchant city-states of western Mediterranean Europe on the other. The first such agreements may have been made by word of mouth alone, for some of the earliest examples are known only from the records of chroniclers. From the 1180s it was common for such agreements to be written down in synallgamatic form and from the 1230s onwards survivals are numerous. It is possible that the count-kings, or their Catalan subjects, made such agreements in the early to mid-thirteenth century. Certainly they had customary trading and residential rights in various Barbary ports by the 1250s.[31]

Their treaties from 1271, however, exceeded the terms of these traditional trade conventions and continued to differ sharply from subsequent agreements made by other Latin states in north Africa. They all had a partly political character and in many cases they imposed tribute or at least some unreciprocated payment to the Crown of Aragon from the north African parties. This tribute went under various guises. In the treaty made between Jaume I and Tunis in 1271, for instance, it appeared as a payment for the loan of a mercenary militia. A similar line was taken in the treaties of 1274, 1309 and 1323 with Morocco and 1309 with Bejaïa. In each case, the payments were for troops or galleys or both. The Tunisian treaty of 1301 represented the tribute as compensation for a despoiled shipwreck. In some cases, after the Aragonese occupation of Sicily, the claim to tribute from Tunis appeared as a continuation or revival of the sums demanded or extorted by Sicilian rulers since Hohenstaufen times: the very 'protection money' which had been withheld by al-Mustansir from Charles of

Anjou, helping to provoke St Louis's crusade. The tribute specified by Pere II in 1285, for instance, was called '*lo trahut de Sicilia*'; it continued to be paid to the count-king Alfons II (Alfonso III of Aragon) even after the separation of the kingdoms, when his brother ruled in Sicily. In many treaties the tribute was perceived as a return on the trade of subjects of the Aragonese monarchs. The treaty with Bejaïa of 1314, for instance, agreed a payment to the count-king of 5,000 ducats a year from the yield of 'the cloths and merchandise which pay duty in the customs house of Bejaïa'. The treaties of 1314 and 1323 with Tunis allotted to the king 4,000 ducats a year out of the dues paid by his subject. In all such cases, the emirs were bound by the treaties to pay the full tribute even if the value of business from the Catalan merchants was insufficient to cover it.[32]

The precedents for exactions of tribute from north Africa may be sought in various directions. It was normal for medieval Hispanic Christian states to mulct Moorish neighbours for protection money. Frequently this tributary relationship was a prelude to conquest. The rights of legitimate 'reconquest' which Hispanic Christian kings claimed from the Moors were universally assumed to extend into north Africa. The Sicilian tribute was specifically invoked by Sicily's Arago-Catalan legatees. And there may have been longstanding commercial precedents for the trading partner-state to reclaim a share of customs revenues from the Barbary ports: as early as 1161, the terms agreed between the Genoese and the Almohads stipulated the return to Genoa of a quarter of the dues paid in Bejaïa. In any event the Aragonese treaties can hardly be read as mere commercial conventions. They represent political stake-claiming, a stage towards the establishment of a protectorate by the count-kings.

The commercial relations regulated by these treaties seem to have been well established by the mid-thirteenth century. In 1227 Jaume I granted the shippers of Barcelona the right of first refusal of any cargo bound for Ceuta. In Tarragona in 1243, a special toll applied to exports to Barbary, though Saracen captives are the only commodity mentioned. By the mid-century, the Catalans maintained consuls in Tunis and Bejaïa. The *funduk* – the community of Catalan merchants – operated in Tunis throughout St Louis's crusade. A list of sailings from Majorca survives for the period 25 January to 18 March 1284; departures from Barbary, leaving once every other day on average, and including some vessels from Genoa and Barcelona, represent two-thirds of the total, although in most cases tonnages are small compared with those of ships making longer runs. Building on these

thirteenth-century origins, the Catalan traders of the fourteenth century, their position enhanced by the political activity of their monarchs,
developed their commerce and entrenched their merchant-colonies
throughout the Barbary coast. By the 1320s, at least 150 Catalan
subjects were making roughly annual trips to Barbary.[33]

Some of them – and probably all those who penetrated the interior
– were Jews. The count-kings had a relatively large number of Jewish
subjects, partly because they attracted and protected them when they
were persecuted elsewhere. They played conspicuous roles in royal
service: until the confirmation of ancient liberties obliged the king to
discharge them from high office in 1284, the brothers Joseph and
Moses Ravaya, for example, were architects of the financial success of
Pere II, liberating him from reliance on representative institutions and
raising money for the conquest of Sicily. Jews had natural advantages
in the Barbary trade. They could elude the restrictions to which
Christian merchants were subject in Muslim cities. They could set up
house outside the appointed quarter. They could gain access to the
markets of the interior, where every European merchant wanted to
trade. Travelling between communities of their co-religionists,
equipped with some manual for Jewish travellers, such as Benjamin
of Tudela's *Itinerary*, they could go far afield unchallenged, even
(when not obliged to wear distinctive garb) unobserved. The fraternal
basis of Jewish family businesses made it possible to maintain
'branches' at both ends of a trade route, in mutually hostile lands. The
Jews were pitiably vulnerable to discrimination and persecution in
Christian countries, but were never successfully excluded from
Barbary.[34]

A remarkable insight into Barcelona's Barbary trade in the fourteenth
century is given by a merchant's manual (analogous to the *Pratica
della Mercatura* and other surviving Italian manuals) compiled in
Catalan, probably in Barcelona, in 1385.[35] Intended, like its Italian
counterparts, to provide instruction in the trader's 'art' it is a self-
consciously didactic work, opening with an adumbration of the perfect
merchant. Almost every noble, even kingly virtue is stressed. The
emphasis on the importance of good faith is reminiscent of the self-
perception presented by the *Book of Deeds* of Jaume I, who kept faith
even with Moors and was taken on trust by them, that only the chivalric
touch seems wanting to make the ideal merchant a regal figure. His
'art' is not an esoteric one. After the didactic section, the work goes
on to convey practical information with concision and clarity. It is an
unusually rich source: 207 types of merchandise are mentioned, of

which 146 are described – far more than in any of the Italian handbooks. The book's title, *Llibre de conexenses de spícies e de drogues ed de avissaments de pessoas, canes e massures de diverses terres (Book of Knowledge of Spices and Drugs and of Information on the Weights and Measures and Capacities of Divers Lands)* portends concentration on spices and on the Levant trade. Indeed, these receive their due attention. But the distribution of the material reflects unambiguously the African priorities of Barcelonese trade. At least seventeen Maghribi ports are mentioned – more than in Italy, Flanders, Castile or the Levant. The concentration on Barbary toponyms is greater than for any other area, save Catalonia and Provence.

But the most detailed revelation of the document is its detailed study of the customs tariff of Tunis and of the commodities traded between Tunis and Barcelona. Two items are conspicuous by their absence: first, Sardinian salt was an important product for Catalan carriers who shipped it all over Mediterranean Europe; yet despite the importance of salt from elsewhere in the Saharan gold trade, none of it seems to have found its way to Tunis and, apart from silver, the only Sardinian commodity demanded in the Maghrib, it seems, was cheese. Secondly, the omission of Barbary wool is equally surprising: it was a traditional export of the region and had played an important part in the commerce of Majorca during the period of Majorcan independence between 1276 and 1343. The only reference to Barbary fleeces in the *Llibre* is slighting: '*aquestes son avols* [these are contemptible]', says the compiler.

Grain is singled out as the most important of 'the goods which go from the said place of Tunis'. This is what one would expect from other sources; grain and fodder were exempt from customs duties in almost every treaty imposed on north African rulers by the Aragonese in the fourteenth century. Throughout the late Middle Ages, the Maghrib remained a net exporter of grain, though the *Llibre* also shows the Catalans carrying a staple starch to Tunis in the form of rice – chiefly, no doubt, from Valencia. Other foodstuffs exchanged were gastronomic delicacies or rare flavourings or aromas, many of them entering Tunis chiefly for re-export: every kind of saffron, liquorice, lavender, pepper, sultanas, cream of tartar, three kinds of nuts and wine. The book's evocation of the fig trade is particularly resonant: Murcian figs from Alicante, white figs from Morocco or Majorca, figs from Valencia or Denia, all imported into Tunis with no mention of re-export, are treated as separate products and subject to different tolls. More than a delicacy, they were a major foodstuff – almost a staple product when grain was short. At a humbler level, Tunis imported cheese and exported oils, fats, semolina and the products of apiculture.

Evidently, Barcelona's biggest market in Tunis was for finished textiles. Sixteen distinct types of cloth are enumerated as well as Alexandrian linen. Leather and cotton were purchased in Tunis. The textile trade supported lucrative exchanges of dyestuffs and other products employed in the textile industry. At least eight sources of dyes are mentioned, together with *gleda*, a gritty substance used for cleaning fleeces. Tunis also required lacquer, hemp rope and paper. Human cargoes were not negligible. The *Llibre* refers to *testes*, which perhaps means slaves (rather as one might speak of 'head' of cattle), and lists 'Christian captives' among the other merchandise with no sense of incongruity. Ransomed Moors are not mentioned in exchange, although they figure in Catalan customs schedules of the thirteenth century. The only other major category comprised metals: the compiler of the *Llibre* expected his countrymen to take silver, tin, lead and copper to Tunis. In exchange, they would export the most lucrative single commodity of the Barbary trade: gold, ready coined in the form of 'Moorish ducats'. Tunis imported gold in the form of thread, but the only other finished metal product to feature among the imports is hawks' bells; these were typical of the small items of truck that might have been traded on from Tunis along the Saharan gold road. Analysis of the commodities mentioned in Aragonese treaties with Tunis yields a similar picture, albeit less complete than that of the *Llibre*, with emphasis on grain and gold.

Further confirmation can be drawn from notarised commercial shipping contracts for Barbary voyages from Barcelona. These survive in considerable numbers from 1239 onwards. In the early years of the trade, it was necessary to take gold to Barbary to make purchases; this is also suggested by the fact that Jaume I began minting 'Arab' coins of gold for the Levantine and Maghribi trades in the 1230s. But evidence of the practice disappears from surviving contracts after the 1270s. Generally the commodities specified in the thirteenth-century evidence are reminiscent of those of the *Llibre*: predominantly textiles, wine, dyestuffs and figs are exchanged for leather, wax and gold. There were, of course, also clandestine trades not reflected in the records: the fruits of contraband and piracy, and above all the illicit sale to Muslims of arms of Christian manufacture. It is reasonable to guess that the arms traffic contributed to the flow, from Africa to Barcelona, of gold.[36]

Despite fluctuations in the precious metals market, gold could almost always be traded with advantage across the western Mediterranean throughout the fourteenth century. The story of the Majorcan Jew who borrowed forty gold dinars, valued at thirty silver Majorcan sous, in Tunis and sold them for fifty sous on arrival in Majorca may not be literally true; but it illustrates the point. The silver price of gold was generally higher on the northern than on the southern shores of the Mediterranean. In 1330, the widely employed north African unit of account, the besant, was reckoned at 1.5 grams of gold or fifteen grams of silver. This ratio of 1:10 may be taken as normal. The comparable norm in Christian Europe was not as high as the tale of the Majorcan might suggest, but in the markets of Valencia, for instance, a ratio of 1:13 was average in the fourteenth century. Towards 1350 it was 1:10.5 in Naples, 1:11 in Florence. In Portugal in 1383 a ratio of 1:11 prevailed. Fluctuations of supply and demand were not necessarily unfavourable to the gold trade. In Barcelona, the gold price of copper and silver fell by about thirty per cent between 1280 and 1330. This reflected the merchants' success in obtaining large quantities of Barbary gold, but it might have ruined them. In fact, however, the effect was to stabilise demand for their merchandise by inducing a general adoption of gold coinage throughout western Mediterranean Europe. Into Sicily Pere II introduced the *pierrale d'oro*. The gold *reial* was coined in Majorca. Even Sardinia, traditional producer of silver, got the gold *afonsí* introduced by Pere III (Pedro IV of Aragon) in 1339. The gold florin became the basis of the coinage of the Crown of Aragon in 1346. The count-kings had a seeming Midas touch. Its source was Maghribi gold.[37]

THE ALLURE OF THE LEVANT

Barcelona's trading empire was a western Mediterranean affair. Beyond Sicily, the outposts of Catalan political strength were few and feeble; Barcelonese merchants were generally unprotected by the awesome power of armies and fleets, unfavoured by the habitual privileges which formed the context of their western Mediterranean commerce. Their commerce with Alexandria and Constantinople was therefore difficult to sustain; but its long duration and regular volume suggest that the effort was worthwhile. The count-kings vaguely waved a flag in the direction of this trade, promising, but never quite delivering help for a crusade; claiming, but never exacting, the allegiance of the Catalan

Company. They even challenged, without defeating, the Genoese in Byzantine waters. The texts which perhaps best express the nature of the count-kings' interest are the millenarian prophecies of Arnau de Vilanova (ob. 1311). Arnau was a prismatic character: an admirer of apostolic poverty, who loved the company of kings; a chiliastic prophet, with a taste for fame and an eye on posterity; a scientist of practical, even empirical mind, who could never resist the esoteric. Dismissed today as 'ravings', his works deserve to be taken seriously. He served as court physician to Pere II from at least 1281, intimate adviser of the king's sons, and *soi-disant* interpreter of the dreams of Jaume II and of the 'black sheep' of the House of Barcelona, Federico II of Sicily. Arnau was therefore well placed to reflect and perhaps to influence the self-perceptions of his masters: he retained the confidence of Jaume until about 1308 and of Federico until his death. He dabbled in every abstruse art. From physic he passed to alchemy and from astrology to divination. This last art had been perfected in Sicily, where Arnau may have conceived his interest in the seminal prophet, Joachim of Fiore, who, nearly a hundred years before, had tried to chronicle in advance the last convulsions of human history: the rise of the Last World Emperor, the conquest of Jerusalem, the advent of Antichrist, the pontificate of an angelic Pope, the cosmic struggle, the Age of the Holy Spirit. From 1289, Arnau was a professor in the University of Montpellier (then a fief of the Arago-Catalan Kingdom of Majorca), in a milieu where Joachimite prophecy was studied and where there were numerous Franciscan 'Spirituals' – followers, that is, of St Francis, who evoked the founder's spirit, transmitted through his testament and the tradition of his friends, and who applied rigorously the doctrine of apostolic poverty. Though a layman, Arnau became saturated in the Franciscan spiritual tradition. Since many spirituals regarded their own movement as the embodiment or prefiguration of the Age of the Holy Spirit foretold by Joachim, these contacts probably reinforced his Joachimism.[38]

In 1292, Arnau began a series of writings which reflect these influences. His *De Tempore Adventus Antichristi* of 1297 – intended as the first part of a trilogy on the Antichrist – was the first of his visionary works to prophecy an eschatological role for the Arago-Catalan count-kings. In the *De Mysterio Cymbalorum*, written not later than 1301, this was refined into a programme: renovation of the church, conquest of Jerusalem, extirpation of Islam, unification with Byzantium, creation of a universal Christian empire with its capital in Sicily. Their crusading failures never fully deflected the count-kings from interest in this programme, or from fascination with the East.

When it seemed unlikely that they would ever make any conquests in the Levant, they campaigned peacefully to acquire some of the relics that sanctified oriental soil. Their piety, and its links with trade, are illustrated by the saga of the body of St Barbara. In 1327 Jaume II (Jaime II of Aragon, r. 1291–1327) wrote to the Sultan of Egypt, requesting a present of relics, including the remains of St Barbara or, at least, a portion of them. In 1328 a favourable reply was received in Barcelona by Alfons II, who, after securing papal approval, sent a gift of gerfalcons and fine textiles with a request that the Sultan convey the body of St Barbara and 'the arms of the Holy Simon' and arrange an exchange of captives. An unfortunate delay occurred when the count-king found that the ship was being dangerously overladen by Barcelonese merchants anxious to ship goods to Alexandria. Neither this, nor nine subsequent embassies, spread over the next two reigns, succeeded in bringing the holy relics out of Egypt, where the shrine of St Barbara remained to attract tourists and pilgrims into the next century.[39]

Trade with the Levant predated and outlasted the count-kings' oriental ambitions. Benjamin of Tudela observed vessels from Greece, Alexandria and Asia in the port of Barcelona in 1160. The first recorded Catalan trader in Acre was there in 1187. Catalan consulates were created in Modon in 1416, Candia in 1433, Ragusa in 1443; the last year was also that of a project for carrying spices to northern Europe via Barcelona. Sailings to Rhodes were common for most of the fifteenth century and into the sixteenth. The records of Levantine trade are most prolific, however, from the mid-thirteenth to the early fifteenth centuries, on routes via Alexandria and Constantinople and, later and more regularly, via Cyprus, Crete and Rhodes. Jaume I asked the Sultan for a consulate and quarter in Alexandria in 1262, and authorised the Consell de Cent to maintain a consul in Constantinople in 1268; it may have been concern for the Egyptian trade that made him withdraw from his promised crusade.[40] But Egypt and Byzantium were too often controlled by hostile powers, too thronged with competitors and, in the case of Egypt, too hedged with restrictions on trade with the infidel, ever to be reliable sources of supply.

Between the 1290s and the last quarter of the fourteenth century, Barcelona's trade with the Levant pioneered a new route through Cyprus which linked up with spice caravans to Beirut and Damascus, where the Catalans had consuls from 1347. The evidence is in commercial shipping contracts recorded by notaries in Barcelona, which reveal both the opportunities and the problems of the trade. Raw cotton and, above all, spices and drugs were demanded from the East. The contracts regularly mention pepper, mastic, incense, ginger, lacquer, cloves and sugar – which was an exotic condiment that formed part of the spice trade. To pay for them, however, was a struggle. Merchants speculatively sent all sorts of goods in the ships: finished textiles, rice, armour, oil, saffron, quicksilver, kohl and 'divers goods'; but even these desperately garnered miscellanea were never enough and almost every bill of lading specifies cash and silver, too. The experience of Joan Benet, whose accounts survive from a voyage he made from Barcelona to Famagusta in 1343, was probably typical. He sailed on behalf of fifteen merchants, who entrusted him with small amounts of kohl, quicksilver, rice, oil and saffron, which he had to sell at cost. The bulk of his outgoing cargo – more than eighty-six per cent – was in coin or silver bars and ingots. He brought back a fabulously rich hoard of exotica: 14,682 pounds of pepper and cinnamon, 12,788 pounds of sugar; 2,862 pounds of ginger, cinnamon flowers and cloves; unspecified amounts of cotton, dyestuffs, mastic, laudanum and borax. The return on the voyage averaged forty per cent before costs. But in the context of an adverse balance of trade, those profits had to be thinly spread.[41]

In and around the 1370s, trade with Byzantium seems to have revived and spread to other Greek ports, including Salonica and Ephesus. But the revival was short-lived. From 1382 to 1415 the documents are silent, and when, in 1415, the notaries' records again allude to trade with Byzantium, it is only to record its collapse; a large number of merchants who had sent a shipper to Constantinople with their cargoes exonerate him for his failure to sell, since they had heard that 'you are unable to shift the goods or the specie and cannot get the right prices for them from the buyers except in long instalments and on bad terms'.[42] The effects of Tamberlaine's rise disrupted commerce in the East, while shortage of capital in Barcelona made voyages ever more infrequent. The greatness of Barcelona's drive for a commercial empire consists precisely in its heroic, barely sustainable quality.

The Commercial Spirit

Neither geography nor any material 'factor' seems adequate to explain Barcelona's medieval commercial revolution. Like her modern industrial revolution, it was an achievement registered against the odds. It is tempting to ascribe it to a 'spirit' of enterprise and adventure; certainly, a marked commercial 'ethos' seems to have been among its effects. Most of the known evidence is late – of the thirteenth and fourteenth centuries. Its clearest exponent was the Gironese polymath Francesc de Eiximenis (c. 1340–1409), at first sight an unlikely encomiast of capitalist values. He joined the Franciscans in his youth; his attachment to the cult of poverty and the distinctive Franciscan vocation is suggested by what is known of his lost works on the seraphic rule; his devotional writing has an ascetic and mystical trend; his vision of Christ is dominated by images of the Passion. He seems, however, in the central years of his career in the 1380s, when he was teaching in Barcelona and Valencia, to have felt called to a mission to the big urban flock to which merchants belonged. This congregation was literate in the vernacular, but not in Latin, and anxious for a more thorough intellectual grasp of its faith than the Franciscans had traditionally offered to their poor congregations, who were presented with emotionally arresting images and morally improving tales. Thus Eiximenis wrote in Catalan rather than Latin and addressed his major work, *Lo crestià*, 'principally to simple laymen without great learning'. It was consciously a work of vulgarisation, largely homiletic in character intended to communicate the *summa* of academic theology in an assimilable form. The work was begun in Barcelona; the section on what might be called political philosophy, the *Regiment de la cosa publica*, was addressed to the city authorities of Valencia, his next port of call, and reflects his experience of the polity of Barcelona. It includes praises of merchants so lavish as to raise the presumption that he must have been extraordinarily satisfied with the audience of the sermons of which early drafts of *Lo crestià* were probably composed. For instance:

> Merchants should be favoured above all other lay people in the world, for the merchants are the livelihood of the land and the treasury of the public weal . . . They are the food of the poor, the arm of all good commerce, and the fulfilment of every matter of business. Without merchants, communities collapse, princes become tyrants, the young are lost and the poor are made to weep.[43]

Eixemenis even went on to compare merchants favourably with 'knights and patricians who live off their rents' who took no care, he claimed, of great charitable responsibilities. For 'only merchants are great almoners and good fathers and brothers to the common weal'. In one sense, this was a truism, for only merchants made a contribution to the public purse related directly to their wealth, since they enjoyed none of the fiscal immunity of the higher estates of nobles and clergy, and the goods they handled incurred tolls roughly representative of their value. In claiming them as great 'almoners', however, Eiximenis seems to be extolling their private virtues, too, and ascribing to them a noble record of private charity and public works. This notion of the essential nobility of a merchant's calling was an important ingredient of the self-perception of Barcelonese merchants in the high Middle Ages. They were called *nobiles negotiatores* if they engaged in long-range commerce, to distinguish them from vendors and peddlers. They liked to live in houses with towers; to judge from thirteenth-century house prices, a belvedere was a most sought-after feature. Their charitable endowments were in the aristocratic tradition of largesse, from the almshouse created with the bequest of 'Robertus the merchant' in 1009 'for the repose of his soul' to the purple altarcloth left by Jaume Albareda at his death in 1258 to the church of the Catalan residents of Bejaïa. The virtues enumerated as proper to the merchant in a commercial handbook of 1385 were based on those of knighthood and even kingship.[44]

Inside their houses, merchants' families led what might be called a selectively luxurious way of life. Their womenfolk had a spendthrift reputation. Eiximenis and his near-contemporary, Bernat Metge, both denounced poor wifely housekeeping as theft from one's husband's estate; satirising feminine vanity, Metge listed 'the foes that accompany a woman to the bath' – exotic unguents and accoutrements, including vulture's blood and kidskin face-flannels 'and innumerable other stuffs which would make you vomit if you heard of them'. But even Metge approved of bathing in the interests, he said, of cleanliness and enhanced female fertility; and on the whole Eiximenis regarded 'the Catalan nation' generally as 'eschewing superfluities'.[45]

The way of life encouraged by this bi-polar scale of values, in which austerity and consumption were both highly prized, emerges from the inventories of late medieval merchants' houses. Guillem Ferrer, whose goods were inventoried in 1398, was a trader to Sicily, Naples and Calabria. He had silver-gilt tableware and a pearl-studded collar. His house, in the traditionally aristocratic carrer dels Lledó had a dining room decorated with arms, reflecting the noble pretensions to which rich merchants were prey. His personal culture, typical of his class and times, is revealed by his books. Almost all of them were devotional aids, richly bound. His two psalters, his anthology of penitential psalms and his book of hours of Our Lady were titles almost universal in bourgeois domestic inventories of the period, but Guillem Ferrer's were written on kidskin vellum and bound in scarlet velvet. His other devotional books, all of which were in Catalan, were almost equally representative, including a narrative of the infancy of Christ and a collection of moral homilies on sin, confession and good exemplars. Highly revealing of the priorities of the sort of man who might have been a member of Eiximenis's congregation was a book called 'The Method which Every Good Layman may Follow in Ordering his own Life and Serving our Lord God'. His only secular titles were 'a big book about medicine' and a 'Breviary of Loves', which, though it had a prayer as a colophon, was probably a book of seculary amatory tales or verse; these were the written counterpart of the lightly gilded little chests in the Museu de l'Art de Catalunya, stamped all over with scenes from *contes fabliaux* and triumphs of love, with the legend, 'Love, have mercy on us, if you please'. His house was spacious, with a terrace – probably an upper-floor loggia – a writing-chamber, a 'chamber newly built' and a room for the slaves; but the henhouse and the business quarters on the ground floor struck more homely and commercial notes. Pere Salelles, at about the same time, lived in more modest circumstances in one of the extramural 'new towns', near the canal that ran north-east of the city walls; but even he had a devotional painting in his bedchamber. Pere Taberner, designated a furrier, which suggested that he was only a vendor or artisan rather than a *negotiator*, had just three rooms including his entrance hall and kitchen, but in his bedchamber, says the inventory, 'there are books'.[46]

If the fortune of Nicolau Bruguera, a rich merchant of the fifteenth century, is typical, the high bourgeois temptation to ape the aristocracy was limited by the sort of 'worldly asceticism' portrayed in these inventories. He felt no compulsion, it seems, to invest his fortune inland in the country. His main rural investments were in a vineyard and a garden with water for irrigation, perhaps intended to supply his table. Rustic property yielded only 18.1 per cent of his income from rents, compared with more than three-quarters from urban property (the balance consisting in interest from an unspecified mortgage). It is evident, however, that he was becoming more and more of a rentier and less and less of a merchant; that was a sort of drift, from active entrepreneurism, to low-risk, unproductive investment habits, which might be thought to characterise a change from a bourgeois to an aristocratic way of life.[47] It had been around for a long time in

Catalonia – Ramon Llull had denounced it in one of his didactic works in the very late thirteenth or very early fourteenth century.[48] In those days, the fabulous profits to be made from trade may have been a more important disincentive than the complaints of moralists: when, for instance, Joan and Raimon de Banyars established their banking business in 1261, Joan took out thirty-three solidi in rent and their total capital was 128½ lliures; when they renewed their agreement in 1264, the value of the rent had increased to seventy-four solidi and the capital to 202 lliures.[49] The vigour of capitalism seems, however, to have responded to opportunities rather than to have created them; in the sluggish commercial conditions of the fifteenth century the drift to a rentier way of life reflected the realities of the market as well as the aristocratic aspirations of the mercantile élite.

THE TENTACULAR CITY

The changes which made a metropolis of Barcelona also sucked the rural life-blood of Catalonia. The great conquests of the thirteenth century – of Majorca, Valencia, northern Murcia, Sicily, the successful conquests, rapidly effected, cheaply retained – relied on manpower drawn from the interior of the Crown of Aragon. They were the work of Aragonese and Catalan warlords and hobéreaus from the zone of mountains. As the centre of gravity of the count-kings' dominions moved towards the sea, the balance of population shifted. By the eve of the Black Death Barcelona contained something like twenty per cent of the population of Catalonia. The countryside had insufficient resources to keep the armies supplied with manpower or, perhaps, the city with food. Barcelona's grain supply was precarious at the best of times. In 1330 the city experienced its first serious famine. 'Maritime' Catalonia could not sustain the imperial career that 'mountain' Catalonia had launched. Never was a city more obviously the victim of her own success. Barcelona evinced the classic symptoms of the monster: corpulence induced by overfeeding, tentacles grown to uncontrollable lengths. As her intended victims slipped from her grasp, she turned to devour those who fed her. Between the hearth counts of 1365 and 1497, the population of Catalonia seems to have fallen by some forty-three per cent. The figures for Barcelona are harder to interpret, but the decline over about the same period cannot have been by more than twenty per cent.[50]

The long, costly imperial experience probably did Barcelona more

harm than good. Her 'era of difficulties' in the fifteenth century was
made worse by war. In the long run she achieved supremacy neither
in the western Mediterranean, nor even in the Crown of Aragon, where
Valencia overtook her in wealth and population in the fifteenth century.
Inside Catalonia, however, the period of imperial adventure coincided
with the establishment of overwhelming Barcelonese economic domination. Cities which had rivalled or exceeded her in their contributions
to the first act of empire-building – the conquest of Majorca in 1229
– like Tarragona and Lleida, were reduced by Barcelona's rise to puny
provincial status over the next hundred years. At the high point, just
before the Black Death, when Barcelona had perhaps over 40,000
inhabitants, Tarragona and Lleida were probably no more than a fifth
of her size. Already the courtly centre of Catalonia, Barcelona became
the principality's unchallenged entrepôt. Only in ecclesiastical affairs
– for Tarragona remained the metropolitan seat and Lleida the university city – was her monopoly of power and wealth imperfect.

The growth that dwarfed these rivals can be traced in a splendid
and confident history of building and 'urbanisation'. At the beginning
of the thirteenth century, growth outside the walls led to the area to
the north-east of Santa Maria del Mar, with houses that reached as far
as the modern sites of the Markets of Santa Caterina and the Born.
On the eastern side of the city, spreading settlement extended as far
as Santa Anna. Over the next 150 years, infilling brought the same
level of urban density to the whole of this area; new settlements – *viles
noves* – almost doubled the built-up area in the north-east around the
vast new foundation of Santa Caterina, along the waterfront to the
south and west as far as the Riera – now the main boulevard known
as the Rambla. In the same period all the major monuments of the
city were rebuilt and a dozen big new foundations added. Early
fourteenth-century records are full of traces of the tension between
neighbours caused by an urban boom. In 1328, for instance, a reclusive
contemplative called Sister Agnes, who had found peace in one of the
most undesirable spots on the city outskirts, found that even her street,
which led to the leper colony, was being invaded. The count-king
ordered these 'vile' newcomers expelled not only because, as Sister
Agnes complained, their presence was distracting, but also because it
was 'not decorous' that such people should live near a saintly woman
dedicated to the service of Christ. In 1329 the count-king himself was
a party in one of these disputes, when an extension to the dependencies
of the cathedral narrowed the street on which his palace stood; his
bailiff ordered the work to stop, but Alfons III let it be resumed when

he had a chance to consider the case. The efforts of the Jews to improve their cramped ghetto in the north-west quarter of the old city incurred further trouble in 1230; some of them had opened ventilators in the ghetto wall to let out the smell from their latrines and sewers, but the stink reached the nostrils of a royal scribe, Climent de Salavert, in his own house, and wafted as far as the portals of Santa Maria del Pi. The reversal of the work was ordered on the grounds not only that it was insanitary but also irreverent.[51]

The growth of the city demanded a new circuit of walls and a new centre. In 1314, the Consell had established two corn markets in order to serve the needs of an enlarged community, but both spaces, one by the north gate, the other by the harbour side, were too congested to cope with the traffic they attracted. In 1320, the Consell therefore decided on a new project of what can fairly be called town-planning: the creation of a vast corn market in its traditional location. Expropriation and demolition of existing buildings on the scale demanded was a complex and costly business, which seems to have got stymied for most of the next thirty years. In 1351 Pere III imposed a new levy on the grains sold in the market in order to provide funds for the project; numerous records of purchases in the area made by the *consellers* in October and November of that year represent a breakthrough in the city's efforts; the series of purchases continued into February 1352. By 1367, when the concerns of the *consellers* were concentrated on the problem of supplying adequate water to the new square, the development seems to have been complete. Although it was outside the old walls, the new plaça del Blat was the acknowledged centre of the city, from where the borderlines of internal administrative divisions were measured. It survived as a major topographical feature, a self-evident 'heart', until 1910, when the via Laietana was driven through it to clear some of the insalubrious of the city's slums and link the new commercial centre of the late nineteenth century with the port.[52]

Despite the vast and widespread scale of building activity and the chaos betrayed by the disputes between neighbours, the history of the plaça del Blat shows that it would be a mistake to think that Barcelona's expansion was unaffected by conscious planning. New building was tightly controlled in one sense, for every addition needed the specific permission of the count-king and contended with the caprice of the *consellers*. And although there was no overall plan, both authorities shared aesthetic assumptions derived from notions of an ideal city which helped to shape the townscape of the time. These assumptions were recorded in the late fourteenth century by Eiximenis. A city should be 'beautiful and orderly', divided – as Barcelona had been since Roman times – into four quarters by straight streets from gate to gate. On each main street should be a spacious square. Notions of rationality, space, clarity, light underlay this vision of the city. The streets and squares pertained to a conception of public spaces as settings for a secular liturgy – the ritual common life of the urban community, elaborated in meetings, processions, disputations, sermons and acts of justice. The fetid sub-world of lepers, prostitutes and other hazards to public health was to be relegated to an extramural twilight zone, downwind of the settled area.

This sort of vision had a real impact on fourteenth-century Barcelona. Although to a modern visitor the Barri Gòtic in the heart of the city seems a charmingly unspoilt example of a typically hectic medieval street-plan, the first of the rationalisations which have scored it with intruded thoroughfares took place in the 1360s, when the Prária Nova was created at the command of the count-king Alfons III and paid for by a special tax levied on the assessed 'benefit' brought by the road-widening scheme to the traders and residents. Rebuilding inside the walls – the cathedral, the episcopal and two comital palaces, the church of Sant Just – involved further erosion. In 1371 the *consellers* declared that new building had to serve the 'beauty of the city'. In 1391 a house was ordered to be demolished because it spoiled a view. Workers responsible for new constructions had to be 'wise and discreet persons'; like all building booms, medieval Barcelona's had its cowboys, whom the planners tried to control or exclude.[53] The explorer in the 'Gothic district' today sees an essentially fourteenth-century city. The cathedral is the dominant monument. Fragments from the thirteenth century survive. The cloister portal is transitional in feel; with its obscure carving of harpies and wild men, dragging a half-naked, pudgy-faced warrior, contrasts with the elegant high-Gothic of the interior, begun in 1298. The chapel of Santa Agata, in the count-kings' palace, was built by Jaume II (Jaime II of Aragon, r. 1291–1307). The first stone of the present church of El Pi was laid in 1322, that of Santa Maria del Mar in 1329.

Not even the Black Death, which killed half the city council and four of the five chief magistrates, could dent the city's confidence or interrupt the building boom. Never was the city so spectacularly embellished as in the reign of Pere III. He built the vaulted halls – more reminiscent of Italy than Spain – of the Saló de Cent in the city hall and the Saló de Tinell in the royal palace, with its martial wall-paintings. In his reign the cathedral choir was lined with gilded stalls. In 1378, at a cost of 17,000 florins, he reconstructed on a larger scale the shipyards where galleys for the Mediterranean war effort had been built since the reign of Pere I; the eight great bays can still be visited, on the frontier of the Raval and the port, housing the Maritime Museum, their height – just right for galley-building – measured by the nineteenth-century ceremonial galley there housed.

The entire urban area was amply enclosed by the most ambitious building project of all: the walls of 1359, which Pere III built to a project of Jaume I's of a hundred years before, when the intention had been to enclose enough land to make the city self-supporting in food during a siege. The new walls skirted the foot of Montjuic and reached the sea by the shipyards. A fragment survives, incongruously guarding the broad, nineteenth-century avenue of the Paral·lel, which represents just the sort of expansive urban ideal to which the rest of the walls were ultimately sacrificed. Pere was an invincibly optimistic monarch who always wagered against the odds: he was the Justinian of the empire of the House of Barcelona, enforcing his rights in Majorca, Sicily and Sardinia in defiance of every consideration of pragmatism; he backed an unlawful successor against the realm and the 'masses' against the aristocracy. The construction of the walls at a time of demographic disaster seems, however, an exceptionally reckless challenge to the force of circumstances, until one recalls that gestures of this sort – gestures of confidence in response to crisis – have been typical of the history of Barcelona and seem, indeed, to constitute a sort of unifying theme that underlies the experience of a thousand years of triumphs and catastrophes. Al-Mansur's raid was followed by a building boom. The original shipyard was built at a time of a naval stand-off that threatened the city's maritime future. The first artificial harbour would be constructed at a time of declining trade. The disasters of the mid-fifteenth century were succeeded by a defiant rebellion, the destructive siege of 1652 by the era of 'the Phoenix of Catalonia', the bombardment of 1842 by new plans for expansion, the tragic week of 1909 by lavish embellishment and unprecedented economic growth.

The optimism of the mid-fourteenth century seems, however, hard to justify with hindsight. Even in the moment of triumph symbolised by the rebuilt walls, Barcelona's was still a fairly modest circuit by international standards, enclosing 220 hectares; this can be compared with other city circuits built at roughly the same period: Siena's enclosed only 180 hectares, but those of Piacenza (290 hectares), Verona (380) and Louvain (395) were all substantially bigger. Brussels, where the walls were completed in 1357, enclosed 415 hectares and those of Paris, in 1370, were even bigger – almost exactly double the circumference of Barcelona's. Even this space took a long time to fill. With the exception of the 1450s, every decade from the 1360s to the 1470s was disfigured by a recurrence of plague.[54]

The first visitation had been in 1333; the obviously exaggerated estimate of the town council's scribe – 10,000 deaths – suggests the bewildering impact of an unaccustomed experience. In 1362, plague was still enough of a rarity to be met with extraordinary measures: the granting of a papal indulgence for its victims. By then, however, summer plagues were beginning to be accepted as a normal hazard of life; in the fifteenth century it was the rarer winter plagues that were most devastating – the toll of that of 1465–6, for instance, which is recorded on a daily basis in the municipal diary, added up to about 5,000. The resilience of the city is demonstrated by the hearth counts. At first sight, they make bleak reading; modest growth can be detected in the last quarter of the fourteenth century, when the spaces enclosed by Pere III's new walls began to fill up: thirteen per cent of the houses were in that area by 1400. Thereafter, however, the overall trend is of stagnancy or decline until the end of the century. Only in the context of the even worse cataclysm of Catalonia as a whole does Barcelona's plight seem less bleak. The principality, which counted over 100,000 hearths in 1365–70, had less than 60,000 in 1497. Barcelona had 6,695 recorded in the count of 1389, 5,765 in that of 1500.

Barcelona must therefore have been drawing population in from a moribund hinterland. Her economy seems to have been ill-equipped to employ and sustain these rootless newcomers. The social disorders of the late fourteenth and fifteenth centuries have to be understood against this background. The loss of economic opportunities took two forms: the decline of trade and the forfeiture of courtly status. As we have seen, oriental trade became stymied in the second decade of the fifteenth century. Only through Rhodes does Catalonia's Levantine business seem to have increased thereafter. The overall picture of decline is given by the plummeting yield of the tolls of Barcelona after the mid-1420s. Between 1410–20 and 1450–60 the duties on textiles and leather goods, for instance, fell by nearly a half; and that was before the dislocations of the civil war that began in 1462.[55]

Loss of trade was exacerbated by the departure of the court. For the spectacular growth of Barcelona in the thirteenth and fourteenth centuries had not been merely commercial in origin. The fortunes of Barcelona had been linked to the favour of count-kings since the tenth century. In one of Europe's most bureaucratically advanced monarchies, in an increasingly bureaucratic age, the status of a courtly centre brought increasing numbers of personnel and hangers-on into the city; it created demand not just on a scale unknown in other cities of Catalonia, but also of unparalleled refinement. The permanent institutions of justice, administration and finance were all housed in Barcelona and attracted money and supplicants from all over the principality. In the last years of the dynasty of the House of Barcelona, in the reign of Martí I (Martín I of Aragon, Martin the Humanist for his literary tastes, also miscalled 'Martin the Humane', r. 1396–1410), the city enjoyed its most lavish spell of comital patronage. Martí set up a proto-university; he brought a fragment of the True Cross to Barcelona from Avignon; he planned improvements to the city which would make the plaça del Rei into a regular *plaza*. He invited the anti-Pope Benedict XIII, Pedro de Luna, to whom the lands of the Crown of Aragon maintained allegiance during the schism of 1378–1415, to make his court in the old palace of the counts. The splendour of the Barcelona of his day is captured in the swirling forms and jewel-encrusted gold of a custodia of about his time, topped by a crown of oriental inspiration, in the cathedral treasury.

Abruptly, however, after his reign, royal favour was withdrawn. The kings of Castilian provenance or birth who ruled Catalonia for the rest of the fifteenth century showed little affection for Barcelona. The first of them, Ferdinand of Antequera (Ferran I in Catalonia, Fernando I of Aragon, r. 1412–16), left in disgust after he was obliged to pay a city fish tax from which the clergy and nobility were exempt, and never kept court in the city again. Alfons IV (Alfonso V of Aragon, r. 1416–58) preferred to live in Naples. Joan II (Juan II of Aragon, r. 1458–79) threatened to move the courtly centre to Tarragona. His successor, Ferdinand the Catholic (Ferran II of Catalonia, Fernando II of Aragon, r. 1479–1516), who was also, for most of his reign, King of Castile and had, admittedly, manifold responsibilities that kept him out of Catalonia, visited Barcelona only six times in the course of his long reign. Although the permanent institutions of the government of Catalonia remained in Barcelona, and although some of them – particularly the Diputació, the executive committee of the representative institution or Corts, and the Audiencia, the supreme tribunal – actually grew as a result of absentee-kingship, nothing, in late medieval Europe, could substitute for courtly status. Barcelona became a royal 'ghost town' with the memories and pretensions of a capital city, but not the reality. When Guicciardini visited the city in 1512, on a diplomatic mission from France, he immediately appreciated that loss of trade and of courtly status were linked in the background of Barcelona's decline: 'Commerce no longer flourishes as in days gone by, for the city is not as wealthy as formerly, especially since the moment when the court moved to reside in Castile.'[56] In the sixteenth and seventeenth centuries the 'widowed city' was a favourite self-image in Barcelonese texts.

THE REDISCOVERY OF THE ATLANTIC

Dynastic union with Castile threatened Catalonia's political independence and distinctive culture; it might, however, have enhanced her economic opportunities by opening up the vast markets of most of the rest of Spain and the maritime empire – bigger even than Catalonia's own – which Castilians were beginning to found in the Atlantic. Catalan traders were willing and, in some cases, anxious to share the benefits of Atlantic trade. A case in point is that of Rafael Font, denizen of Barcelona, who was a towering figure in the sugar trade of the Canary Islands in the early sixteenth century. All the Catalan traders in the islands in his day seem to have been business associates of his. He was classified by the governor of some of the islands as among a detested group of 'men so rich that they can well wait awhile without prejudice to their estate' for the recovery of debts he owed them. His business was based on a traditional Barcelonese pattern: importing textiles and exporting sugar; in 1505–7, however, he introduced huge quantities of gold and silver, insured in Barcelona, into the islands and advanced large sums to sugar producers. This may have been part of an attempt to pre-empt much of the sugar production, at least of Tenerife. He was obliged to operate, however, at the sort of disadvantage inflicted on all Catalan subjects in the dominions of Castile – vividly instanced when he was prosecuted in 1503 for 'extracting bullion from the realm' when he tried to move some of his profits directly to lands of the Crown of Aragon.[57]

The kind of restrictions that impeded Rafael Font's operations in the Canaries were multiplied in America, where formal prohibitions – however easily evaded – discouraged Catalan settlers and direct trade was banned. When Catalans were admitted to American commerce – via a Castilian port – in 1526, sporadic attempts to export Catalonian products to America were handled by growing numbers of Catalan residents in Seville, where the monopoly of the New World trade was first confined, and, later, in Cadiz. In the last quarter of the sixteenth century contracts for this sort of activity became numerous, perhaps because the use of Barcelona as a staging post on the bullion-route from Seville to Genoa gave the New World an unwontedly high profile in Barcelona's commercial scene.[58]

The civic iconography of sixteenth-century Barcelona was dominated by Hercules, the legendary founder, who established for the Renaissance city a classical pedigree. In the seventeenth century, Hercules yielded to Neptune. The displaced god suited a value-system that deified ideal prowess, which had prevailed in Barcelona during the supremacy of the patrician-class of *ciutadans honrats*, with their aristocratic airs and connections and investments in land. He gave way to the new or renewed prestige of commercial wealth. Barcelona's maritime vocation was pursued with renewed energy. Yet the seventeenth century produced few new transatlantic initiatives, though in 1637 the Catalan missionary Jaume Opí founded the settlement of Barcelona in Cumaná and in the 1680s Catalan Capuchins undertook the evangelisation of Guyana. The despatch of two ships a year directly to the Indies, if royal licence could be secured for such an infringement of a Castilian privilege, was one of the projects mooted by Feliu de la Penya for the economic regeneration of Catalonia in the same decade.

Barcelona's opening to the Atlantic finally came about as the result of a crisis. Denied access to the Spanish Atlantic empire, the Catalans had cultivated relations with British colonies in America. Long-range trade was a matter of the exchange of Catalan brandy for Newfoundland cod. The carriers were British or North American. War with England in 1739 froze the trade; by the mid-1740s the merchants of Barcelona were desperate. The first recorded recourse to direct trade with the American colonies was on a small scale: almond oil, usually consigned for Cadiz or Amsterdam, went direct to Vera Cruz on small vessels in 1743 and 1744. This suggests that the constraints on direct trade were economic as well as political: American products were small in bulk and high in value, including cacao, indigo, cochineal. The brandy that was Catalonia's most suitable product for the colonial trade had to be exported on a vast scale to make the return trip worthwhile, which meant in turn that the capacity of returning ships would be seriously underemployed. In 1745 the first effort to put together a viable mixed cargo on a big ship was organised by a consortium of leading merchants. The total value of the sailing was over 60,000 pesos. It fell into English hands at sea, but the venturers recovered much of its value from insurance and from negotiations with the London firm that bought the prize and sent it home with a profitable cargo of English textiles and china. The result was, on balance, encouraging. The next vessel to attempt the route carried cargo worth more than 100,000 pesos. The *Perla de Catalunya* (the soubriquet of *Nossa Senyora de Monserrat i Sant Antoni*) did not sail until after peace with England had been signed; but it is to the conditions of war, not the coming of peace, that the opening of Barcelona's direct trade with America must be ascribed.[59]

The cargo was extraordinarily diverse. The most detailed part of the records relates to a consignment of eight cases of books, containing 1,115 volumes. By far the greater part were multiple copies of theological textbooks, catechisms and the raw material for sermons, but there were titles intended for lay members of the Catalan community in New Spain: four copies of Feliu de la Penya's history of Catalonia, one of Zurita's chronicles of the Crown of Aragon, fifty of Serra's history of Montserrat, together with a hundred engravings of the shrine. The books were a good business, realising more than two-and-a-half times in Mexico what they had cost in Barcelona. Half the total cargo, in value terms, was brandy; nearly 5,000 pesos' worth was accounted for by nuts (almonds, walnuts and pine kernels). But industrial products were well represented: over 20,000 pesos in metal products, including some raw iron and steel but much fine cutlery, and a similar amount in textiles. The balance was mainly made up of smaller quantities of paper, glassware and candles. The overall return of thirty-six per cent for the merchants taking part seems an extraordinary success: unrecorded overheads reduced the profits, and the transport costs had been severe; but the experiment was amply justified. Unofficial direct sailings to America immediately became an established part of the commercial scene in Barcelona.

In the middle of the next decade, the Royal Company of Barcelona began trading directly with Santo Domingo, Puerto Rico and Margarita on privileged terms: cargoes had to be registered at Cadiz en route but not unloaded. Exports were duty-free. The Company was allowed to carry a further, limited trade to the far shore of the Caribbean. But under-capitalised and outflanked by unofficial private initiatives, the Company was no more than a curtain-raiser for free trade between Barcelona and the New World. In 1765, restrictions were lifted on trade to the Antilles and, later, to Louisiana; in 1778 the whole American empire was opened up. The investors in the Royal Company were active merchants who were able to benefit from the abolition of its privileges. Nevertheless, the unrestricted admission of the Catalans to the New World trade was equivocal in its effects. The Company had contemplated the founding of colonies to create permanent demand for Catalonian goods in America. Barcelona might have become the parent of a 'New Barcelona', which might have endured. The huge but wildly fluctuating inflows of cash from transatlantic trade would have been smaller, under the monopoly of the Company, but might, in the long run, have been better assimilated by Barcelona's economy.

As it was, the figures, however disfigured by war, represented a sudden and short-lived bonanza for Barcelona. In the years of peace between 1784 and 1792, exports to the New World climbed, with some fluctuations, from over fourteen million reals to nearly fifty-six million. The value of precious metals flowing into Barcelona over the same period increased by an even greater proportion, from over ten million to near forty-nine million reals. War impeded the trade but until the disaster of Trafalgar it remained robust. The basis of the trade was always brandy but Barcelona's industrialisation was stimulated, too. Over 37,800 pairs of shoes and boots went in 1792, over 48,000 pairs of scissors, 3,843 dozen hats, 214 umbrellas of local and eighty-two of foreign manufacture. Some of the proceeds were eroded by inflation, some consumed by a spending boom; but increased demand from one side, reinvested capital from the other, tugged and pushed at Barcelona's nascent and growing industries.

Commerce from beyond the Straits of Gibraltar already accounted for thirty per cent of Barcelona's trade in 1772–3. Few new shipping initiatives were to be directed towards the Mediterranean until the steamship era. The notable exception was the attempt to develop Barcelona's old Levantine and Maghribi routes. Treaties between Spain and the Ottoman Empire (1782), Tripoli (1784), Algiers (1786) and Tunis (1791) created opportunities for a renewal of commerce; but the ill-matched markets of the partner-states had a limiting effect. The Barcelonese launched a profitable grain trade based on cheap Maghribi supplies, but had little to offer in return as their textiles were underpriced by northern European manufactures. Much of even this modest trade was alienated to foreign carriers. An obscure scandal of 1802, when the American consul was accused of forging American papers for Catalan vessels bound for oriental ports suggests that foreign status could be an advantage. When the routes of Atlantic commerce were severed by a series of disasters from 1796 – war with England 1796–1802, Napoleonic invasion 1808, American revolutions 1810–24 – Barcelona's shipping had no well established role in her home waters to fall back on.[60]

The Steamship Age and the Artificial Port

By the dawning of the steamship age, Barcelona's seaborne trade was so far decayed – 'reduced to simple *cabotage*', according to the *Diario de Barcelona* in 1831 – that the new invention could appear more an opportunity than a threat. The city's first steamship factory went into production in 1836. The reach, however, of early steamship navigation from Barcelona was severely limited. The official city Guide of 1842 advertised regular sailings only to Tarragona, Valencia, Alicante, Cartagena, Almeria, Malaga and Palma and – outside the realm – to Gibraltar, Port Vendres, Marseilles and Genoa.

When the Suez Canal project was mooted in the 1850s, Manuel Duran Bas called for radical improvements to the port to enable Barcelona's long-range shipping, still sail-bound, to switch to steam; the prospect he urged was a competition with Genoa and Marseilles, which Barcelona could hardly have aspired to before. Ferdinand de Lesseps himself saw the canal project as a fillip to 'that great industrial city of Barcelona, which I love as a second fatherland and where all the best memories of my career and happy home life are focused'. Because Lesseps had been French consul in Barcelona, and the Empress of the French was of Spanish birth, Barcelonese observers at the opening of the canal felt particularly privileged, almost proprietorial. On 17 November 1869, the steamship *Pelayo* of Barcelona was the fortieth vessel through the canal, carrying aboard representatives of the Spanish navy whose own vessel, the *Berenguela*, was unable to sail till the following day. The din of their greeting, with gunfire salutes, flags and cheers inspired the correspondent of *Época* with a sense of how frightening a naval battle must be. At Ismailia, 'it was enough to be a European to be offered whatever one wanted'. Lesseps himself was particularly gracious 'when his guests were speakers of our language' and the crew of the *Berenguela* went away well feasted after serenading the Empress Eugénie.[61]

Duran Bas was right to forecast that the canal would transform the prospects for Barcelona as a trading port. The exploitation of these opportunities depended, however, on heavy investment in the improvement of the artificial harbour. The slow beginnings of the creation of a port date from an era of decline. Alfons IV had ordered work to begin in a decree of 8 December 1438, at a time when the volume of traffic was still buoyant, but when the lucrative cargoes, with the increase in wealth and population that followed them, seemed to be monopolised by Valencia or lost to non-Catalans. Though the need to improve the harbour was tackled in an optimistic spirit, resources were sparing and progress slow. The first stone was sunk near the convent of Santa Clara on 2 August 1439. The builders' efforts were outpaced by the destructive effects of the weather and the silt. In 1477 the Consell de Cent was complaining that all the work so far had been useless. A new steering committee was appointed, the project resited and on 20 September 1477 the king himself toppled the first stone of the new construction, marked with the sign of the cross, into the water. The engineer summoned to take charge fixed a limit of three years on the work; by 1484, with no end in sight, and the silt still building up around the mole, the Consell decided to build no further than the Isla de Mayans, only a little more than a hundred metres from the shore. The results were unsatisfactory: in 1495, part of the quay collapsed; in 1497 an old canal which debouched into the harbour was diverted in an effort to reduce the silting; meanwhile, discussion opened on the siting of a third mole.

No major new work was undertaken, however, until 1590, when the Consell and the technicians who advised the king were at logger-heads over whether to extend the mole or build a new one. The city fathers chose the former course in defiance of the king's engineers. By 1602 the extended mole was 177 metres long, and the storms still invaded the harbour, sinking three ships, for instance, in 1605; and the silt went on accumulating, closing the harbour mouth in 1616.

It was obvious that the problems of the harbour could only be met by a combination of dredging and building with constant effort and at fearful expense. By the 1660s, after the destructive political conflicts of the mid-century, when commercial projectors were beginning to recall 'the Catalan Phoenix' from the ashes, the political will to do something definitive and the capital investment required were at last forthcoming. In 1697, the mole was declared complete, at 200 metres long by thirteen wide, after the expenditure of 300,000 ducats. The result hardly seemed an improvement. Seventeen ships were lost in the storm-lashed harbour in 1715, when part of the mole collapsed. A further 'completion' was celebrated in 1723, and the work dragged on, like a popular singer's farewell, encored at increasingly long intervals. But though the harbour was never fully satisfactory, it was capable, with constant attention, of handling sufficient shipping to restore Barcelona to the first rank among Spanish ports and to an important place in Mediterranean trade. The eighteenth-century sequences of improvements can be said to have come to an end in 1822, with the completion of the last work to be done without the aid of steam dredging. By then, the mole had grown to 418 metres long and 33.44 wide, rising two and a half metres above the level of the sea.[62]

Hardly was the old harbour complete when Barcelona was surprised by the steam age. The first effect of steam power was on the dredging of the sand bar. In 1828–30 nearly fifty million cubic feet were dredged, creating a channel three metres wide. The transformation of Barcelona harbour into a refuge for heavy craft was celebrated in 1832 with the arrival of the forty-gun frigate *La Perla*. Barcelona's industrial growth, however, was such a stimulus to trade in the mid-nineteenth century, that demand for a modern port, equipped to handle ships of the world's heaviest tonnage, was soon irresistible. Josep Rafó's project of 1859, coinciding with the plan for the enlargement of the city commissioned by the municipality, and with the excitement of the future Suez Canal plan envisaged 3,274 metres of new docks and nearly two and a half million cubic metres of dredging. The project dominated the development of the port almost until the end of the century, when the floating dock system invented by Clark and Stanfield for Barrow-in-Furness, which had already been adopted for constructions as far apart as Valencia and Vladivostock, was taken up by Barcelona. In the ten years after its completion in 1903, the tonnage handled by the new floating dock rose from 43,551 metric tons to 226,085. Bilbao handled heavier volumes of goods, because of the nature of the heavy industries of the Basque country, but Barcelona remained ahead in terms of value. Her trade was dominated by the demands of her industry; between 1926 and 1931, for instance, her raw cotton imports exceeded in value those of all other goods put together. But it gradually became a commerce that linked most of Spain to most of the world.

With the recovery of her commercial role, Barcelona paradoxically lost part of her maritime identity. From 1848, when the railway opened, the port area was a grimy wasteland, cut off from the city by the tracks that led to Mataró. Barcelona turned her back on the sea or, as Joan Maragall said, seemed to 'flee' from it. At the cost of a piece of industrial-archaeological vandalism – the uprooting of Spain's oldest railway – the open embrace in which the great esplanade of the Moll de la Fusta enfolds the sea has now been restored by the most radical urban reform programme of recent years. Café-shades and potted trees have sprouted from the concrete. The change owes nothing to 'conservation' or historical reconstruction, everything to the tyranny of economic pressure. The spaces once devoted to the dockside needs of manufacturing industry have been colonised by 'leisure activities' and 'service industries'. The realm of producers has been conquered by consumers. The restaurants are there already. The artificial beaches, the Olympic village and the marinas are on their way.

III

'More Spanish than Yourselves':

Barcelona and Spain

> *On ets, Espanya? No et veig enlloc.*
> *No sents la meva veu entronadora?*
> *No entens aquesta llengua, que et parla entre perills?*
> *Has desaprès d'entendre an els teus fills?*
> *Adéu, Espanya!*

(Where are you, Spain? You're nowhere to be seen,
By me. And can't you hear my thundering voice?
Or can't you understand this language, perilously
Uttered? Or is it that you don't want to hear your
                                                    sons?
Farewell, Spain!)

> – Joan Maragall, 'Oda a Espanya'

> *Podrás dirlos, oh vila,*
> *La llansa la he penjada,*
> *Pus lo temps de mas guerras ja ha pasat.*
> *Y al Lleó de Castilla*
> *La guardia he confiada*
> *De mon escut ab sanch de un rei pintat.*

(Oh, town, you can tell them,
My lance laid to sleep,
That I've finished with fighting for good,
To Castile's guardian lion
Entrusting the keep
Of my shield, daubed with majesty's blood.)

> –J. Rubió i Ors, 'Lo gayté de Llobregat'

Es, pues, Barcelona la ciudad de España que más
desmiente las imputaciones de algunos escritores

extranjeros, empeñados en divulgar nuestra desidia,
abandono, pereza, falta de industria, y otras
gracias con que nos favorecen.

(Barcelona, then, is of all Spanish cities that which most belies the
aspersions of certain foreign writers who have made it their business
to spread images of our inertia, indifference, lack of industry and other
such compliments which they deign to pay us.)

– A. Ponz, *Viage de España*

The Emulous Capitals

'The trouble with Barcelona,' a distinguished Spanish statesman
once said, 'is that once or twice in every century we have to
send an army to besiege her from Castile.' There was truth
in this (as in all good jokes), which can be measured by the number
of times Spanish troops have been used in Barcelona to suppress
movements, in whole or part, of defiance of the Spanish state. In the
revolt of 1640–56, Catalan leaders abjured not only their place in the
Spanish monarchy but also their allegiance to the king; Barcelona was
the focal point of resistance and the scene in 1652 of a particularly
bloody and destructive siege. In 1705, Catalonia, asserting the status
of a sovereign principality, joined an international alliance against – in
effect – the rest of Spain and was forced into submission by a gruelling
siege of Barcelona in 1713–14. Of the many civil disorders that had to
be suppressed by troops during the nineteenth century, those of 1842
and 1856, in particular, were motivated in part by distinctively Catalan
causes: the demand for protectionist tariffs and the resentment of
political changes determined in Madrid. All the disturbances of the
early twentieth century took place against a background of agitation
in favour of a privileged status for Catalonia within the Spanish state:
the riots of the 'Tragic Week' of 1909, when control of the streets was
lost to the mob, were not concerned with specifically Catalanist issues
but came at a time when the Catalanist cause was accumulating
triumphs at the polls and any demonstration of discontent in Barcelona
was seen in Madrid as a threat to the unity of Spain. The last conquest
of Barcelona by a 'Spanish' army in 1939 came in the course of a civil
war waged, *inter alia*, by doctrinaire centralists against devolutionists
and separatists of different hues. In the hundred years before autonomy
was secured by the constitution of 1978, it had been proclaimed

unilaterally four times from the balcony of the Palau de la Generalitat.

Catalonia's past and potential statehood implies the status of a sovereign capital for Barcelona. The conflicts of Catalonia with Spain have been underlain by the rivalry of Barcelona with Madrid. This rivalry has always had a life of its own distinct from the history of Catalan nationalism. As the Barcelona paper, *La Vanguardia*, pointed out in 1881, one cause of Barcelonese resentment was that Madrid 'pretends that she is the whole of Spain';[1] in other words, she aspired in Spain to the sort of cultural and political hegemony enjoyed in France by Paris. Paris has also been Barcelona's favourite role-model for the last hundred years and more. Barcelonese contempt for Madrid's alleged cultural poverty – an attitude sustainable until the 1970s – has tended, moreover, to be accompanied or outweighed by resentment of pan-Spanish centralist politics. In the same year of 1881, the brilliant publicist of Catalan causes, Valentí Almirall, was the author of a pamphlet which proclaimed, in its title, 'War on Madrid'. Its pages, like those of Almirall's newspaper and all his references to the capital in speeches, are infused with hatred not just of the rival city but also of the régime it symbolised, which wavered between inefficiency and oppression. 'Madrid is a town composed – with some exceptions – of parasites who live on the proceeds of office, or who aspire to do so, a centre of immorality, of unproductive speculation, of traffic in political and administrative jobbery.' The rest of the country had been left to 'praetors and proconsuls' – perhaps a rather flattering designation for most nineteenth-century provincial civil governors and captains-general in Spain. The influence of Madrid had restrained enterprise, enervated industry, fostered inefficiency, favoured the undeserving and spread corruption. What could Catalonia expect from Madrid? Almirall asked. 'For them, commerce, education, the arts – every manifestation, in short, of the energies of mankind – are just so much fodder from which to extract the life-blood that keeps them going from one day to the next. How can we expect measures for the promotion of industry and the creation of wealth from men who see the budget as nothing more than a meal-ticket for their gang?'[2] Between the lines of these complaints, the age-old fiscal basis of Catalanist resentment of the centre can be detected: the monstrously greedy capital city, the outstretched tentacles, the fat, slippery periphery. Barcelona had always tended to practice centralist politics of her own within Catalonia, of which she proclaims herself the 'head and hearth', but could never cheerfully endure them from Madrid.

'DIFFICULTIES' OR DECLINE?

Even as part of the Spanish monarchy, Catalonia remained a nominally sovereign principality until 1716. By then Barcelona's status as a capital had been eroded more or less steadily for 300 years. Castile and the Crown of Aragon (of which the Principality of Catalonia formed part) had a single sovereign continuously from 1516; but already for just over a century before that, Catalonia had been ruled by kings of Castilian provenance whose priorities, as we have seen, reflected their foreign origins and the diversity of their realms. Foreign rule was foisted on Catalonia by the Holy Spirit, invoked by an anti-Pope. The last count-king of the House of Barcelona died in 1410 leaving no obvious heir apart from a grandson disqualified by illegitimacy. Pedro de Luna, who, reigning from Perpignan as Benedict XIII, had lost the allegiance of most of the rest of Christendom, asserted the authority still accorded to him in the Crown of Aragon by convoking an assembly of saints and jurists, representatives of the constituent dominions of the crown, to elect a new king by divine inspiration. For fifty-six days they listened to the advocates of six candidates, all of whose claims were flawed in law. The most influential vote in the electoral college was that of the Dominican preacher Viçent Ferrer, whose acknowledged sanctity may have swayed some of his colleagues in favour of the candidate he selected. His choice in turn was probably influenced by the interests of the anti-Pope, who wanted the richest and militarily most successful of the candidates to be beholden to him as king. Thus Ferdinand of Antequera, who was Castilian-born and Castilian-speaking, and whose claim, contrary to custom, was staked through the female line, was elected to inaugurate a new dynasty. Three representatives in the male line of the blood of the old counts were passed over. One of them, Jaume of Urgell, was of unimpeachably Catalan credentials and seems to have had, in strict terms of law and custom, the best right to succeed: there were impassioned demonstrations on his behalf in the streets of Barcelona, and he seems generally to have been the most popular candidate in Catalonia. But the anti-Pope's influence had stacked the electoral college against him and he, perhaps believing that justice would prevail over interest in an assembly sanctioned by God, refrained until too late from objecting to the system.

The outcome was accepted at the time without seriously threatening the peace or unity of the Crown of Aragon. The unsuccessful candidates were bought off. The new king, with his aura of success and

divine approval, was not regarded with any chauvinistic abhorrence
in the realm accustomed to cross-border marriages. Still, the Catalans
would have preferred someone else and two of their representatives
in the electoral college had voted for defeated options. Ferdinand's
accession has therefore been resented in modern times as a 'lost
moment' of Catalonian history, when the principality's long-term
prospects of power and independence were seriously, perhaps fatally,
compromised. The sterile debate on whether Ferdinand was 'endorsed
by' or 'imposed on' the Catalans can still be followed in the correspondence columns of the Barcelona press.

Like most alleged turning points, however, this one probably only
confirmed the way things were already going. Despite her extensive
Mediterranean empire and her claim on the alliance of the other
dominions of the Crown of Aragon, Catalonia looks, with hindsight,
unfitted for peninsular hegemony in the fifteenth century. The kingdom of Castile was favoured by her geographical position, with outlets
to both the Mediterranean and the Atlantic; by her strategic position
within the peninsula, dominating interior lines; by her relative weight
of resources in manpower and land, the unity of her command, the
fiscal exploitability of her subjects. In demographic terms, Castilian
preponderance of 'peripheral' Spain increased without a break from
the fourteenth century to the nineteenth. The very nature of dynastic
politics made it likely that all the Christian realms of the peninsula
would ultimately become part of a pan-Spanish monarchy. The distribution of resources made it inevitable that such a union would be
dominated by Castile. In the fifteenth century, Castile and Catalonia
seemed to pass one another like fairground riders on adjoining ferris-
wheels – on the rims, in a contemporary image, of counter-spinning
wheels of fortune. The 'rise of Castile' from a poor and war-torn
kingdom on the periphery of Latin Christendom to become the dominant power in both the western Mediterranean and the Atlantic, with
the beginnings of a vast and unparalleled global empire, coincided
with what historians have called Catalonia's decline.

Writing in the late eighteenth century, Antoni de Capmany dated
the 'decadence ' of Barcelona from about 250 years before. He blamed
it on the discovery of 'both Indies', the conquest of Egypt by the Turks
and the depredations of the Barbary pirates. Barcelona's greatness was
mercantile and relative: when new oceanic routes transformed the
nature of European commerce, she remained largely penned up in the
Mediterranean, unable to compete with the Atlantic ports which
eclipsed her; at about the same time her access to the Levant was

impeded by the Ottomans, her home waters in the western Mediterranean ravaged by corsairs. This neat thesis was attractive, as long as it remained untested by critical scrutiny and quantitative research.[3]

A later generation of historians linked or identified the decline of Barcelona with the 'decline of Catalonia', a concept invented to explain the relative ineffectiveness of Arago-Catalan arms and navies in fifteenth-century wars and the apparent stagnation of the imperial growth that had been so spectacular in the thirteenth and fourteenth centuries. Peninsular hegemony passed definitively to Castile, maritime preponderance to Genoa and commercial ascendancy within the Arago-Catalan world to Valencia. Catalonia, who had once inspired the militant chauvinism of Muntaner and created a great empire of her own, became a small and restless province of the emergent 'Spain' of the reigns of Ferdinand and Isabella.

Yet, like the similar problem of the 'decline of Spain' in the seventeenth century, that of the decline of Catalonia in the fifteenth has to be treated cautiously. What is remarkable about the achievements of fifteenth-century Catalonia is not that they should have been slowed or arrested but that they should have continued at all. They included the definitive pacification of Sardinia (1442), the reconquest of the mainland kingdom of Naples (1443), the recovery of the counties of Roussillon and Cerdagne after their temporary alienation to France (1449) and the sustaining of a long, somewhat intermittent campaign of intervention in the politics of Castile, which culminated in the self-defeating triumph of the reign of Ferdinand and Isabella; a count of Barcelona was king in Castile; but the centre of gravity of power in the peninsula was shifted forever towards the centre. Catalan experience in the fifteenth century seems too mottled with short-term checks, leaps and lurches to justify the use of a sweeping term like 'decline' except in a relative sense: especially in the late fifteenth century, the neighbouring kingdoms of France and Castile were developing the means to mobilise unprecedented strength.

Barcelona's fifteenth century, however, was at best an 'era of difficulties' – progressive exhaustion, ultimate prostration, redeemed only by the extraordinary mental resilience of an indomitably optimistic ruling class. One can see resolute civic spirit etched into the faces of the élite depicted, for instance, in Lluís Dalmau's 'La Verge dels Consellers', painted in 1443 to project a magnificent image of the city magistracy in the intimate company of heavenly protectors. On the left, St Eulàlia presents the chief *conseller* and two colleagues; the other *consellers* are presented on the right by St Andrew, whose feast marked the day of the annual election. In the background, behind the angelic choirs, idealised city-scapes line the shore. This sort of confidence saw the city fathers through the projects and troubles recounted in previous chapters: the attempted building of a port; the checks to commerce; the recurrent plagues; the struggle of Busca and Biga (see above, pp.29–33).

In 1462, however, Barcelona faced a rebuke more scathing than any of these. In part, the civil war which broke out that year was another round of the familiar factional strife. Its dominant character, however, was political and 'constitutional': the issues tried were to raise, for the first time in Catalonian history, the problem of the political relationship of Catalonia – and *a fortiori* of Barcelona – with the rest of Spain. In particular, one party in the conflict defended the immutability – or at least the distinctiveness – of Catalonia's customs, laws and institutions against a party prepared to compromise them in the service of a prince whose standards of political propriety were derived from Castilian models. In one sense, the war of 1462–73 was the first of Barcelona's wars with 'Spain'.

The difference between the traditions of Castile, which dominated the perceptions of the count-king Joan II, and those of Catalonia, which informed the thinking of the Consell of Barcelona, were admirably expressed in the exchanges between the contenders before the war broke out. Ostensibly, the controversy was over whether the count-king could hold prisoner his son and heir, whom he wished to exclude from the succession. Underlying this was a deeper division over the limits of royal power and the nature of the constraints upon it. When Joan spoke of his 'majesty' and his accountability 'solely to God' he was using 'absolutist' language which had been formulated, originally, in Italy and France and which had penetrated Castile in the early fifteenth century without so far, however, having any significant influence in Catalonia. When the Consell of Barcelona retorted that they had 'laws and privileges made by contract, conforming to the laws of God and man', they expressed an alternative theory of monarchy limited by contractual obligations and irrefrangible laws. When the count-king relied on 'a law in Castile which is called the law of Spain', they replied that 'the Catalans already have their own laws and customs, which are very different from those of Castile'.[4] The rights of the heir to the throne gave the count-kings' adversaries a clear and just cause around which to unite. The prince's death in September 1462 broke that unity. Those who had rallied to him in the expectation that he would soon be king – for his father was neither young nor well befriended –

found their situation transformed. Most of the 'natural' leaders of Catalan society, however, remained implacable. Joan was a terrible radical force. He tampered with the laws of succession; he made an alliance with the traditional French enemies of Catalonia; he appeared to encourage the peasants against their lords and the urban poor against the patricians. In Barcelona the Consell identified the royal cause with that of the Busca (above, p.29). In February, 1462, the Queen, as Joan's regent in Catalonia, received a petition of *artistes* and *menestrals* calling for a new *sindicat* – the revolutionary institution which had usurped power in 1453. The first act of the war was in effect the execution in May of members of the pro-Busca faction in the patriciate who were suspected of plotting with her. At the same time the Count of Pallars, with the authority of the Diputació and Consell, marched on Girona, intending at first to expel and later – when passions escalated and the stakes were raised – to imprison the regent. Of this, as of later Catalan revolts, Barcelona was the 'head and hearth', the treasury and the sword. With much of the country indifferent or inconstant, and the count-king even shorter of resources than the city, the conflict would be won by the side that showed greater endurance: neither was strong enough for a knock-out blow. The insurgents' problems deepened as they began to run out of two vital resources which their war effort required: money and pretenders to the throne. Most of the 60,000 lliures they raised in Barcelona in 1462 had been spent by the end of the following year; thereafter their campaigns were crippled by caution and all their means were spent and overspent by 1465.[5] They needed rivals for Joan II's throne who could both aid their cause and legitimate their authority. But the heir whose claims they had backed before the war was dead. The search for substitutes drove the rebels to ever more desperate expedients. In August 1462, Enrique IV of Castile agreed to be their patron but, finding it an unprofitable position, withdrew before the end of the year. Prince Pedro of Portugal, who was descended from an unsuccessful claimant in the contest for the crown of 1421, and had no fortune or prospects in his own country, was a tireless but luckless successor, who died in 1466. The Diputació then secured the services as figurehead of René of Anjou, whose claims were similar to those of Pedro and who sent his son and heir to represent him; but when the latter died in his turn in December 1470, the evidence seemed irrefutable that God was on the side of the old count-king; sixty-four at the start of hostilities, he had outlived or outlasted all his adversaries, recovered from blindness in the course of the war and never renounced a line of his rights or a jot of his vigour. He was still hated in Barcelona, where his supporters were equated with 'spreaders of the plague'; since plague had reputedly claimed 5,000 lives in the winter of 1465–6 this was as profound an expression of loathing as could be formulated. In the rest of Catalonia, the drift to Joan's banner gathered pace. Justifying his defection, the Bishop of Girona confessed that he wanted to escape the 'derision' which Catalonia's many changes of allegiance had provoked. By the early summer of 1472, the city was surrounded and alone. In October, reduced 'to eating bread made from beans', the Consell accepted Joan's promises of pardon. His victory was advertised by a comet – a more dignified augury than the beached whale which presaged the death of his predecessor.[6] Scattering assurances of doubtful value, he entered the city on 17 October in the atmosphere rather of a *joyeuse entrée* than of defeat and devastation. The impact of the defeat was felt over the next generation. Canny entrepreneurs had fled during the war, to the enrichment of Valencia and Naples. They did not return. Building stagnated. The city could not afford to repair the storm damage of 1482 and 1483. The next hearth-count, in 1497, showed Barcelona still some 1,500 hearths short of the level of 1464.[7]

The new count-king Ferdinand, who succeeded his father as Ferran II in 1479, blamed the Barcelonese for their own plight. It was because of the squabbles of the citizens (he wrote to the *consellers* in November 1490), the usurpation of government by a single faction and the consequent maladministration that the city had 'come to such severe depopulation and ruination'. The *consellers* were equally convinced that the policy of the crown was responsible. The main cause of their troubles was the scale of forfeitures of rebel property after the revolt of 1462, which Joan II had failed to return as promised and which Ferdinand continued to retain, only finally relinquishing them in return for a heavy subsidy. On his accession he had received the city's pleas, in terms which contrived to be pathetic and menacing at once. 'Today no trade at all is practised in this city; not a bolt of cloth is seen; the cloth-workers are unemployed and the other workers the same . . . and all the time the men of property are deprived of their rents and goods: who then will give work to the artisans?' The king was told that the skilled men were all going off to seek work in Provence, Majorca, Naples and Valencia 'for here they cannot find the means of life . . . And of all the troubles we are suffering, the worst is this: for we see our city turning into something no bigger than Granollers' – a village on the approach to Barcelona – 'and the lord king takes no heed; but it rather seems, with all due respect, that he pays more attention to the private interests of his counsellors'. This almost treasonable language was conveyed through an intermediary. The following year the *consellers* repeated the same analysis, without the direct criticism of Ferdinand, in a letter to the king himself. 'This city of yours,' they wrote, 'is now abandoned by most of its people and is being emptied, day in, day out. The reason for it, sire, is that for a long time the men of property . . . have received nothing in rent so that today, having spent all their capital, they are reduced almost to beggary and in consequence can provide no business for the workers. And so they all go looking for the means of life in other places and this city is being widowed.'[8]

The effects of the withheld forfeitures were exacerbated by the king's threat to introduce the Inquisition, which had a further depressing influence on trade, because of the commercial importance of citizens of Jewish ancestry, and the Inquisitors' notorious interest in the heresies of converts and their progeny. The city's envoys pleaded with the king to keep the tribunal out of Barcelona, with its secretive procedures, its network of informers, and its daunting powers of sequestration and confiscation. The introduction of a prerogative court within Catalonia was contrary to the laws of the principality, but they preferred to urge the less fastidious reason that the Inquisition would cripple Barcelona's already impoverished economy. 'The little sustenance and means of survival which this city still has,' they were instructed to say, 'derives from the small amount of trade practised by those who are known as *conversos*, in whose hands rests today the greater part of the wealth of the city; and it is thanks to the business they carry on in, for example, coral, cloth, leather and other merchandise that many and various workers are kept and survive.' The mere threat of the Inquisition drove many of its potential victims into exile in Perpignan, Avignon 'and other parts'. The arrival of the tribunal seemed to the *consellers* to justify their gloomiest expectations. On 20 November 1484, they complained that the news of the king's final decision had 'brought as great distress to everyone, from the greatest to the least, as if they [were] already seeing this city totally destroyed and lost – as it certainly will be if this Inquisition goes ahead.' The city was being deserted and the exchange 'emptied within the space of a few days'; many fugitives 'in their fear have had their possessions transported to other parts'. Among the first exiles was one of the most respected citizens from among the *converso* community, Anton de Bardaxí, described by the *consellers* as 'a man of great wisdom and prudence, of whom nothing could be suspected contrary to the Catholic faith'. Barcelona, after all the depletions of the war and post-war years, could ill afford to lose such men.[9]

The city fathers who saw the introduction of the Inquisition as an attempt to erode their jurisdiction were, in part, probably justified. Ferdinand the Catholic was the embodiment of the success of his father's policy of promoting his dynastic interests in Castile. He was in Aragon when news of the vacancy of the throne reached him in December 1474. Wrapped in anonymity, cloaked against the cold, he rode full pelt for Segovia with only a few attendants, to press his claim. Sustaining a personal challenge against the superior rights of his own wife, he agreed a contract of joint rule with her only just in time to join forces for a four-year war of succession against a third pretender. Once established on the throne, he committed Aragonese resources to conquests on Castile's behalf in Granada and, later, in Navarre. Along with Castilian priorities he inherited some, at least, of his father's enmity towards Barcelona.

The context of his hostility, however, may not have been as commonly supposed. The most influential study of the subject,[10] now over fifty years old, included the assumption, which all historians made at the time, that Ferdinand was a 'modern' monarch – the founder, indeed, of the 'modern Spanish state', who pursued 'centralising' policies consciously intended to impose unity on 'Spain' and to make institutions uniform – or, at least, more homogeneous than formerly – throughout his realms. This, if true, would have provided an explanation of his conduct towards Barcelona. It seemed to be contradicted, however, by another assumption widely current at the time, that Ferdinand was an abettor of 'the rise of the bourgeoisie' – modern precisely because he favoured the towns against the aristocracy, whom he was thought to have 'disciplined' or domesticated. In the present state of our knowledge it seems unlikely that Ferdinand had any cosmic political strategy. He had neither the power nor the imagination to challenge the natural and traditional sources of devolved power in his dominions, but was willing and able to manipulate a variety of political stratagems to cajole or compel obedience or cooperation. This mastery of the rules, rather than the code, of power made him one of the idols of Machiavelli's *Prince*. Utterly dependent on aristocratic passivity or support, he tended to target the towns in attempts to increase royal jurisdiction. In that sense, Barcelona was one victim among many and the deployment of the Inquisition was a characteristic device. The most insidious methods at his command, however, involved the manipulation of factional rivalries and the exploitation of princely patronage to buy support or to promote his creatures. These, in effect, were precisely the methods on which he relied in suborning the municipality of Barcelona.

Ferdinand was fortunate to be able to exploit the long history of factional strife in Barcelona, which had surfaced in gang warfare, the struggle of Busca and Biga and the origins of the civil war. In particular he benefited from the behaviour of the initially preponderant faction of Pere de Coromines, a genuine patrician who tried to exploit the language of Biga tradition. Patrician attempts to impose further limitations on access to the ranks of the oligarchy were probably just self-interested, not class-motivated. The effect was to incline the men on the fringes of the élite – leading professionals, *artistes* and *menestrals* – to support the main rival faction, led by the lawyer, Jaume Deztorrent. Factional strife, as in the confrontation of Busca and Biga, again acquired the appearance of class struggle. The Deztorrent family had been associated with the Busca but their faction, like almost all those of late medieval urban partisanship in Spain, was an interest-group bound by ties of kin and business rather than by common principles or policies. The king loaded Jaume Deztorrent and members of his family with honours and offices of profit under the crown; those who were *ciutadans honrats* he elevated to the ranks of the nobility. As a result, the Deztorrent clan could buy and bully its way to control in the Consell: and Ferdinand secured a compliant city by means as thorough as, and less costly than, his father's confrontationalist approach. Without any serious opposition from the cowed or corrupted council he was able, from 1490 until his death, to exercise a veto over the lists of candidates for offices in Barcelona. After his death the crown, once having restored control of the lists to the city, was unable to reassert anything like the same power again until nearly a century and a half had elapsed and another war between Barcelona and the crown had been fought. Ferdinand's Barcelona was no battleground of conflicting principles: this was a struggle neither of 'Catalanists' with 'centralists' nor of a 'bourgeois' with a 'feudal' class, but an old-fashioned power-struggle won by an alliance of practical politicians.[11]

Why, on Ferdinand's death, did the crown surrender the key to its authority in Barcelona? Ferdinand's successor was his grandson, the future Emperor Charles V (Carles I in Catalonia, Carlos I of Spain, 1516–56). He seems to have had some personal liking for the city, which he favoured disproportionately as a place to visit and stay during his frantically peripatetic life. At the start of his reign, however, he was probably actuated by no more than the impulsive generosity characteristic of a young man, nurtured in chivalric values, with a keen sense of the obligations of kingly largesse. In subsequent years, not only did he manage his relations with the city without vetting the candidates' lists, but also appears largely to have refrained from exercising the crown's right to create *ciutadans honrats*. This was an exceptionally important right of patronage, a means not only of rewarding supporters but also of increasing the numbers of reliable creatures qualified for candidacy in the lotteries of civic and provincial office: he may have created as few as three, compared with twenty-eight elevated by his successor.

RENAISSANCE AND RECOVERY

Charles's light touch was reciprocated by a quiescent Barcelona. In general, over the sixteenth century as a whole, city and crown made few demands of each other. Considered from one point of view, over the past 500 years and more, the history of Barcelona has consisted in periods of aggressive self-assertion alternating with eras of *enrichissez-vous*. The sixteenth century was one of the latter. It was a long haul back to prosperity after the disasters of the late fifteenth century and economics had priority over politics.

The success of Barcelona's collective project of reconstruction is suggested by the unanimity with which late sixteenth-century travellers praised the splendours of the city. Some of this material has to be treated with care. Every history of Barcelona, for instance, quotes with approval Don Quixote's praise of the 'treasure house of courtesy, the refuge of strangers, the hospital of the poor, the homeland of the valiant, the avenger of the injured and the abode of firm and reciprocal friendships, unique in its position and beauty', without allowing for the facts that the context of the passage is full of irony in a highly ironical work, and that Don Quixote suffered a humiliating experience in Barcelona. On the other hand, the Don's opinion, even if ironically reported by Cervantes, was commonly held. Prince Maximilian of Austria thought Barcelona's deposit bank, the Taula de Canvi, comparable with the Banco di San Giorgio of Genoa – the most solvent institution of Mediterranean finance. Hendrik Cock, visiting the city in Philip II's entourage, thought it 'as good as any city in Spain'. For Lope de Vega, it was a city of love and money, with 'a thousand ladies at the balconies and a thousand gallants in the streets'. 'Great Barcelona' served Spain as a splendid façade serves a house, in his opinion. The terms of these praises suggest financial and commercial recovery, as well as the urbanity of a rich way of life.[12]

The most circumstantial account of this period is perhaps that of Thomas Platter, student of Montpellier, who visited the city in 1599. Part of the motive of his journey was to see King Philip III of Spain (Felip II in Catalonia, r. 1598–1621) receive his bride, Margaret of Austria; but reputedly refusing a subsidy from the city of 20,000 crowns, the king preferred to grant the honour to Valencia: this was the first hint of an era of renewed acerbities between city and crown. Platter's disappointment, however, was mollified by the delight he found in the town. Everything he recorded seemed to reflect industry and luxury. The vast walls of the arsenal made this 'one of the strongest places in Spain'. He watched a newly built galley slide down the slipway of the shipyard. He attended the Palau de la Generalitat, where the façade, completed about twenty years before, was the most conspicuous Renaissance monument in Barcelona; there he found himself in 'the most beautiful chamber in the world'. On the esplanade, used then as now to 'breathe the air and sharpen the appetite', he prepared his visits to the pastrycooks and restaurateurs and to the commercial wine cellars where samples of sherry, malvasia, canary and other wines of France and Spain were served with biscuits as a *dégustation*. He admired the theatres, where chairs were supplied by the children of the hospital and collections taken for the poor, and the splendid hospital itself – whose buildings on the carrer del Carme still afford much the same aspect today – where daily gifts were taken in of wine and meat. He marvelled at prostitutes who behaved like honest women and cobblers' wives 'who excelled noble ladies in vanity'. When on a visit to the university, he took part in the defence of a doctoral thesis, he was presented, like the other disputants, with a gift of gloves of perfumed kidskin – the present commonly given to contestants in a joust. And lamenting the expense, he bought luxuries in the shops and markets of Barcelona, including 'decorative little slippers' with heels so high that women needed assistance to walk in them.[13]

The recrudescence of display was favoured by economic conditions and social change. From the 1570s, Barcelona's place on the bullion-road from the quays of Seville to the banks of Genoa created a new source of wealth. From beginnings discernible in the previous century (see above, p.79), the reception of Renaissance moral philosophy helped both to enlarge the ruling élite and to change their self-perception. The distinction between aristocracy and upper citizenry

became blurred. Demand for education rocketed. And the rich surrounded themselves with an assorted garniture of chivalric life and
Renaissance taste.

One of the first makers of Barcelona's Renaissance was the early
sixteenth-century Archdeacon Lluís Desplà, who decorated his official
residence – it now houses the municipal historical institute – with his
personal coat of arms. His chapel had an altarpiece painted by Barto-
lomé Bermejo, perhaps the most accomplished of the Hispano-Flemish
painters who preceded the Renaissance in Spain. Desplà, however,
also shared the latest taste in aesthetics and lined the cloister of his
house with inscriptions and classical bric-à-brac from city building
sites and from the barely excavated ruins of Empùries. The effect
must have resembled, on a smaller scale, that of Michelozzo's courtyard
in the Medici palace or the patio of the Afán de Ribera palace in
Seville. In 1524, the *consellers* met daily to hear readings from moral
philosophy – one of the subjects of the humanist curriculum – and
commissioned a master to lecture to them on Aristotle's *Politics* in the
Casa de la Ciutat. Later in the century the legend 'Senatus Populusque
Barcinonensis' was inscribed over the door of the chapel in the same
building, not merely as an antiquarian allusion but as a stake claimed
in a classical notion of virtue.[14]

Nobility – these transformations implied – was attainable through
virtue, and virtue through study of the classics. When the Jesuits
opened their college on the Rambla in 1544, demand soon induced
them to open their doors to lay pupils – 140 of them in 1576, 160 in
1599; in 1585 the scholars performed poetry recitals and learned
disputations for the king and the school fête of 1616 was attended
'by learned nobles and the city magistrates'. A pair of fake Roman
inscriptions on the bases of two columns in the Casa Gralla expressed
the essence of the new ethos of display in a mock-classical epigram:
'*Privatae voluptati, publicae venustati*' – 'for private pleasure and
public adornment'. Such accents continued to define the tone of
high-life in the city in the next century. Pau Ignasi de Dalmases, a
newly ennobled patrician who made his fortune from having cloth
made up by cheap rural labour, remodelled his recently acquired
palace in the carrer de Montcada to accommodate his books, display
his decorations in honour of Neptune and house his learned circle of
friends, formally constituted as the Academia dels Desconfiats. A
Barcelonese writer of 1688 even thought it was 'better to make oneself
noble than to be born noble'.[15]

Once humanists had redefined nobility, invidious distinctions between 'old' and 'new' families, or between landed and urban wealth could at least be blurred, if not obliterated. It was normal for *ciutadans honrats* to be ennobled by the purchase of baronies of the gift of sixteenth- and seventeenth-century kings. Rural aristocrats moved into town; by 1639, according to a muster-roll drawn up to maximise the enforcement of military obligations, a quarter of the Catalan nobility lived in Barcelona. As aristocrats colonised the city, *ciutadans honrats* moved their fortunes into the country. In 1635, the assets of Miquel Joan Magarola, a *ciutadan honrat* and judge of the highest court in Catalonia, were overwhelmingly in rural property (including a recently purchased lordship) which yielded nearly two thirds of his fixed income. Although the average return on commercial ventures was ten per cent and that of mortgages only five per cent, the *ciutadans honrats* of the early seventeenth century preferred the low risks and high prestige of a rentier income and, in particular, of investment in the land.[16]

A curious product of the symbiosis of the rural and urban aristocracies was the revival of annual jousts from 1565, connected, like the contemporary revival of chivalry in England, with the cult of St George. The new order founded to renew the practice was the Confraternity of Sant Jordi, whose first statutes offered only a brief justification: the exercise of arms was the noblest and best in the world, serving to defend the common weal and to be the right arm of justice; Catalonia, exposed to enemies by land and sea, had particular need of it; and it was fitting to perpetuate a custom venerable through the glorious deeds of forbears. New statutes of 1573 included a more detailed exposition, which explained that it was through neglect of arms that 'the Spanish nation' had been conquered by Carthaginians and Romans, despite its superior valour and fortitude. Similarly, it was mastery of the practice that enabled Spain to reverse the process and subjugate its former conquerors. These practical and antiquarian arguments may have convinced those who formulated them; in reality, however, though the confraternity took some genuinely useful training – foil fencing, for instance – its role was soon diverted into that of enhancing civic occasion with spectacle. In 1601, the canonisation of St Ramon Penyafort was celebrated by a mock *paso honroso*, 'fought' by quadrilles dressed as Aztecs, Albanians and Turks; at the conclusion of the festivities a huge model phoenix was set alight, revealing the image of St Ramon in blessing, emerging from the smoke. For the procession of 1609 the leading figures dressed as Moors and Turks, for that of 1611 as Ethiopians. The jousts celebrated in 1630 for the

Queen of Hungary were fought between 'gypsies' amd 'negroes'. At every tourney there was a prize for the 'best gallant', voted by the ladies. In terms of social function, this exotic mummery served to bring the citizen-cavaliers together with those who belonged formally to the noble estate, the Braç Militar. From the time of the first chapter of the confraternity, members of three ranks can be distinguished: titled nobility, gentlemen accorded the courtesy title of Don and, almost as numerous, the *ciutadans honrats*.[17]

THE CHASM OF THE CARRER DE LA LLIBRETERIA

In an incident famous or notorious in the annals of Catalonian banditry, on 30 December 1613, the charismatic robber-chief Barbeta surprised a mule-train bearing silver to the crown's Genoese bankers. This foreign bandit – probably of Italian origin – had established a surprising rapport with the Catalan peasants among whom he moved 'like a fish in the sea', and seems also to have forged links of mutual respect and profit with well-to-do elements in Barcelona. Encouraging local villagers to help themselves to as many silver bars as they wanted, Barbeta told the Genoese commissioner that it gave him 'more pleasure that these people should get rich on the wealth of the Genoese, than that I should carry off anything for myself'. The social alliance that sustained banditry embraced members of other classes too: the rural aristocrats to whom the bands could supply useful services; the corrupt officials whose extortions they could abet; the deep-rooted totemic brotherhoods whose feuds they fought; and otherwise respectable Barcelonese financiers who 'laundered' silver bars pillaged by countrymen who could not dispose of them. 'A large part' of the money stolen in Barbeta's raid, according to the Genoese commissioner, 'is believed to be in Barcelona, in the hands of people who have good connections in the city and are treated with deference'.[18]

Complex cross-currents like these made early seventeenth-century Catalonia a genuinely ungovernable province of the Spanish monarchy, where royal administration had little or no role. Anything the viceroys did might threaten to upset the delicate balance of potentially violent forces, which only inertia could guarantee to preserve. Campaigns against banditry were the usual set-piece forays by which viceroys proclaimed their energy; but while the crown was unwilling to waste resources merely to contain the bandits, the extinction of so useful an institution could hardly be endorsed by Catalan society as a whole. In an age when to be 'a very good Catalan' was held to be 'a defender of the country's privileges', vice-regal vigour, however estimable the cause, was bound to be ambivalent in its effects. As long as the principality was prosperous and the monarchy undemanding, the equilibrium of the rickety structure of government could be preserved. Broadly speaking, that was the situation that prevailed in the later sixteenth and early seventeenth centuries. In the 1620s, when the flow of bullion eased, and the Mediterranean world was affected by recession, the economic conditions of stability began to fade. At the same time, the resources of the monarchy were put under terrible strain by the problems of global defence at a time of falling resources. The need to spread the burdens of empire more equitably – especially between over-taxed Castile and under-taxed Catalonia – or, at least, to make the Catalans pay for campaigns against their own bandits, was increasingly apparent and increasingly difficult to shirk.

In Barcelona, the short walk along the carrer de la Llibreteria, which separated the civic centre from the palace complex where the viceroys lived, became a bridge over a political chasm. Its depth could be measured in the growing number of disputes over legal immunities, limits of jurisdiction, fiscal privileges and protocol which mounted up between the council and the viceroys. An index of royal exasperation is the numbers of *ciutadans honrats* appointed by royal prerogative; thirteen in the second decade of the century, twenty-two in the third and eighty in the fourth. It was galling to see, emerging repeatedly from the lottery, names of such 'enemies of the royal service' as Jeroni de Navel – ambitious, pedantic, with a hereditary grudge against the crown – whom the luck of the draw placed in a commanding position at a critical time. By an agreement of 1599 between the king and the city, the royal nominees, while eligible for election by lot to civic offices, were classified in an inferior category and treated with less deference than the *ciutadans de matrícula* who inherited their status or were coopted by their peers: snubbing the crown was not just a civic vice but a social institution. Royal supporters were enclosed in a status ghetto.[19]

The crown's attempt to procure a compliant administration was not necessarily part of a plan to subvert the rights of Catalonia, or to reduce the whole Spanish monarchy to the rule of uniform laws and institutions. Rather, it was a response to intractable problems at a time of international emergency, an attempt to bypass the fiscal blood clots that kept Barcelona's wealth in her veins; an effort to promote coherence of command in the interests of collective defence. In the traditions of Catalonian constitutional thought, however, it could never be said that 'necessity hath no law'. Allegiance was owed to the king as prince in Catalonia, not king in Spain, and allegiance to the laws of the land and the privileges of the city took precedence, in Barcelona, over any wider responsibilities that might be thought to attach to civic office. In 1632, the *consellers* were willing 'to keep the whole world waiting and the eyes of the whole monarchy fixed', while Catalonia's subsidy for the defence of the realm was deferred pending settlement of a dispute over protocol.

The 'privileges' (*privilegis*) and 'rights' (*furs*) or liberties which meant so much to Barcelona were never systematically codified – though compiled in haphazard collections called the '*Llibre vert*' and '*Llibres vermells*' – and are difficult to define. Castilian models, and the different nuances of Castilian thinking, which could not be translated directly into Catalan, tended to mislead policy-makers in Madrid into misapprehensions about the sort of traditions they had to deal with in relation to Barcelona. The result was a dialogue conducted at cross-purposes. In Castile, the *fueros* of a city normally consisted in a charter granted by the king, and revocable at royal will, which might confer immunities and exemptions on the community – from billetting, or certain forms of recruiting, for instance, or certain taxes or the jurisdiction of particular tribunals, royal, seigneurial or ecclesiastical. The same document or set of documents might also confer rights on the citizens, such as the right to hold a market or fair, to exercise justice collectively within (or, in some cases, in restricted areas beyond) the limits of the city, or to elect their own town councillors, or some of them. The greater part of most *fueros*, however, and the entirety of many of them, were administrative regulations which were not always to the community's advantage, but rather tended to displace power into the hands of royal representatives or nominees. In Castile, in short, civic liberties were a negotiable commodity, revered but not sacralised.

Barcelona was not analogous to any Castilian city. As the capital of an ancient sovereign principality, her identity was bound up with the juridical status of Catalonia as a distinct and equal partner in the crown of Aragon and, separately, in the Spanish monarchy. Her liberties were not, in many cases, granted by the sovereign prince as an act of grace, but governed by the Constitucions – the laws, irrevocable except by the representative assembly of Corts, which limited royal authority in the principality. Whether it was a matter of resisting billetting, or withholding recruitment levies, or building unauthorised fortifications, or retaining criminous citizens for trial in Barcelona, or refusing the crown's claim to a fifth of the city's revenues, or – most contentious of all – insisting on the *consellers'* right to wear hats in the king's presence, 'each privilege added to the power and prestige of Barcelona, and the currency of prestige was worth as much as the ducats demanded of Barcelona by the king'.[20]

The period of mounting tension in the 1620s and 1630s coincides with the supremacy of Philip IV's (in Catalonia, Felip III, 1621–65) chief minister, the Count of Olivares. In consequence, Olivares has often got the blame, especially from Catalan historians. He proposed means of distributing the burdens more equitably among the king's subjects, which threatened the Catalans with a backlog of debt from years of undersubscription. His demands of Catalonia may have been excessive, because he seems to have been misinformed about the size and resources of the principality. It is evident, too, that he was willing, if baulked, to use force against the Catalans and reduce their laws 'to conformity with those of Castile'. That is not to say that he was primarily interested in radical reform, only that he was prepared to countenance it in pursuit of objectives of imperial defence.

Velázquez's most famous portrait of Olivares shows him in a typical baroque pose, twisting in the saddle of a rearing war horse. In an adjoining room of the Prado, another equestrian portrait by the same artist depicts Philip IV, sedate, even inert, his baton relaxed, his dreamy countenance fixed on some distant vision. The contrast between these two images forms the basis of the received view of Philip and his minister: a sacral figurehead, complemented or controlled by a restless dominator, who was literally convulsed – for many contemporaries observed the jerkiness of Olivares's gait and gestures – by his 'passion to command'. By extension, Olivares has been seen as impetuous and destructive. In one tradition, he appears as an intellectual rigorist, who failed because history would not submit to his inflexible logic. In another, which is particularly popular in Catalonia, he was the incarnation of authoritarian radicalism, bent on crushing non-Castilian Hispanic identities or replacing the traditional polity with 'modern' absolutism. He was obviously no fool; therefore the disasters of his years in power, which left Spain in the throes of apparent disintegration, have been attributed to knavery or madness. Much documentary evidence has disappeared, increasing historians' reliance on court gossip: this in turn has encouraged a vision of the period in terms of 'personalities' rather than 'issues', which may well be appropriate but which tends to favour the transmogrification of a figure like Olivares into a fantasy-character of imaginary stature, a hero or bogey.

The real Olivares was a cautious, consciously 'prudent' decision-maker with what his best-informed biographer has called an 'ingenious but unoriginal' mind. His reformism was of a traditional stamp. He aimed not to subvert the nobility in favour of a predatory bourgeoisie but merely to simplify bureaucratic procedures, emasculate factions and improve crown finances. His vision of a less disparate Spanish state was inspired not by Castilian nationalism but by the need for enhanced efficiency in the face of war; and his *ambizione de dominare* was rippled with a genuine desire to retire among his books. Risking redundancy, he sincerely sought to educate the king into 'being his own favourite'. He was neither knave nor madman, but a tragic figure, flawed by hubris and foiled, in his own view, by 'fortune' – or, as he more often said, by God. The Spanish monarchy of his day was tottering from the effects of resources overreached. The magic of deficit finance, which had kept the monarchy going in good times, could not be sustained in bad. Not all Olivares's relentless energy could arrest the decline of income and of morale. His tendency to blame defeat on divine displeasure with himself was, in the circumstances, pardonably egocentric. Any work that was not thrust upon him he took upon himself. He ruled Spain by the same sort of tentacular, sleepless habits as Philip II had developed before him.

Olivares acted on a vast stage, simultaneously masterminding campaigns from Bahia to the Baltic. Yet his own world of experience was surprisingly small. One observer attributed his exaggerated esteem for Spain to his ignorance of foreign countries. He lived and thrived in that warped, cramped microcosm, the royal court. His ascent began when he kissed the heir apparent's chamber-pot and reached its climax when he was granted the right to dine, once a year, at the king's own table. He was the unrivalled master of the rites and passages of the palace, and almost monopolised access to the king for nearly twenty years. Yet even on this 'home' ground his power was limited by practical problems. To acquire his creatures, to instal them in key offices and to retain their loyalty were all long, arduous processes. Olivares was never safe from the vengeance of enemies or the inconstancy of friends. Towards the end of his career, amid defeat abroad and revolt at home, he became obsessive about his power base. He retreated into a 'bunker', reshuffling sycophants, imprisoning – even, perhaps, assassinating – opponents and manoeuvring on paper non-existent armies, fleets and funds. When his break with his royal master finally came, in 1643, it was less, perhaps, because that complaisant king had lost confidence in his handling of the crises of Catalonia, than because he could no longer endure the stifling atmosphere. Olivares and Catalonia were not as important, each to the other's fate, as Catalan historians have commonly supposed.

Although, in hindsight, the contest of Olivares with Barcelona in the 1630s seems a conflict of Titans, or destined to end in some bloody *Gotterdämmerung*, the chances are that if left to follow the course it had assumed by the middle of the decade it would have been amicably resolved. The crucial issue was money, and Barcelona had often shown herself willing to pay for privileges. In 1635, however, war between Spain and France widened the scope of the differences between Olivares and Catalonia. Issues which had formerly concerned Barcelona only – from whose cause the smaller, jealous towns of Catalonia actually dissented – now became confused with the unpopularity of the war throughout the principality. Catalonia resented the loss of her trade and the interference with her comfortable tradition of contraband. Above all, consistent with the laws and traditions of the principality, it seemed intolerable that she should billet troops and pay costs for a war which did not – at least initially – threaten her own frontiers. The monarchy looked so different from Madrid, whence Olivares surveyed it with an all-seeing eye. From the perspective of Barcelona, the fate of the King of Spain's other dominions was a matter of fraternal concern, but not of vital interest. 'The Catalan,' Olivares said, 'ought to see more of the world than just Catalonia.'[21]

His hopes that the Catalans 'once attacked or provoked by the French will turn out gallantly' were put to the test in 1639 when, partly by his own contrivance, the French invaded Catalonia. At first, however, the campaign went badly and Madrid blamed the Catalans: they deserted in droves; they declined to take supplies to the front without payment on the pretext that it was against the Constitucions; the *consellers* of Barcelona were deliberately withholding help in order to extract more privileges from the crown; Barcelona behaved unpatriotically in refusing to raise the sacred banner of Santa Eulàlia. There was justice in all these accusations, though the Catalans themselves were more aware of their sufferings, their sacrifices and their eventual hard-won victory. The *consellers* of Barcelona emerged with no credit at all, having been forced to the last effort that brought success only by a riot of the common citizens. The course and outcome of the campaign convinced Olivares that the Constitucions must be circumvented if an efficient war effort was to be mounted and a conclusive victory won.

His decision to billet an army in Catalonia at Catalan expense during the winter in readiness for the campaign of 1640 may have been militarily justifiable but it was also a conscious provocation to the Catalans. Some communities refused to accept the troops; punitive measures got out of hand and as fighting between peasants and soldiers spread it became evident that the royal army was unable to get the better of the insurgents. There was much sympathy for the peasants among the people of Barcelona, though the oligarchy was not yet, it seems, prepared to approve the movement of resistance; in May 1640 fierce demonstrations against a royal flotilla that put into port deterred the commander from landing to make the usual courtesies. Soon afterwards, peasant insurgents made two forays into Barcelona. The first was on 22 May when they entered through a suspiciously unclosed gate with the declared intention of releasing an imprisoned member of the Diputació: he was particularly identified with the anti-billetting cause and his arrest had been ordered by Madrid, apparently *pour encourager les autres*. As the peasants meekly left immediately afterwards, the incident gave the impression in Madrid that the Barcelonese élite was allowing them to do its dirty work. In Barcelona, the experience suggested that the peasants could be managed. Their second incursion, however, followed a very different course.

On 7 June a party from the countryside got into the city among the peasants who traditionally gathered there for the feast of Corpus Christi. Although they had departed after their previous intervention, in the time-honoured tradition of medieval jacqueries, with acclamations for the king and denunciations of bad government, they had been reported as threatening to kill the viceroy, the Marqués de Santa Coloma 'and other traitors'. Knowing that it would be impossible to exclude them from the traditional festivities, the city waited apprehensively. Santa Coloma, who had no forces of his own, and depended for his protection on the municipal guard, was afraid that this time the peasants, inflamed by resentment and emboldened by success, would execute their threats.

'My life will be in great danger,' wrote the viceroy. 'I will run the course with a brave heart.'[22] Finding, however, that the *consellers* seemed tepid in their guarantees of his safety and that he could not trust his guards, the viceroy attempted flight; his discretion was justifiable, for the insurgents had begun a selective massacre of judges of the court of the Audiència and other royal servants and appointees.

He reached the shore in safety and secrecy, but, fearing that his departure would mean the abandonment of the city to the rebels and the escalation of the conflict, he hesitated, fatally. Chased by a mob along the shore, he was unable to reach the galley that awaited him. Some of the rebels – allegedly led by a surgeon – commandeered a cannon and kept the vessel at bay with a shot. Staggering from the heat and unwonted exertion, driven by a hail of stones and shot onto the rocks of the shore at the foot of Montjuic, the viceroy stumbled or slipped, collapsed in a dead faint and was stabbed to death where he lay, defended only by two servants. Three bishops and a number of noblemen, who had attended him when his flight began, had scattered for safety.

Far from conniving in this peasants' revolt, the oligarchs of Barcelona seem to have been as shocked and fearful as anyone at the excesses of the mob, especially as most of the common people seemed sympathetic to the insurgents or, at best, indifferent. The day after the bloodshed, noble residents and other leading citizens turned out in force to police the town and the *consellers* managed to lead the peasants out by a ruse, claiming that Girona was being attacked by the army. In some ways, the peasants seemed biddable; on their first incursion, they had been turned back by the pleas of the Bishop of Vic, whose ring their leaders kissed and whom they cheered to the city gate. During the Corpus riot, the Franciscans had quelled them at one point by exposing the Host and, but for the intervention of 'demonic spirits', it was thought that the bishops and *consellers* might again have led them out of the city before any irreparable damage was done. In reality, however, the peasants were like the 'spirits of the vasty deep'; they could be adjured but not directed. Beyond the walls of Barcelona, the jacquerie was assuming proportions and frenzy which not only eluded the control but threatened the survival of the Catalan élite.

What were denounced as demonic spirits in the town were heard as angelic voices in the countryside. Inspired by the evidence of divine favour that brought success against regular troops, the peasants called themselves the 'Christian army' and defended their cause in the old-fashioned language of millenarian revolution. Their anonymous leaders were called the 'Captain-General of the Christian Army' and 'Governor of the Arms of Christ'. The pamphlets they published in June were issued on behalf of 'the great army' of 'the rustic and simple, moved by the Holy Spirit'. Their threats were directed with equal acerbity against the royal servants who had infringed the Constitucions and against the urban oligarchs who had failed to act against these traitors.

Barcelona was singled out for particularly strong condemnation; she had 'forgotten God's cause' and brought the wrath of God down on the whole principality. Writers of letters and diaries in the city sensed the menace of a Bagaudae revolt, led, it was claimed, by criminals escaped from the galleys.[23]

Barcelona was faced with an invidious dilemma; neither side in the rural conflict represented her interests. The royal army was barely more disciplined than the peasants and threatened the Constitucions. The insurgents, nominally a 'Catalan camp' of defenders of the principality, were an anarchic monster, subversive of all order. The balance of terror favoured the peasants. Barcelona, according to a report made by an informant of the viceroy, 'has to go along with the rest, instead of leading them as was formerly the custom'. The city made an attempt to align itself with the peasants in late June, when the atrocities of the garrison of Perpignan, who bombarded the town in the course of a quarrel over the terms of billetting, elicited a relief force from Barcelona, 1,200 strong, in support of a peasant army of 4,000 men. The appearance of legitimacy was contrived by persuading the new viceroy, the Duke of Cardona, to approve and, indeed, accompany the expedition. It left the peasants unreconciled to the city, which seems to have come under attack from the insurgents several times in the succeeding weeks.

In these circumstances, what most members of the Catalan élite really wanted was some third force, which would protect them both from the menace of the peasants and from the threat to the Constitucions. Traditional recourse to the clemency of the king seemed out of the question. The revolutionary discourse of 1640 in Catalonia inherited the medieval convention that the king was good and only his *consellers* bad. The entrenched position of those *consellers* – especially the hated Olivares and his henchman of sinister reputation, Jerónimo de Villanueva – made reconciliation with the crown seem almost impossible in the immediate future. Direct negotiations with France were the only practical alternative.

Probably initiated by a relatively small group of conspirators within the Diputació, overtures to the French could have been conceived in a variety of ways and there seems never to have been any sort of consensus about the intended objective. For some of the leading figures in the approach to France, it was a frankly treasonable device, an act of vengeance on a régime hated sometimes for patriotic and sometimes for private reasons. The conspirators' first envoy, for instance, Francesc Vilaplana, disgraced for a juvenile homicide, had led a bitter life, in the intervals of exile as a criminal and evasion as a deserter. Pau Claris, his uncle, was a canon of Urgell – a chapter that collectively pursued rebellion in the course of a vendetta against its bishop – destined, by his respected gifts, his social connections and his rhetorical skill, to be the effective organiser of a party of secession from the Spanish monarchy, he was the John Pym of the Catalan revolt, who might have been won by the court had his talents been appreciated. The Fontanella family, who became the mainstay of the pro-French party in Barcelona in the 1640s, had been alienated by Joan Pere de Fontanella's failure to achieve a place in Catalonia's supreme tribunal, the Audiència, whose offices were royal gifts. Francesc de Tamarit had also inherited a grievance against the crown, from his father, who had suffered imprisonment, exile and material loss under Philip II.

Whether prompted by private or patriotic motives, recourse to the French could be seen as a measure of practical prudence, either to prevent a French invasion or to meet an attack from Spain. This seems to have been widely feared after the murder of Santa Coloma: a punitive expedition against Catalonia was discussed in Council in Madrid at that time, though the decision to use force was not taken by Olivares until 31 July; by then outrages against royal authority had accumulated to an intolerable level all over Catalonia and the conspirators of Barcelona were already deeply implicated with the French. Olivares hoped to avoid the inevitably ruinous consequences of a civil war by accumulating an army as a threat, by which Catalonia would be coerced into modifying the Constitucions 'which obstruct good government and the administration of justice, and which stand in the way of uniformity with the other kingdoms of the crown'.[24] The representative assembly of the principality was therefore to be summoned to a meeting under the mouths of Castilian guns. The Diputació in Barcelona anticipated this manoeuvre by summoning the assembly in its own name: if not an outright abjuration of the authority of the crown, this was an act of unambiguous rebellion. On 10 September the rebel assembly opened. On the 17th, the Consell of Barcelona rather hesitantly expressed its willingness to accept French tutelage. On the 24th, the conspirators' envoys, now with some claim to represent Catalonia, proposed to their French counterparts an alliance 'in the war with which this Principality is threatened by the ministers of Spain'.[25]

The ambiguous terms of this offer suggest that, like the roughly contemporary 'Great Rebellion' in England, Catalonia's was reluctantly espoused. An anonymous but representative diarist in Barcelona blamed the king's bad counsel for 'the greatest sorrow this Principality of Catalonia has suffered', which was 'to have been obliged to rely upon a foreign prince, moved by necessity, and to have had no other recourse . . . May God and most holy Mary be pleased to return us to the grace of our father and lord, Philip.'[26] Many localities failed or refused to subscribe men or money for defence, which came to rely increasingly on a French army of occupation. Not until the masters of the rebellion in Barcelona had concluded their formal alliance with France did Olivares send in the threadbare forces he had gathered for an invasion. Their advance through the southern part of the principality was virtually unopposed. When the royalists reached Tarragona, commitment to the revolution waned even in Barcelona. The war was prolonged by a coup inside the city by the partisans of France, who turned against the fainthearts and pro-Spaniards the violence of a mob infuriated by failure and apprehensive of royalist revenge; in the last week of December the mob ran wild, murdering 'traitors', opening the prisons and firing the houses of the proscribed. All goods should be had in common, they were said to have claimed, because our father Adam died intestate.[27] During January, negotiations between the conspirators of the previous summer and the French commissioner, Duplessis-Besançon, produced the formula 'for the preservation of this province': Pau Claris declared Catalonia a republic under the government of the King of France 'as in the time of Charlemagne, with a contract to observe our constitutions'. Duplessis took control of the city and command of its defence. On 26 January, he turned back the advance of the Spanish royal forces in a pitched battle within sight of the walls.

French rule in Barcelona was far more offensive to traditional susceptibilities than anything known before the revolt. It has often been supposed that French supremacy relied on the large minority of French immigrants – probably more than ten per cent of the population – who had gravitated to Barcelona, as to other Catalan towns, in large numbers, especially in the second half of the sixteenth century. Most of the 'French', however, were Catalans of at least the second generation. They had, in most cases, come from southern France and spoke languages similar to Catalan. Their assimilation had been painless and they are unlikely to have felt beholden to the culture of Paris or the rulers of the land they had left. Their presence may help to explain the fragility of loyalty to Spain but not the adhesion of the city to the cause of a traditional foe. What does seem to have sustained the French position was the collective war fever of a beleaguered community, which made a sane word an act of treachery. Continued peasant unrest created the feeling of a beleaguered city almost throughout the twelve years of French mastery. Not for the last time in Barcelona's history, a seige mentality favoured political extremism and fanaticism; fear of what lay outside the walls led to the rule of terror from within. The peasants' next invasion of the city caused a permanent change in Barcelona's institutions of government. In May 1641, a few score of the rural insurgents, accompanied by a city mob, marched on the city hall intent on the elimination of 'traitors'. They were stopped in the street of the silversmiths by guildsmen who used their counters and shop fittings to make a barricade. At the time of the next election of *consellers*, the Consell offered no resistance to the crowd of guildsmen demonstrating for the addition of a sixth *conseller* to the strength, to represent their interests. A modest revolution had been salvaged from the defeat of anarchy. The adscription of a representative of a relatively low estate of men to the ruling council was to be the most enduring consequence of the war of the 1640s, and one which marked Barcelona out from most other Spanish and Mediterranean cities.

Sources of tension with the central institutions of the state did not end with the substitution of Paris for Madrid. The city's jurisdiction continued to be infringed in emergency conditions; conflicts over billetting in the countryside continued with French, as with Spanish, troops; the mob's cry in the streets was still, 'Death to bad government!' The appointment of Michel de Mazarin as governor in 1648 provoked a characteristic wrangle over whether he was entitled to enter the city on a litter; classic disputes over the Constitucions animated the years from 1648 to 1652 when the French troops, in their indigence, were obliged to live off the land without making the payments due under the law. Marshal Brézé's complaint that the Catalans seemed 'incapable of understanding their own best interests' might have been made by Olivares.[28]

Relations between citizens and French proconsuls were exacerbated by incessant French fears of 'Castilian' conspiracy. The first anti-French broadsheets were posted in November 1640, and there was another poster campaign in April 1641. In 1642 the Bishop, and in 1643 the vicar general and many other clergy, were expelled for refusal or suspected mental reservation when challenged to swear allegiance to the king of France. A conspiracy unmasked in 1645 ended with the imprisonment of the president of the Diputació and the execution of two of its high officials. In 1649 the arrest of exiles returning with official leave alienated even some fervent partisans of France.[29]

Rule of a disaffected city in a climate of suspicion drove the French to increasingly onerous methods of control. Their surrogates in city government were the Fontanella clan and their affinity, excluded before the war, implicated in the totemic rivalries of the ruling class and resented by other members of the natural élite. Reliable instruments of French rule themselves, they were capable of commanding loyalty in a small circle and provoking hostility in a large one. The French controlled access to office in the city and the provincial government by exercising over candidates' lists a veto which was contrary to the Constitucions. Above all the indigenous organs of government they erected a council of war and introduced Frenchmen into positions of influence, again counter to the Constitucions; the viceroys, turned over even more rapidly and amid more recriminations than under Spanish rule, were always French or, in one case, Italian. From 1645, Barcelona had a French bishop who, presiding over a privileged network of informers, always fearing assassination, was one of the most efficient agents of repression. This structure of government was rickety not only because it was deeply resented, but also because nobody believed it would last. Rumours that France was prepared to return Catalonia to Philip IV as part of a general trade-off and peace – rumours justified in the event – caused a scramble among influential Catalans to anticipate the return to Spanish allegiance. This in turn made French interlopers determined to exploit the province while they could, for all it was worth. Barcelona was colonised by French merchants – at least 140 of them: the spearhead, perhaps, of growing French commercial and financial penetration of Spain in the late seventeenth and early eighteenth centuries.[30]

French domination of Catalonia was only secure while the Spanish monarchy was over-extended on other fronts. In 1648, however, peace with the Dutch gave Spain a respite just when France, afflicted with war-weariness and a royal minority, was distracted by civil wars of her own. The plague of 1650–4, which reputedly claimed 30,000 lives in Catalonia, sapped the will to continue the struggle and gave moralists a scourge for troubled consciences. By mid-1651 most French garrisons had gone from south of the Alps and the recovery of Barcelona was being planned in Madrid. In August, a siege by land and a blockade by sea was begun under the overall command of Don Juan José of Austria. He had no wish to beat Barcelona too severely, for the monarchy was more concerned to devise a lasting settlement than to win a quick victory; nor were his forces strong enough to risk a direct assault. Both sides settled to a long process of attrition, knowing that time favoured the besiegers and only a French counter-attack could bring relief.

A French force did fight its way through to the city under the Count of La Motte Houdancourt in April 1652. It was strong enough to prolong the conflict without affecting the result. The plate of the churches and private houses was commandeered to make coins with the legend *'Barcelona Civitas Obsessa'*. The blessed sacrament was exposed everywhere to animate morale. The garrison was reduced 'to eating grass'. On 28 September the Consell told La Motte they could resist no longer. He replied that horses and fodder were still left in the square. They pointed out that Mataró had fallen; he warned them not to listen to rumours. The Consell approached the other sources of authority in the city – the cathedral chapter, the rump of the Diputació, the assembly of the noble estate – and, in permanent session until unanimity was achieved, gradually procured general agreement to treat with the king's commander. Don Juan received their messenger with tears in his eyes and told him to take his own tip from a chestful of silver. He promised to treat the citizens as brothers 'just as the king would as a father'. On 13 October, two days after receiving the formal submission of the *consellers*, he entered the city in triumph, in a green coat with silver braid and a hat with green feathers. The *Te Deum* in the cathedral was followed by illuminations and dancing in the streets.[31]

THE AGONY OF THE CONSTITUCIONS

Don Juan intended this festive atmosphere to inaugurate an era of oblivion, symbolised in an almost universal pardon. He was the architect of a restoration which left the status quo almost unimpaired. The main changes that modified the pre-war government of the city had been introduced by the French: the admission of the *conseller* of the lower artisans and the supervision of candidates for office by the sovereign authority. Barcelona could – had the king and Don Juan wished – have been reduced to 'absolute' government. On 14 November, the Council in Madrid proposed the abolition of the Consell and its replacement by a small corporation under the chairmanship of a royal nominee; the construction of a fortress with a permanent royal garrison; and the transfer of the power of creating *ciutadans honrats* to the crown. Philip IV, however, preferred to proclaim respect for the Constitucions. The crown did attempt to influence the politics of

the city by heavy use of a traditional prerogative, elevating more than
250 citizens to be *ciutadans honrats* during the next three decades; in
partial consequence, perhaps, Barcelona was to show, in the next civil
war, astonishing depths of loyalty to the Habsburgs.[32] On the other
hand, reversion to the status quo raised the danger of another round
of conflict. What Barcelona most needed to ensure her future stability
was a long period of peace and prosperity. In fact, in the second
half of the seventeenth century, she got hardly a breathing space.
Civic-minded optimists and economic projectors, led by Narcis Feliu
de la Penya, had hardly begun their efforts to revive the 'Catalan
Phoenix' before the French wars of the 1670s to 1690s exposed her
lands to more campaigns and the city to another siege. The locust
plague of 1687 devastated the province and only spared the city after
the *consellers'* vow to the Virgin of La Mercé. Barcelona had still not
reconstructed her stake in stability when, in 1700, King Charles II
died, leaving no direct heir. The rival claims of powerful pretenders,
Habsburg and Bourbon, plunged the succession into the crucible and
Europe into war. Unresolved issues between Barcelona and Spain,
which the restoration of 1652 left pendant, came to dominate Catalonia's attitude to the conflict.

Barcelonese adherence to the Habsburg cause – not just the fact but
also the ferocity of it – is one of the most beguiling problems of the
War of the Spanish Succession. Merchant communities would usually
rather fight shy than fight. The Catalans could only profit from this
new war if it was kept off their territory. Memories of the Habsburgs
were imprinted with images of conflict and disaster, whereas Bourbon
rule began in a blaze of promise. In 1702, at the Corts celebrated in
Barcelona for the tendering of allegiance at the start of his reign, the
Bourbon candidate, Philip V of Spain (Felip IV in Catalonia) had
sworn all the traditional oaths and granted new and potentially exploitable privileges to the Catalans. The terms of the declaration he
subscribed were virtually a Catalanist manifesto; the principality was
'free and independent', voluntarily associated with the other peoples
'of the Catalan nation, who speak the Catalan tongue' in Valencia and
Majorca, and with the Crown of Aragon. The territory of Catalonia
was defined as including the counties of Roussillon and Cerdagne – an
implicit acknowledgement, on Philip's part, of his obligation to attempt
to prise the lost counties from his grandfather's clutches. The new
king's material generosity to the Catalans was correspondingly lavish;
he granted Barcelona the status of a free port and opened the trade of
the New World to two ships a year. To the nobility of the principality

PMA

Miró's *Dog Barking at the Moon* (1926). Joan Miró i Ferra was born in Barcelona in 1893, and studied in the Cercle Artistic de Sant Lluc by the Els Quatre Gats café. He lived in Paris from 1920 to 1932, adopting Surrealism by 1924, but continued to spend summers in Montroig. He returned to Barcelona in 1932 and collaborated with the avant-garde organisation Amics de L'Art Nou.

A wild man in combat and a griffin devouring prey: Romanesque carvings from the gate of St Ives in the cathedral. Most work of the Romanesque period in Barcelona was smothered by triumphant rebuilding in the Gothic style during periods of prosperity in the thirteenth and fourteenth centuries.

AM

St George, patron saint of Catalonia, depicted on the façade of the Palau de la Generalitat by Pere Joan (fourteenth century). As well as inspiring the long survival of the cult of chivalry in Barcelona, St George became a symbol of Catalan identity and a focus of mediaeval nostalgia in modern times.

AM

GEORGE WRIGHT

DOMINGO

The cathedral cloister, though it looks dramatic here, is one of the most charming corners of old Barcelona, with its diminutive scale, shady palms and grazing fowl.

The cathedral, which houses the tomb of St Eulàlia, looks dominant when suitably photographed, but is really a building of self-effacing position. The west façade was added to the fourteenth-century building in 1882. The broad aisle windows visible here and the absence of exposed buttresses are typical of Barcelonese Gothic.

Gothic Bridge of Sighs over the carrer del Bisbe.

The Ajuntament, or City Hall, the focal point of Barcelona's tradition of civic independence, is behind this austerely classical façade an ancient Gothic building. The political campaign which preserved its Gothic character, and adorned even the classical façade with statues of mediaeval heroes (discernible in the niches on either side of the main door), was a *cause célèbre* of nineteenth-century Barcelona.

Fifteenth-century *consellers* from the *Book of Privileges* of the Gardeners' Guild. The art of such books demonstrates guildsmen's civic pride and anxiety over status. The appearance of the *consellers* confers both prestige and legal authority on the gardeners' confraternity.

'The Virgin of the Consellers' (1445), by Lluis Dalmau, the first Spanish painter known to have studied in the Netherlands, shows realistic portraits of the *consellers* for that year at the Virgin's feet, with the celestial protectors, St Eulàlia and St Andrew (on whose feast the *consellers* were elected), and an idealised cityscape in the background.

IM

AM

IM

Charles V before Barcelona, reviewing the expeditionary force bound for Tunis in 1535. Flemish tapestry in the Royal Collection, Madrid. After the period of 'difficulties or decline' in the fifteenth century, the reign of Charles V helped to stimulate Barcelona's recovery by restoring the priority of Mediterranean policies.

IM

(Above) Firing of the old Inquisition Tribunal and Prison in the Palau Reial (carrer de la Tapineria), 1820. Liberal propaganda surrounded the collapse of this moribund but symbolic institution with heroic and romantic images of released captives and triumphant warriors.

(Bottom left) Part of the Masque organised by Barcelona's guilds to celebrate the visit of the future King Charles III, 1731. The float on wheels represents the Temple of Poseidon, the large ship in the foreground that of the Argonauts. The occasion combined reconciliation with the Bourbon dynasty and celebration of Barcelona's maritime traditions with a display of civic loyalty.

Massacre of friars and other acts
of sacrilege during the riots of 1835.
As well as clerical targets, the rioters of
that summer chose the army and police,
and practised Luddism.

IM

The defenestration of General Bassa in
the riots of August 1835. Engraved for
a popular market thirty years later, the
scene has become romanticised, with the
rioters in heroic poses and dress which
reflects a wide social mix.

IM

Building barricades from uprooted paving-stones to defend the approaches to the plaça de Sant Jaume in an anonymous painting of 1843. The shops include well-known commercial names of the period, including that of the jeweller Francesc Clarà and three bookshops: Caspar, the widow Gorchs and Francesc Font.

Through the colonnades of the plaça Reial, Barcelona's most harmonious square, the street-lamps designed by Gaudí can be seen. Here, a hundred years ago, the first pavement cafés, which still dominate the life of the square, took the conventions and atmosphere of bourgeois life out of its domestic shell and on to the streets for the first time.

IM

PÉREZ PUIGJANÉ/DOMINGO

PÉREZ PUIGJANÈ/DOMINGO

The academic, sentimental and heroic monument to Columbus, erected for the Universal International exhibition of 1888, was designed by Gaità Buïgas and topped by a statue by Rafael Atché. It weighs 233 tons and incorporates a complex and extensive iconographical scheme in praise of Catalan contributions to the discovery of America, as well as a lift to the top.

IM

(Above) The Café Torino of 1902 –
winner of its year of the city's prize for
the best building – was perhaps one of
the most evocative corners of Modernist
Barcelona. Gaudí and Puigi i Cadafalch
contributed to the design by Richard
Capmany, and writers and artists
gathered to drink the vermouth first
popularised here by the Italian
proprietor, Flaminio Mozzalama.

(Right) Shop-signs in Barcelona are
among the most conspicuous works of
art of the *art nouveau* era, like the well-
known Chinese dragon of the Pla de la
Boqueria, which presides over a square
where the site of the old city gate of
Santa Eulàlia opens onto the Rambla,
opposite the city's central market.

(Bottom left) The skyline of Barcelona
with smoke rising from the fires lighted
by rioters during the Tragic Week of
1909. Almost all the eighty buildings
fired were direct dependencies of
religious orders.

GEORGE WRIGHT

RH

Gaudí's Casa Vicens
in Gràcia, carrer de
Carolinas, designed
in 1883, is a good
example of the
architect's early,
angular style, heavily
indebted to Moorish
traditions, which also
informed the richly
ornamented interior.

AAA

(Left) The spires of Gaudí's
Sagrada Familia, rising above
what Dalí called 'tender doors
of calves' liver', have come to
symbolise Barcelona. The organic
appearance of the buildings, the
paraboloid curves and the distant
but unmistakable Gothic
inspiration are representative of
Gaudí's art.

(Right) Gaudí's Casa Batlló
(1904-6) (paseo de Gràcia, 43) has
been described as a 'piece of lustre
ware, responding constantly,
diversely to reflections of the sun'.
Its balconies, architraves and
eschewal, inside, of straight lines
have made it for some
commentators a beacon of *art
nouveau*, its shimmering façade,
to others, a symbol of what Dalí
called Gaudí's 'creative bad taste'.

AA

Pérez Puigjanè/Domingo

AAA

(Above) The Parc Güell is a favoured spot for leisure-seekers in Barcelona today – a product of the wealth, patronage and civic philanthropy of the Güell family, and of the genius of their favoured architect, Gaudí. On the park's hillside location, these cavernous arcades support a sunlit upper storey.

(Top right) The willowy lines, bulbous 'jaws' and fantastic chimneys of Gaudí's Casa Milá (1905-11) (paseo de Gràcia, 92) are well displayed in the photograph, which also shows the characteristic shape of the main intersections of the Eixample road system. Though lampooned in its day, this was perhaps Gaudí's most revolutionary building, technically as well as aesthetically, planned with great freedom thanks to the use of a structural steel frame instead of supporting walls.

(Bottom right) An early photograph of the Casa Milá tries to minimise its 'unbuilt' look. Notice, however, the trunk-like pilasters, dune-like overhangs and encrusted vegetation.

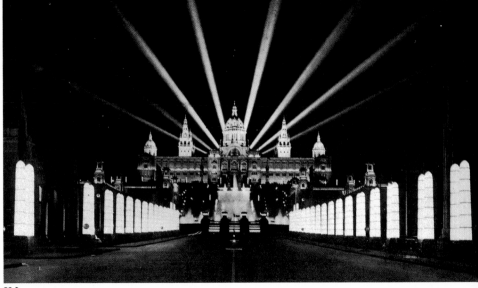

IM

Barcelona's International Exhibition, eventually mounted in 1929, was originally conceived as a celebration of electricity. The fan-tail of the searchlights which illuminated the focal point of the exhibition campus, the Palau Nacional of Montjuic, and the dramatic lighting of the fountains and avenue of arcades in the foreground, echoed this theme when the event opened at last, twelve years late.

The Olympic stadium in Montjuic, originally built for the Universal International Exhibition of 1929, has been remodelled by Alfons Milà and Frederic Correa to accommodate the 1992 Olympiad.

Pascal Rondeau

he scattered titles with an open hand, including leading citizens of Barcelona in the spree.

Even this most favoured élite responded guardedly, because Philip had, it was thought, already betrayed signs of an arbitrary disposition and an untrustworthy nature. Before coming to Catalonia, he had imposed a new viceroy on the territory at a time when, by the strictest interpretation of the law, having not yet exchanged oaths with his subjects, he had no power to do so. The new viceroy had compounded the offence by appointing professors to the university in despite of the right of nomination of the Consell de Cent. The envoy despatched to complain, Felip de Ferran Sacirera, was briefly gaoled in Saragossa. When the king arrived in Barcelona, the same man was chosen to join the deputation sent out to meet him. The city could hardly have addressed a clearer message of caution to the king.

The royal arrival was celebrated with due pomp, but also with a notable reserve on both sides. The equivocal reception committee included not only Ferran Sacirera but also three other figures who seemed calculated to be offensive to the king: Josep Galceran de Pinós, whose father had been one of the most unremitting champions of resistance during the last revolt; Joan Llinars i Farell, who had been a hero of the struggle against the French besiegers of 1697 and who had publicly blamed faint-heartedness in Madrid for the submission of the city; and Joan Baptista Reverter, who had placed his legal expertise at the service of the city in the dispute over the university appointments. These four met the king outside the city, near Martorell, to remind him of the *consellers'* privilege of wearing their hats in the king's presence. The monarch's meeting with the *consellers* was dramatically staged; the king advanced through the outskirts of the city, gathering in his wake deputations of worthies – the professors of the university, the city clergy, the representatives of three estates. As he approached the gate of Sant Antoni, the trumpets brayed for silence; the warders and mace-bearers in blue and crimson taffeta emerged to make way and in stately procession the *conseller en cap* and five other *consellers* followed, representing respectively the city patriciate and the higher and lower guilds. At the king's command, they uncovered their heads. The crowd waited with bated breath to see whether he would issue the traditional command, 'Be covered'. Into the silence, the *conseller en cap* inserted his speech of welcome; the party kissed the king's hand. The *consellers* exchanged glances; a murmur arose in the crowd; to cover it, the trumpeters struck up, while the still hatless *consellers* took their places in the procession, the *conseller en cap* at the king's side, and rode into the city. In a society so attuned to the nuances of deference, the king's silence on this cherished privilege, which had been so bitterly contested and so triumphantly secured, seemed ominous.

Even had Philip's reign not begun with a series of offensive gestures, he would still have had to contend with deep-seated hostility to his cause. The French, who still fancied themselves – at least their king did – as 'protectors' of Catalonia, were almost universally loathed in the principality; they had deserted Catalonia in the last revolt, according to the version of events cherished by Catalans; they had seized the Catalan lands of Roussillon and Cerdagne, and had then turned their arms against their erstwhile allies in the wars of 1673–8 and 1680–97. Castile was hardly better loved than France, and the Catalans were still awaiting their reward – in the form of a greater share of offices throughout the monarchy – for their loyalty and sacrifices in the recent wars. The Catalan nobility felt itself deliberately run down by the non-replacement of expired lineages and the 'Sabine ravishment' by which heiresses had been lost to Castilian marriages. By the beginning of the eighteenth century, the last duchy in Catalonia, that of Cardona, had passed into the hands of a Castilian house.

Against this background of resentment the concessions of 1702 were insufficient to buy Catalan loyalty. In the following years, Philip's government committed new outrages against Catalan susceptibilities. In January 1704, a new viceroy was sworn in who appeared the embodiment of Castilian imperialism. Francisco Fernández de Velasco presided over a series of blunders calculated to arouse apprehension in Barcelona, where no historical precedent was ever forgotten. The sending of Catalan troops to Portugal recalled a *casus belli* of 1640, when Olivares had provoked a rebellion in Portugal by demanding Portuguese troops be used against the Catalans. A cherished privilege was transgressed – the Catalans' right to serve only in defence of their own homeland; the expulsion of a Dutch resident, Arnau Jager, who had married in Barcelona and become thoroughly assimilated by Barcelonese society, served the cause of the king because Holland was a member of the 'Grand Alliance' of his enemies, but was contrary to Catalan law. Among Velasco's nominees for election to the Consell dels Cent was a Tarraconensian, whose provenance made him ineligible; an attempt to intrude a citizen of another town filled the Barcelonese with disgust and led to the rejection of all the royal candidates. Catalonia remembered with affection the viceroyalty of Prince George of Hesse-

Darmstadt, who fought in the Habsburg camp and whose agents excited pro-imperialist conspiracies against Velasco.

Despite the naturally peaceful inclinations of a mercantile élite, many of the leading members of Barcelonese society were disposed to respond to Velasco's indelicate rule with violence. Many of them were the sons of fathers who had fought Madrid in the 1640s and 1650s. They owed an obligation of honour to memories dating from those years. Psychologically inclined to fight, they were also ideologically equipped. It was an almost unquestioned assumption that Catalonia was a sovereign state with a right, in principle, to secede from a monarchy which was thought of as confederative. The theory of contractual monarchy, which late seventeenth-century fashion made familiar, seemed ideally to fit the historical experience of Catalonia, and of the other component-states of the crown of Aragon, where royal authority was explicitly dependent on observance of the *Constitucions* and where, according to the contractualist version of Catalan history, the sovereign prince had commonly been elected, back to the time of Charlemagne.

Nevertheless, the repudiation of King Philip, however vexatious his rule, would have been unthinkable but for the circumstances of the war. The need to maximise resources and suppress conspiracies drove Velasco to ever more impolitic excesses. In July 1704, the failure of an imperialist coup in Barcelona evoked from Velasco a savage response and, in the citizens, longings for a change of rule. By 1705 – the decisive year of Catalonia's change of allegiance – it looked, moreover, as if the allies would win the war. Everyone likes to be on the winning side, especially a commercial community for whom money spent on warfare is a reluctantly made, high-risk investment. Catalonia was caught in an uncomfortable crossfire, between the French frontier and the English 'lake' in the western Mediterranean, where the British navy could wreak havoc on a hostile coastline and dictate the terms of trade. At the end of the war, when Barcelona was fighting on alone, the inhabitants were inclined to blame the English for inveigling them into the imperialist alliances with promises. The trick was performed, almost equally, with implicit threats. On 20 June 1705, when representatives of 'the Most Illustrious, Famous and Renowned Principality of Catalonia' signed a treaty with England in Genoa, the guns of British ships could be heard in Catalan waters. Catalans came later to see the episode as a typical instance of Albion's habit of acquiring by bribery or intimidation an ally she would later abandon. From the Catalan point of view the sixth clause of the treaty was the most important, by which England guaranteed that 'now and in the future the Principality of Catalonia shall keep all the graces, privileges, laws and customs which severally and in common her people have enjoyed and do enjoy'. This revealed the decisive motive on the Catalan side; after the failed coup of 1704, Velasco had begun, under cover of the war effort, to dismantle the traditional institutions of Catalan government: only a change of allegiance, it seemed, could safeguard the precious heritage. Appetite for war in Barcelona *vient en mangeant* and the Barcelonese, shy imperialists at first, would become the most committed and tenacious partisans of the Habsburg cause. They joined the allied cause in a calculating spirit but clung on when it was hopeless and all the other allies had withdrawn. They dared beyond hope, endured beyond reason, and reaped the usual reward of that sort of heroism: defeat. Bourbon victory became almost inevitable after 1711, when the Habsburg pretender succeeded to the Imperial throne: the powers of the Grand Alliance would not fight to put the Emperor Charles VI on the throne of Spain. The Catalans, however, found it impossible to adjust to the new circumstances; their stake was too high to abandon without seeing the contest through.

The example of the siege of 1652 was fatally misleading. It encouraged the Barcelonese to believe that the liberties of Catalonia could be ventured again. In the negotiations which brought peace to most of the combatants in the War of the Spanish Succession, Catalan partisanship of the defeated Habsburg coalition brought no rewards, and not even any guarantees, for Catalonia. The Habsburgs' English allies adopted a nakedly perfidious course, insisting that Queen Anne's honour must be saved, but encouraging the Spaniards to make a token concession to Catalonia's 'ancient rights' and exact a satisfying vengeance later. Charles VI, vowing never to desert the Catalans, authorised the evacuation of his forces from Catalonia without securing any but the most perfunctory assurances from his enemies. Barcelona's decision to fight on alone was a calculated risk: if the bloodshed and destruction of 1652 were to be re-enacted, so might the outcome, the renewal of the *furs*. The imperial troops gathered for embarkation during June 1713. By the end of the month French observer was convinced that Barcelona would commit an act of despair: 'The inhabitants are more senseless than ever, capable of extreme folly'. A spy warned the Castilians that the city fathers 'would sooner die or become Moors than surrender'.[33]

There was surprising unanimity among the leaders of society in Catalonia and, in particular, in Barcelona in favour of continuing the war. Even the pessimists spoke approvingly of the example in self-immolation of Lucretia. The meeting of Catalonia's representative assembly, the Braços, at the end of June and beginning of July, was held in a charged atmosphere of national sacrifice. The noble estate vacillated and the clergy withdrew on the grounds that they were incompetent to vote on a matter of war; but the commoners' estate, the Braço Real, voted for war by acclamation at dawn on the 9 July and carried the rest with them. The withdrawal of some of the higher clergy to the enemy camp only heightened the religious fervour in which the spirit of resistance was being expressed; and, in a city in which popular politics had always been decisive, the leading *consellers* who would have preferred a prudent course soon suppressed their objections. On 23 July, the citizenry gathered at the shrine of the Virgin of Mercé to witness the image's solemn receipt of a petition begging her favour in the coming fight. In 1687 she had warded off a plague of locusts, and if in 1696 she had failed to respond to a similar petition to grant issue to King Charles II, that was 'because of the inscrutable secrets of divine providence'.

Outside Barcelona, resistance crumbled in the central and southern parts of the principality. By late August, the city was isolated, except by sea. In the hinterland, only the rural guerillas known as Miquelets were sustaining resistance. The conflict was prolonged through the summer and winter, however, by the fanaticism with which Barcelona was defended, and the faint-heartedness of the enemy's attack. Philip V was not anxious to crush the productive potential out of his subjects. He wanted the city squeezed into surrender, not battered and sacked, and underestimated the warlike resolve of the merchants and *menu peuple*. His grandfather, Louis XIV, who had the material power to break Barcelona at will, was urging an even softer policy: he fancied himself as the protector of the Catalans and wanted a well-disposed community on his borders; he incessantly urged Philip to show 'clemency' to the Catalans by conceding their privileges and negotiating with the Barcelonese. The King of Spain, however, was adamant that the Catalans should have 'no more privileges than the Castilians', partly in the interests of state efficiency and partly out of a politic disinclination to reward dissent. His field commander, the Duke of Pópoli, hardly seemed serious about the siege, assuming that Philip and Louis would keep his army intact, whatever the cost, and that time favoured the Bourbon cause.

Certainly, the Barcelonese had no allies in the offing, except in their own imaginations. Their appeals to England, being couched in moral terms, evoked no response, except from a Parliamentary opposition who saw the 'disasters of the Catalans' as fodder for a good debate. When a British squadron briefly appeared off Barcelona during the siege exciting the hopes of the populace, the commander delivered, with expressions of sympathy, only a demand for payment of the city's war debts to its British creditors. The Emperor Charles, whom Barcelona continued to hail as 'sovereign', inflamed resistance by promises of help, repeated in the spring of 1714. But he took no action. Barcelona was the victim of the inertia of European diplomacy. None of the ex-combatants of the War of Succession could or would re-enter the fray merely to improve her terms of surrender.

The city was not well defended. Some 10,000 men were available to man the walls at the start of the siege, but most were untrained civilians. The core of the trained force was the Coronela, a traditional urban militia, tough in defence but unwary at such affairs as sorties and surprises. There seem to have been no more than 2,000 regular troops, many of them German deserters from the withdrawn imperial force, detained by sentimental connections in the city or induced by the promise of pay. The city was fortunate to find a commander of valour and ingenuity in Antoní de Villaroel, a professional soldier of Castilian parentage, who had distinguished himself in the Bourbon cause before deserting to the imperialists, frustrated by his own in-expertise in court intrigue. Having been inspector-general of infantry in the last weeks of the imperialist regime, he accepted command from the Catalan estates on 11 July; in supervising the defences, raising morale and leading sallies he was insuperable, though for his preferred strategy of breaking the siege by a major enveloping sortie, means were lacking. He was effectively military supremo, but in a siege the distinction between civil and military authority becomes blurred, and for Villaroel, as for most officers in analogous circumstances, his civilian partners proved difficult and irksome.

As the siege went on, the fervour of the government grew more intense and its forms more revolutionary. Executive responsibility was in the hands of a *junta* of thirty-six, appointed by the estates and divided into committees charged with maximising resources for the defence. The city council remained in office, too: on 30 November, to the evident alarm of some of the incumbents, a new election by lot was held amid allegations that some councillors were profiting from war shortages; the result was suspiciously favourable to the old guard, almost all of whom remained in office. In December the *junta* of thirty-six was replaced by a new *junta* of twenty-four. The permanent organ of the estates, the Diputació, remained in session, exercising, for the most part, only its judicial role; but its failure to support a general uprising against the Bourbon forces in the countryside in January provoked mob indignation: on 26 February it dissolved itself, handing over its powers to the city. Alongside a reconstituted and more radical *junta* of twenty-four a committee of eighteen popular representatives waged a campaign for the moral rearmament of the defenders, the elimination of profiteers, the enforcement of austerity and expulsion of the gypsies. Through all these changes, Villaroel had to struggle to retain military responsibility in his hands; only his repeated threats of resignation kept the zealots at bay.

The fanaticism of the defenders was fanned by prophetic voices and the exploiters of popular devotion to saints and images who were hijacked in the cause of all-out struggle. The voice of '*El Despertador de Barcelona*' was one of the loudest in denouncing faint-hearts. In May, when the reception of an envoy from King Philip seemed to offer a brief hope of peace, priests were ordered to conduct a plebiscite in the confessional to establish what the people really felt. The findings of this curious public opinion exercise of a predemocratic age were predictable. Resistance was 'the service of God'. The people would fight on as an act of faith. The twenty-four declared the Barcelonese 'instruments of God for the liberty of the entire Monarchy of Spain' – an interesting formula, which shows that they were capable of conceiving the campaign for the *furs* as part of a more generalised struggle of 'liberty' against 'despotism'. The king's envoy departed, advising his master to bombard the city into submission. Not for the last time, Villaroel tried to use his influence for peace: the imminence of Louis XIV's intervention, and the arrival of the Marshal-Duke of Berwick with crushingly superior forces, were now an open secret, expected almost daily. The twenty-four, however, wrote to Berwick to warn him that they would not be intimidated by his reputation. They might be vanquished by irresistible strength, they admitted, but they would 'make the streets run with blood' rather than surrender. The rule of populist fanatics and visionary priests thrived on short rations.

Berwick arrived in July with orders to spare women, children, the aged, convents and churches but not to concede the ancient privileges. He wrote loftily to Philip, enjoining him to be merciful to a population that seemed to be 'sick . . . possessed by some irrational rage.' As his forces built up and the heat mounted, the atmosphere inside Barcelona grew febrile. On 30 July, the authorities ordered collective vows to put the city into a state of grace. No jewellery was to be worn; public spectacles, including the theatre, were suppressed; 'profane and costly fashions' were outlawed; the clergy were 'requested' to have the Sacrament permanently exposed and the Rosary continually recited in public. On 3 August the councillors assembled to perform penance in public after confession. On the 15th, the problem of the search for allies was declared to be over: a 'celestial alliance' with St Eulàlia, whose banner flew from the ramparts, was to serve the city's needs. A muster on the last day of the month showed only 6,215 men still fit to serve.

At the start of the siege, Barcelona had been well stocked and Majorcan supply-ships had successfully run the blockade. By now, however, hunger was straining morale. In the first week of September, the aged and infirm and those otherwise disqualified to fight were allowed to leave the city and beg for mercy and sustenance from the besiegers. But when the authorities assembled to debate whether to hear Berwick's call for surrender on the 4th, they returned, by an overwhelming vote, that 'they do not even wish to hear, much less entertain any proposal from the enemy whatsoever'. On the grounds that it was unreasonable to refuse even to listen to the enemy's proposals, and that further resistance would merely shed needless blood, Villaroel issued his last threat to resign. His aide takes up the story:

> I found him in the company of Colonel Ferrer. He asked me if I yet knew what resolution the commune had taken in response to his last message. I replied that it grieved me much to see the state to which matters had sunk, and that his departure was inevitable since the authorities had already nominated his successor. Anxiously, he asked me whom they had chosen. 'The Virgin of Mercé,' I replied, and showed him the order. And I can certainly say that that resolution took him by surprise.[34]

Although the image of the Virgin evinced no unwillingness to assume command, Villaroel agreed to carry on as her deputy so as not to demoralise the defenders.

The last days of the siege saw many unavailing acts of heroism, but on the 11th, with the guns of the further redoubts turned in on the city and with Villaroel wounded in combat and under the surgeon's knife, a group of officers defied the civilian authority and approached Berwick directly for an accommodation. The Marshal remarked that 'a king does not make terms with his subjects'; the military envoys warned him that the citizens' leaders would rather die than surrender, but on the 12th the commune, after an agonised debate, agreed to treat, provided the terms of surrender were not formally unconditional. The last stages of the negotiation are shrouded in the obscurity of conflicting accounts. Berwick made no written promises, but may have guaranteed to the citizens their 'honour and lives' and personal property within the city; the rest, including the precious *furs*, were to be 'left to the King's clemency'. Writing his chronicle of the reign in Madrid, the Marqués de San Felipe could conceal neither his satisfaction nor his desire for revenge. 'This is what the unyielding pride of the Catalans, their faithlessness and treason, had brought them to . . . Those were not wanting who advised the King to raze the city to the ground and stand a column in the midst of it. There could be no chastisement too severe for a city that had been the cause of so much evil and that had deprived the Monarchy of so many realms.' He was still thinking of the events of 1640–58 and the losses of the Netherlands, Portugal and Roussillon.[35]

The Sweets of Defeat

The first act of the 'repression' that accompanied Berwick's occupation of Barcelona was the banning of the old permanent institution of the Corts, the Diputació, the symbol of Catalonia's ancient right to autonomy. Ironically, Berwick was suppressing a body that no longer existed. The Diputació had already dissolved itself, resigning its powers into the hands of the city. Exposed as an anachronism, the ancient government had been a victim of the jealousies of the politics of the beleaguered community, a sacrifice to the exigencies of the siege. The severities of the repression were felt more keenly by nineteenth-century historians than by those who suffered them at the time. The 'nationhood' they extinguished was as yet barely felt by the Catalans themselves. The abolished 'liberties' were most keenly regretted when they represented fiscal immunities and economic privileges. Yet their loss coincided with the start of an unparalleled era of prosperity, an economic resurgence which adorned the city and expanded its limits. The fawning adulation for the Bourbons expressed by the Barcelonese in the eighteenth century never lost its tone of apology for the excesses of the war, nor its air of special pleading; yet it represented a genuine sentiment. Bourbon rule may have been repressive in its origins, but it was congenial in its effect. Barcelona's response to Bourbon conquest was summed up by words ascribed to one of the five administrators

appointed by Berwick on the day after his victory; to a cleric who
wished to formulate a reply to the decree dissolving the Diputació, he
is said to have observed, 'Where there are no means of resistance, there
is no point in reply.'[36]

During Berwick's occupation, vindictive measures were few. On 2
October he expelled the preachers who were blamed for igniting the
morale of the besieged city; they had 'a reputation as spiritual men'
which they abused 'by causing great harm with their false doctrines
and enticing the people, by means of false revelations, to believe that
it was God's will to give them a miracle in their last extremity'. This
was a remarkable tribute to the persuasive powers of the two dozen or
so priests expelled. A few days later the military leaders of the rebellion
were shipped off in irons, accused of conspiring at the bedside of the
wounded Villaroel since the fall of the city. They were paraded in
triumph through the streets of Alicante before being locked in the
castle, from where Berwick hoped, as he wrote to the King, 'never to
see them emerge'. In fact, none seems to have been incarcerated for
long. Villaroel felt exceedingly sorry for himself; if his clandestine
correspondence out of the castle were discovered, 'my torments would
be doubled, if there be any worse than I already suffer'. His only
crime, he thought, 'was to have performed punctiliously my obligations
of honour to my master . . . and I do not know why I have been
forgotten in Vienna'. In reality, his services were well remembered
and, ultimately, well rewarded. The final settlement between Philip
V and Charles VI in 1725 brought his release and retirement to
Vienna with a Habsburg pension. Together, the clerics and generals
constituted a small class of victims of political persecution. When the
tower of the prison of Barcelona collapsed from neglect in January
1715, the city wits were titillated. It did not matter, reflected the most
savage of them, because the whole of Catalonia was now a prison. The
fact remained that there were no political prisoners in custody at the
time.[37]

Apart from disputes over the billeting of troops, typical of every
occupation, friendly and unfriendly alike, the other act of repression
directed specifically against Barcelona in the aftermath of the war was
the building of a citadel to overawe the city. It came to be hated –
more, perhaps, as a waste of space than as a symbol of submission. Its
demolition was at last undertaken by the city authorities during a brief
period of political instability early in the 1840s, and completed only
with the coming of the First Republic and renewed Catalan autonomy.
For more than a century in the meantime, however, it remained to

offend Barcelonese susceptibilities. At the time of its construction, the offence most deeply felt, it seems, was pecuniary: 800 dwellings, housing over 4,000 people, had to be demolished to make way for it. The cost of compensation, and of the unstinted effort of construction – the entire fortification was erected within seven months – had to be borne by the city. Apart from the feeling of being under the surveillance of an intruded garrison, specific injuries inflicted on Barcelona by the Bourbon 'terror' are hard to find. The administration, though backed by military force, remained in the hands of local notables appointed by Berwick and confirmed in office from Madrid. Arbitrary arrests seem to have been few and confined to the first year of the occupation. Uncompensated confiscations of property were limited to those who had held office during the 'rebellion', and to extramural property, consistent with what is known of Berwick's promises at the time of the city's submission. The most conspicuous victim was, perhaps, the University, whose faculties, except for medicine, were removed, ostensibly for reasons of security, to the 'signally loyal' country town of Cervera. The teaching of grammar was turned over to the Jesuits and the old University premises, after temporarily housing nuns removed from the site of the new citadel, was turned into a barracks.

On the other hand, the Catalans in general now had an indefeasible reputation for political and fiscal intractability. They were 'always on the lookout to dodge the yoke of justice'. Their objective 'in all ages past' was 'to achieve the remission of taxes and imposts' so 'that they feel nothing more acutely than liability to fiscal exactions imposed by royal authority alone'. This was scarcely more than the truth. José de Patiño's advice to Philip V went on to reflect the conviction in the Bourbon ranks that the recent war had been fought against the collective insanity of their opponents. 'They are passionate about their fatherland,' he wrote, 'to such a degree of excess that it makes them desert the use of reason'; and, he added, as if in proof of this assertion, 'they talk only in their native language'. In the circumstances of 1716, Patiño could be excused for concluding that their pride had been 'cast down' but had henceforth to be held down by force. 'They now respect justice and the precepts of your majesty, not out of love or affection, but under constraint of superior force.' Quiescence and obedience, 'which the country needs because of the sort of place it is and the temper of the natives', had to be 'affianced' to the force of arms. 'A strong arm will always be present to sway and support the ministers of justice.'[38] If it is excessive to speak of a repressive regime in Bourbon Barcelona, it is fair to recall that there was a repressive state of mind

in Madrid. Perhaps the most remarkable consequence of the defeat
was the rapidity with which Barcelona got over it. In the death-throes
of the siege, the spirit of resistance seemed indomitable; just before
the professionals' surrender the commune had summoned the people
to a last stand which seemed to be a consciously self-immolatory act.
Yet a few days later Berwick was writing that it seemed 'incredible
that so profound a calm should succeed so much uproar, all in the
next instant'. The shops reopened on 14 September; the inhabitants
watched the victorious troops, from their houses and shops, or from
the roadside, as if at a peacetime parade. The city escaped from trauma
into oblivion as a matter of official policy. One of the *consellers'* last
orders after the capitulation was that everyone should return to his
normal work and refrain from speaking of the past. There were
occasional lapses: in 1760, the Audiència tactlessly recalled the events
of 1714 when decreeing a ban on the wearing of arms; in the same
year, Barcelona's deputies at the Spanish legislative assembly joined
representatives of other parts of the former Crown of Aragon to defend
the old constitution against the enlightened despotism of the king. On
the whole, however, oblivion was upheld, because, as the council
of state in Madrid observed in 1760, 'prudence dictates that those
happenings be sedulously expunged from memory, and not intemper-
ately recalled'.[39]

The first profit-takers of Bourbon rule were the collaborationist
aristocracy and patriciate. Their palaces and villas can still be seen.
The finest of them, the Palau de Comillas, now houses the Generalitat
bookshop on the Rambla. Its building history began when Pere de
Castellà i Desbac – created a marquis by Philip V on the king's first
visit to Barcelona in 1702 – was granted the right of opening doors
and windows in the fortifications of the city's south gate. The Rambla
was an old waterway used in the Middle Ages for races and horse fairs.
The present palace was erected in 1774, when the transformation of
this unkempt boulevard into the main artery of the city marked the
triumph of a policy of *enrichissez-vous*, made palpable by enlightened
town planning. With its flattened pediment and its defiance of its
original surroundings, the palace might have looked like a model of
intrusive rule; the Marquesses of Moja, however, had it decorated
inside with largely fictional scenes of the participation of their ancestors
in great events of Catalonian history.[40] Around the corner, the palace
of the Comte de Fonallar enhances the grandeur of the expensive shops
in the carrer de Portaferrisa. The Palau Mercader, with its baroque
courtyard and virtuoso staircase, where the supports of the arches are

deliberately severed, and the elegant house of the Baró de Castellet, which now houses part of the Picasso Museum, demonstrate how the purses of the collaborators were fat enough to bounce back from the disaster of 1714.

The wider reach of Bourbon prosperity is apparent in the surviving fabric of major public-spending projects of the second half of the century: the restrainedly classical façade, the heroic interior decoration of the Llotja, the headquarters of the merchant community, the rational layout of the urban reforms of the period in Barceloneta, in the north-east corner of the dockland, the Rambla and part of the Raval. The destruction that accompanied the defeat of 1714 left Barcelona literally, physically diminished, because of the loss of population and the razing of seventeen per cent of the city's housing stock to build the citadel. By the mid-century, however, the need to replace the lost accommodation was keenly felt; the model suburb first proposed by the engineer Verboom at the time of the building of the citadel was at last authorised, and begun in 1753. Within thirty months, eight of the proposed sixteen streets of Barceloneta were completed, intersecting at right angles, lined by low blocks, in contrast to the rickety towers of the old town; low building was a convenience to the residents and the police authorities alike. The rational design, based perhaps on French and Sicilian experiments, owed nothing to Barcelonese tradition but was to prove a blueprint for the future. The uniform dwellings or seventy square metres each represented an attempt to put into reality the vision with which Pere Pau i Montaner decorated the ceiling of the Llotja, where crowned Prosperity clothed Nakedness, while Industry and Commerce urged the scourging of Poverty and Disaster. The same faith in rational solutions, imposed from above, characterised the debate between Francesc Canalls and other early amateurs of urbanisation over straightening the kinks in the Rambla and tidying the seamy Raval.[41]

Continuously underlying Madrid's policy towards Barcelona in the eighteenth century was the conviction that the obedience of the Barcelonese could be bought. Indeed, this was openly acknowledged in the city. Francesc Romà Rosell, in a protestation of loyalty of 1766, declared that the object of government was 'legitimate authority, absolute but gentle rule, bread and honest amusements'. The government itself did not actually provide any modern equivalents of the ancient *divertissements* of the circus, but, in addition to the regular pageants that marked religious festivals, the city council did lay on spectacular processions for royal visits in which floats bore guildsmen

omenfolk or representatives of parishes arrayed in *tableaux*
presenting the loyal virtues of citizenship and the material
Bourbon rule. By fostering commerce – the 'fifth element'
na, as one official called it in 1720, after earth, air, fire and
w... the new regime liberated the 'industrious, laborious and
optimistic' spirit of the Catalans and kept them suppressed by surfeit,
contained by contentment.[42]

The outcome of the War of Succession favoured Barcelona because
the monarchy lost the industrially advanced provinces in the Netherlands and northern Italy that outclassed Catalonia and held her industry back; and the foreign policy of the new reign, which concentrated
on the recovery of Sardinia and Sicily – achieved by 1721 – restored
the sources of supply that industrial development demanded. During
the same period, the government began to shift the burden of taxation
on trade away from domestic producers to foreign competitors. In the
second half of the century Barcelona's abundance was of the stuff
of childish dreams, with the cheapest grain and the most copious
sweetmeats in Spain, where the number of *chocolatiers* increased
sixfold between 1729 and 1770. Their products were the long-term
sweets of defeat by the Bourbons. The consumption of chocolate was
surrounded with rituals of social differentiation and images of wealth.
In the Museu de Ceràmica, eighteenth-century painted tilework in
honour of the chocolate cult shows cups of the stuff being offered by
bewigged gentlemen, on bended knee, to sumptuously attired women,
beside the fountains of a pavilioned *hortus conclusus*.[43]

A further, perhaps more remarkable consequence, was Barcelona's
first experience of industrialisation. The *chocolatiers'* expanding trade
was almost matched, for pace of growth, by others producing more
durable goods. Their guild was founded in 1779 – just a century and
a quarter after the first chocolate mill was opened; by then, other more
traditional crafts were in the throes of a decline that marked the
displacement of workshops by factories and the old relationships
of master and apprentice by the new social fabric of owners and
employees.

The Hierarchy of Work

In the late eighteenth century, Antoni de Capmany, who wrote about
Barcelona from the comfort of a career made in Madrid, stressed the

honourable nature of an industrial occupation and contrived to make the heritability of the artisanate seem like an aristocratic characteristic. The Barcelonese in general, however, were slow to recognise the nobility of work or ascribe honour to a manufacturer's trade. Suppliers of luxury goods to an aristocratic clientèle had been accorded the courtesy of a noble corporate designation in guilds dignified with the style of 'magnificent colleges of *artistes*'. But this introduced an invidious distinction into the ranks of Barcelona's artisanate, which the favoured groups were anxious to preserve, especially as the status of '*artistes*' carried a privileged role in the government of the city, above that of the excluded *menestrals*. Contempt was passed on down the line, as far as the despised professions, whose guilds were unrecognised by the authorities and played no part in civic life: the ironmongers, wool-carders, butchers, tavern-keepers and grinders – trades exercised by Italian immigrants, gypsies and mulattoes. The notion of heirarchy was too entrenched to be challenged; when the silversmiths supplicated for enhanced status in 1707, their petition endorsed a system 'which follows the example of celestial glory'. Their request failed on the grounds that silversmithery was a 'mechanical art' like that of the ironmongers or locksmiths.[44]

At the top of the hierarchy, members of a 'college' like that of the purveyors of drugs, spices and *confiserie* affected quasi-aristocratic habits, with their genealogical records that were kept from 1565, their shared membership of prestigious parochial confraternities with merchants and patricians, their service on civic bodies and among the ranks of the *consellers*, and their endogamous breeding. Clans and *droguers* had the market sewn up – the Ramonda family marrying with the Ballesteros and Pi, the Sanmartí with the Roca and Pujol. A hundred years after Charles II declared nobility compatible with the calling of a merchant, Charles III made a similar declaration about the reputedly 'vile' trades: the occupations of ironmongers, tailors, cobblers, carpenters 'and others of this sort' were 'decent and honour-able'. They 'made vile' neither the individual who exercised them nor the other members of his family, nor did they disqualify a man from election to municipal office.[45]

In one sense Barcelona did not need this lesson; the lesser guilds had an established place in the carefully articulated civic hierarchy. An industrial mentality, however, in which business and manufacture were esteemed for their own sake and accorded a high place in the common value-system, was still in the making. While members of the relatively humble cloth-dressers' guild, for instance, enjoyed the right

s and were obliged to prove their 'purity of blood', mer-
excluded from the ranks of *ciutadans honrats*. Part of the
ıs that noble status conferred fiscal immunity in an already
d society. In 1709 the city fathers took the view that
had more in common with the artisans than the patricians:
if they were freed of taxes, billeting and military service, only the
lower classes would be left as the 'atlantes of the commonwealth'.[46]

Merchants who procured ennoblement in the eighteenth century
were so few as to be celebrated, and none more so than Antoni Gispert,
the son of a courier of the exchange. He chose a career as linen
merchant, while his more adventurous brother, Joan Pau, scorned the
established trades and set up in business independently. But while
Joan Pau got rich quickly and wielded the influence of wealth, it was
Antoni who rose to an elevated social position through service to the
city and province in the Junta de Comerç and the Companyia de
Barcelona. His admission to the ranks of the *ciutadans honrats* was
for his contribution to the campaign to abolish the export tax on
textiles in favour of a new protective imports tariff – an objective dear
indeed to the citizens of Barcelona. For twelve years from 1765 he led
and largely financed the campaign, 'not,' he claimed, 'for personal
interest but only for the good of the fatherland . . . The principality
groaned under this yoke, lamented its hurt and implored its relief.' He
recalled immodestly, 'This repeal, which will be memorable forever
in Catalonia, created the most celebrated epoch of her prosperity.'
By elevating him to their own rank, his social superiors certainly
acknowledged that it was a service of exceptional merit.[47]

In the 'lost world' of pre-industrial Barcelona, manufacturing was a
mainstay of the economy; but it was confined to the intimate society
of the workshop and the master's home and regulated not by the
impersonal 'market' but by the collective morals of rich and powerful
guilds. A visitor to the Museu de l'Història de la Ciutat can see the
sort of images which dominated the mental world of the guilds: their
art reflected professional pride and devotion to the patron saints; the
book of privileges of the shoemakers is decorated with a huge but
elegant bronze-gilt slipper with tapering toe, pressed into the leather
binding; the silversmiths' pattern books record, in meticulous drawing,
the 'copyright' of rival masters to thousands of designs, each inscribed
with the master's name on a scroll and, if the design was actually
effected, the legend '*Me a fet en obre*' ('He hath fashioned me as an
object'). The gardeners' book of privileges, begun in 1453, is flanked
by the busts of their otherwise obscure advocates, Saints Abdó and

Senen, and the gaudily painted wooden box in which the guild preserved their relics, like any religious community. Everywhere the
images of the saints are reminders that the guilds doubled as devotional
confraternities. Evidence of their prestige and wealth can be found
around the city today: the shoemakers' palatial hall, for instance, in
the plaça de Sant Felip Neri, decorated with lions in honour of the
patron, St Mark, who made a convert of the shoemaker of Alexandria,
St Anias; the graves of the guild masters, with the same emblem, in
the cloister of the cathedral.

A particularly sumptuous example of eighteenth-century decoration
survives on the guildhall of the silk weavers in the via Laietana. The
most important members of the guild may have been embarrassed by
the role they had to play in the masque that greeted the Infante Carlos
– the future Charles III – in 1731. These rich and solid citizens had
to dress as 'bandits or Turks' while lesser artisans cavorted in the role
of 'Chilean Indians' – the most barbarous of the king's subjects.[48] This
was an irony consciously contrived to entertain the crowd, for in the
eighteenth century, while the guilds' economic and religious roles
remained intact, their civic role and contribution to the government,
their pomp and public profile were perhaps greater than ever before.
So many traditional institutions were abolished and degraded after the
War of Succession, that the guilds, with their long and respectable
roots in civic life, appealed increasingly to the government as an aid
to the control and regulation of the city. In some ways, the most widely
representative institution of eighteenth-century Barcelona was the
Junta General de Collegis, Gremis i Communs – a body of two or
three hundred individuals, representing seventy guilds. It assembled
at the order of the city council or captain-general, to validate potentially
unpopular acts, quell public unrest or affirm the festive character of
civic or state occasions. The announcement of a new tax, such as the
defence imposts of 1744, 1770 and 1793–5; the proclamation of billeting arrangements; acts of loyalty to the state, such as the proclamations
of kings or the reception of royal visits; acts of civic defiance, such as
the homage to the liberal deputies exiled in May 1820; emergencies
such as the suppression of riots in 1766 and 1773; the election of the
permanent representatives of the guilds to the town council: these
were all occasion for the summoning of this large assembly, which
also, increasingly, summoned itself to lobby for its own demands,
addressed to central government, and especially for Barcelona's favourite cause, protective tariffs.[49]

If, as is commonly supposed, the strength of the guilds inhibited

of old industries, there is no evidence that it depressed
new ones. Cotton manufacture benefited precisely from
e practices in other textile trades. Eighteenth-century
o Barcelona 'preferred factory life to subjection under the
the guild-masters'. The most conspicuous feature of the
statistics of the organisation of work in the period is the growth in
numbers of *vagos* – workers unattached to guilds – relative to the
declining numbers of guildsmen. The bridle-makers' confraternities,
allied in a guild dedicated to St Stephen, had 108 members in 1729,
forty-seven in 1808 and twenty-seven in 1814; the decline occurred
during a period when the population of the city trebled, and was at its
most acute at a time of war and high demand for harnesses. In the
textile industry, which was directly affected by reorganisation into
factories and the drafting of less skilled labour, the decline was even
more spectacular. The cloth-dressers, whose numbers had fluctuated
in the seventeenth century owing to war, had a normative strength of
700; by 1825, the guild had only three members left, who had neither
studios nor workshops and were too old to work. Not all organisations
were so dramatically affected, but most were transformed by the ageing
of the membership and the lack of new blood. The carders ranged
from twenty-eight to sixty-five years old in 1719, and from fifty-one
to seventy-eight years old in 1793. The cloth-dresser's average age was
forty-seven in 1725 and sixty in 1770. In the early part of the century,
relatively young men – usually of around thirty years old, but often
still in their twenties – had commonly sought and obtained admission
to a mastership; their disappearance opened a generation gap in the
government of the city.[50]

Writers of the late eighteenth century sensed the weakening of the
guilds and mourned their passing. In a work of exculpation for riots
in 1766, Francesc Romà Rosell blamed the indiscipline of guildless
workers for the trouble.[51] The corporate system represented 'order
and good customs'. Its breakdown would sow confusion and disquiet.
The guilds, in a work commissioned by themselves, were praised for
the contribution they made to public order, tax collection and military
service as well as the adornment of the city. Capmany's history,
published in 1761, was full of nostalgia for the guild life of the middle
ages. The author's main concern was to demonstrate – somewhat
against the evidence – Barcelona's record of loyalty to her kings; hence
the gratuitous praise of Philip V, the long list of eulogies addressed by
the city to medieval monarchs, the honour roll of citizens who provided
ships for royal expeditions down to the sixteenth century. His next

most important concern was to vindicate the guilds as loyal, honourable and socially beneficial. At the time, they still seemed strongly entrenched; Capmany's excessive protestations betray his awareness that they were under threat.In the new century the guilds were gradually replaced by mutual societies, or limited themselves to their social, pious and ceremonial traditions. The silversmiths distributed 36,000 soup rations during the war of 1796–1802 and 4,600 helpings during the cholera epidemic of 1834. In 1803 the seamen gave twenty-five lliures in dowries to twenty-eight poor brides. The wigmakers set up their charitable fund in 1800, the carpenters theirs in 1814. The *vagos*, whose coming had deprived the guilds of economic control in Barcelona, were fed and clothed and inexpensively wed by courtesy of these guilds in time of need.[52]

THE INDUSTRIOUS NATION

The Catalans' renown as a naturally 'industrious' nation, which goes back to the Middle Ages, has been universally acknowledged since the late seventeenth century. Before that date, however, there were some to dispute it. Duplessis-Besançon regarded their reputed 'industry' as a euphemism for greed. 'They are very slow and indolent in all their affairs and content themselves with working their lands only to keep alive, without bothering with commerce outside their own neighbourhood. . . . They show little capacity for business . . . Their principal vices are idleness and avarice, wanting to profit from everything and do nothing.' Native Catalans would not admit such a characterisation of any but the remotest backwoods of their country. The appraisal of another enemy of Catalonia, or at least of Catalan liberties, about a hundred years later, reflects their perception of themselves: 'as to their genius, they are industrious and indefatigable in the pursuit of any perceived advantage, and more ready to save than to spend, even on necessities'; their province, according to this source, was 'vastly fruitful thanks to the industry and application of the inhabitants'.[53]

This sort of appraisal became the commonplace of observers, foreign and native alike, until the present day. When Alfonso XIII returned to Spain from exile, he chose to do so through Barcelona and to visit the National Organisation for Industrial Development (*Fomento de la Producción Nacional*) where he proclaimed Barcelonese industriousness as a model for the whole of Spain. The stereotype of the 'go-ahead and enterprising' Catalans worked its way into popular fiction. Yet the tension between the 'industriousness' and 'greed' first observed by Duplessis-Besançon remained. When Barcelona's industrial revolution came, it was under-capitalised and relied on protectionism.

A strong literary tradition unites – sentiment for sentiment, sometimes word for word – the work of the industrial apologists of nineteenth-century Catalonia. The message was pretty well fully armed by the time of Antoni Gassó's *España con industria, fuerte y rica* of 1816. The inherent virtues of industry – strength, wealth, civilisation and progress – qualified the Catalan economy for special treatment. Industry anywhere was a benefit to Spain as a whole – indeed, Gassó presciently observed, the only means of survival as a great power in a modern world. The Factories Commission (*Comisión de Fábricas*) of 1837 sketched 'a wretched picture' of a nation without industries, 'of misery, emigration and brutalisation'. Characteristically, blame for Spain's industrial backwardness was put on free trade, of which Spain had hardly any experience; this was another coded demand for protection. The same prejudice underlies the praises of industry uttered in Catalan submissions to the Cortes in 1870. Industrial nations 'always enjoy advantages which lead sooner or later to the domination and absorption of those which limit themselves to a purely agrarian economy; and what Spain needs to develop her output and wealth are . . . factories and internal markets, which increase demand for raw materials a hundredfold and limit transport costs'.[54]

Catalan idealisation of industry was nearly always qualified by the fear of foreign competition. In a satirical portrait of Barcelona of 1854, Martí Angelón pictured a character intended to represent the manufacturing class, who suffered from congenital rickets, watched his spending anxiously and spent all day reading the tariff laws and all night discussing them in the café with his friends.[55] Protective tariffs are the crutches of every lame economy. The campaigns for them in eighteenth- and nineteenth-century Barcelona were perhaps the most consistent feature of the city's history. They united all classes and helped the city survive the social tensions of industrialisation. They demonstrated the weakness of Barcelona's industries and the limitations of her economic base. In as far as they were successful, they tied the city to Spanish markets, confirmed Barcelona as a Spanish port and Spanish city and cemented the political unity of the Spanish state at the expense of Catalan identity.

Once, when the rest of the world was mercantilist, Barcelona had favoured free trade; in 1599, for instance, the *consellers* petitioned against taxes on the circulation of goods on the grounds that 'according to the *Constitucions* of this principality, trade is frank and free and every sort of produce can be freely bought and sold'.[56]

The assumptions of Francesc de Gilabert, an early seventeenth-century projector, were classically mercantilist: bullion must be kept inside the realm; grain should not be imported by Barcelona, which ought to feed itself entirely from the Catalonian hinterland. Yet, in most cases, he thought the economy of Barcelona would benefit from the relaxation of tariffs. Barcelona's precocity, however, in the cause of free trade did not last. In the eighteenth century, when the rest of the world was converted to the cause, Barcelona abandoned it. While the other clauses of the liberal creed were enthusiastically espoused, this was rejected. Fear of competition was already inhibiting the earliest moves towards industrialisation in the late seventeenth century. Feliu de la Penya, busily trying to raise money for hosiery factories and searching out old Catalan recipes for dyes, felt frustrated partly by lack of capital – 'there are no great fortunes in Catalonia', he said – but chiefly by the stranglehold on trade lost 'through our neglect' to the English, Dutch and French. In 1693, the Santa Creu cloth manufacturing company was formed to exploit Flemish expertise. Catalan traders made so much, he complained, out of the traffic in foreign textiles of inferior quality, that they did all they could to prevent the growth of the native industry.[57]

The protective measures introduced under Bourbon rule seem to have been aimed specifically at fomenting the textile industries. A ban on foreign silks was introduced in 1718 and periodically renewed. In 1726, in an anachronistic revival of a sumptuary law, the government banned the use – though not the importation – of some luxury cloths made abroad. In 1729–30 this ban was extended to trade in, as well as use of, the offensive articles, and inclusion of cotton helped to stimulate the rise of Barcelona's first 'modern' industry – the first, that is, to be organised in factories rather than *ateliers*. From 1728, a series of exemptions from the obligations of civic office or from the payment of certain dues, shows that the government was trying particularly to favour large-scale entrepreneurs. In 1750, for example, Bernat Glòria and Rafael Guardans were granted a right to export their wares at half the normal duty, because they had perfected a dyeing technique which enabled them to employ up to thirty-eight workers in each of six workshops; they also had a cotton factory, which fed the dyeshops with work.[58]

Boosted by protectionism, supplied with raw materials and cus-

tomers by the American trade, the cotton industry was the infant
prodigy of Barcelona's early industrialisation. In 1768, there were
twenty-two cotton factories, by 1773 at least fifty-five, employing on
average about 130 workers each; smaller workshops, employing about
fifty workers each, accounted for another thousand jobs. Output
trebled between 1768 and 1784, then doubled again by 1792. This was
the basis of the favourable impression made by Barcelona on *fin de
siècle* travellers. As one approached by road, townie villas – one of
them, the Can Carabass, survives today in an otherwise unattractive
suburb – and the intensity of road traffic, 'announced greatness from
afar', as Peyron found in 1779; from 1784, the city council's physicians
harried new factories outside the walls on grounds of public health.
When Arthur Young drew near in 1787 he found more activity than
anywhere else on the road since Paris. In a town which already had a
reputation as 'a little England inside Spain', he heard 'the noise of
business' everywhere and observed 'an active and developed industry'.
The model factories produced cotton: Simeon Lebret, for instance,
produced 120 *arrobas* of cotton thread a day on his thirty jennies; but
factory organisation was spreading to other textiles, too. Joseph Townsend in 1786 was particularly impressed with the Bernis woollens mill,
which employed 350 workers producing cloth for the American
market.[59]

The industrial advances of the last quarter of the century were
registered amid generally accelerating economic indicators, preceded
by a period of preparation. The leading historian of eighteenth-century
Catalonia has dated the principality's economic recovery from about
1743. Droughts in Urgell from 1748–53 made fortunes for Barcelona
grain importers. In 1749 direct trade with America began. In 1756 a
chartered company was founded to manage the Indies trade. In 1758
the Junta de Comerç began its task of fomenting trade and manufacture
together; the promotion of factories was 'one of the principal missions
with which the king had entrusted us'. In 1775 a magistrate, complaining of the cost of the luxuries of Barcelonese life, in which an official
could not allow himself to be outdone by members of the commercial
classes, claimed that the real value of his salary had been halved since
1720. In 1778, trade between Barcelona and the Indies was freed of
most remaining restrictions and the total volume of trade through the
port trebled in the next fifteen years. Wages, which had begun an
inexorable rise in 1761, took off from about 1780: from a base line of
100 representing the mean of the years 1737–1750, they had risen on
average to 114.4 in 1780 and 199.7 in 1797. This was double the

rate of increase registered during the same period in Madrid. The population of 1716 – doubtless an artificially low figure because of the effects of the siege that ended the War of Succession – had doubled by 1770, according to census figures, and increased by a further twenty-five per cent by 1787, according to a minister's estimate.[60]

The End of Social Peace

One consequence of the growth of the city and the beginnings of an industrially-based economy was the forfeiture of social peace. In 1766 riots against high corn prices and the government's fiscal and manpower demands were blamed on the 'vagabond' labour that had penetrated the city, without joining the disciplined craft structure of the old guilds, in order to exploit the growing opportunities for casual work and extorted 'alms'. More riots in 1773, provoked by a recruiting campaign in which the city was obliged to levy 'quotas' from among its residents, had a strong anti-clerical flavour, despite the rioters' appeal to the bishop to intervene on their behalf; some of the *revoltés* were drawn from the indigent jetsam that naturally battened on the clergy for help and turned nasty when its demands exceeded the church's means. Bishop Climent left a picaresque description of

> the beggar-folk known as *murris*: people with no fixed abode and no sense of religion. They wander about in mixed bands of men, women and children. They live more from robbery than beggary, for they thrust themselves on the households of priests and working men, who find themselves obliged to shelter them at night and give them what they demand. And when I asked some of the constables why they do not arrest people who by virtue of the mere fact of being vagabonds are obviously indictable, they replied that they did not dare, partly because they are so ferocious and partly because, when some of them had been brought to this city under arrest, they were soon back at liberty and burned down the homes and houses of those who had arrested them.[61]

The Catalan countryside was providing Barcelona with the makings of a mob.

Food riots of late February and early March 1789 seem to have mobilised more people, drawn from a bigger social range and including elements of a genuine urban proletariat. All the observers who had left accounts call the insurgents simply 'the people'. A French intelligence agent's report implies that the rioters included many householders; it was not an anti-clerical mob, for at one point a dangerous mood was calmed by the intervention of a Capuchin armed only with a crucifix, despite complaints about the irreverent language used by the rioters. At another moment, the mob spared the house of a suspected grain speculator for fear of setting fire to her neighbours' homes by contagion.

Not until after the struggle against Napoleon, during which the common people got plenty of lessons in civil disobedience from their betters, were the excesses of street violence observed by a reporter who was both critical and sympathetic. The anonymous of the *Succesos de Barcelona* was probably a *petit bourgeois* whose prejudices were strongly liberal and anti-clerical. He was aware of the wider European context of constitutional struggle, identifying with the Greeks against the Turks and the Belgians against the Dutch. Yet, though he wrote in a sort of Catalan – idiosyncratic and somewhat Castilianised – he had a great feeling for *'la nostra amada España'* (*sic*) as well as *'la afligide Barcelona'*. The events he wrote about came at a time of terrible trial: the last plagues of the Middle Ages were joined by industrial disease; the dislocation and insecurity of life in an industrialising society exacerbated the plight of the poor for whom, in post-war conditions, there was little work. In 1821, a drought and an epidemic of yellow fever paralysed trade and industry. Day-workers were fed by the *ajuntament* from the proceeds of a tax on pigs and employed on repairing the pavements and the decayed channels of the water supply. In January 1822 the customary optimism no longer appeared in the declarations of the *ajuntament*: 'Long, uninterrupted years of good fortune will be needed if Barcelona is ever to recover any part of the brilliance and opulence which once made her one of the most celebrated cities of this peninsula . . . We can take it for a fact that in the capital of Catalonia the prosperous star of fortune has been eclipsed forever.' The struggle in Spain at large between constitutionalists and absolutists, together with the loss of American markets as a result of revolutions in Spain's colonies, was 'obstructing the sources of our prosperity'. The poet Aribau, who was working for the Junta de Comerç at the time, witnessed 'the springs of Barcelona's wealth drying up'.[62]

In these circumstances the anonymous of the *Succesos* witnessed the French invasion in defence of absolutism, the seige of Barcelona from July to November 1823, and the repression which followed. He was rather vague about the nature of the 'hatred and tyranny evinced towards the poor liberals' who were 'resolved to die in defence of our sacred constitution'; but some were killed, some left in poverty. The

French ships departed, carrying off booty and captured guns and trophies, leaving chaos in the streets. Amid murders and robberies 'every man governed himself, so that it resembled the tower of Babylon [*sic*] where all were misunderstood'. The liberal bourgeoisie were the victims of a holy alliance of 'barbarous monks' and 'despotic friars' with the 'vile *canaille*'; the liberals' conviction that their own employees were innocent and that a *déclassé* mob was manipulated by the clergy recurred in most cases of riot in Barcelona during the next half-century. Just over ten years later the liberals got their revenge in the next big social confrontation in the city, accompanied and perhaps provoked by the same natural afflictions: summer heat and lethal plague. In September 1834, cholera killed capriciously and liberals selectively, executing clerics and ultras. Thousands fled the city every day.[63]

In July the following year, the radical politicians were able to mobilise rioters for a further reckoning with their surviving enemies. On 25 July, five houses of religion were burned down 'and afterwards', according to the anonymous, 'everyone wandered round the streets perfectly calmly, admiring the great conflagrations and the dead friars in the streets'. On 5 August the military governor, General Bassa, was shot inside the government building, flung dead or dying over the balcony and carried to be burned on a pyre formed of the files of the commissariat of police. The anonymous hailed this as 'a day of judgement, a day of glory'. He insisted that the mob was well disciplined and that 'there was order in the midst of disorder'. In reality, the crowd was out of control and pursuing vendettas of its own. Most ominous from the point of view of the bourgeois masters of this revolution was the incendiarism deflected from the monasteries to the factories. On 27 July arsonists attacked the Bonaplata factory which made machines for the textile industry – 'a model school of industrial method'. The owner's son got special permission to use the militia unit he commanded to defend it and three city newspapers raised money from their readers to help rebuild it. This response was the rally of the classes that elected the revolutionary Junta; the electoral college was composed of six guildsmen, three manufacturers, three merchants, three nobles and landlords and eighteen militia commanders, who were drawn from 'good' commercial and industrial families.[64]

The anonymous's justification of the rebellion exactly reflected the objectives of this leadership; he wanted power for 'progressive' politicians and protection for Barcelona's industry. 'Because of our having no happy government or happy representatives we were miserable in Spain for so many years and now that Spain has a good government we can mock all the nations of the world.' Spain had formerly been 'the laughing-stock of all nations' and her troubles had allowed the French and English to steal her trade 'and also to introduce goods into Spain, as a result of which we suffered great deprivation'. The anonymous evidently identified good government with tariff protection. Like other Barcelonese liberals, he would be disappointed; the liberal governments of the new era in Madrid tended to be suspiciously anglophile and dangerously interested in free trade.[65]

'Smoke from the Volcanoes'

Barcelona's industrial beginnings in the eighteenth century were conspicuous, but small. The economy that supported the city's trade was still overwhelmingly agrarian, and even in manufactures, industrialisation had made only selective inroads. Barcelona's industries were uncompetitive, by international standards, and dependent on the fragile, protected markets of Spain and her empire. Grape brandy and wine, nuts and cork were the most conspicuous items on the quays of the port; agricultural profits seem to have risen faster than those of trade, perhaps inhibiting industrial investment. During the period 1792–1821, war, disruption and economic lurches kept growth in check. In the first half of the nineteenth century, the increase of population in the city, though substantial at forty-five per cent, was greatly exceeded by that of Catalonia as a whole, where numbers doubled. Not until 1832 did the city's population recover its pre-war level of about 112,000.[66]

This was not just a temporary blip caused by war. Barcelona's problem was structural. Only the emergence of a vast metropolis could bring economic specialisation to the hinterland and nourish Barcelona's further industrialisation in turn. Catalonia was traditionally an area of dense population, diverse character and economic decentralisation. Industry was attracted to hinterland towns by cheap labour and available water-power. The making of modern Barcelona would therefore genuinely be a process of conurbation, in which, while Barcelona grew outwards to absorb much of the rest of industrial Catalonia, the hinterland towns grew to meet her.

The chief impediments to industrialisation were poor communications and lack of natural resources. Communications could be improved if sufficient capital investment were forthcoming. Lack of resources – especially of coal – was an insoluble problem. The use of coal was opposed by physicians in the city on health grounds in the 1770s and 1780s, but speculators in English coal were still able to make huge fortunes in the Barcelona market. The Junta de Comerç put a lot of money into a mine at Llansá, because private venture capital could not be raised: in 1787 the operation had to be closed down when the product was found to be useless; the extraction of Gironese coal was a frequently mooted project but it seems never to have been realised on a large scale. The limited scope of an industrial revolution dependent on expensive foreign coal and iron remained apparent in Barcelona throughout the nineteenth century; the city would have been an industrial monoculture, reliant on textiles, but for the sort of heroic efforts that created and sustained a metallurgical and engineering sector that was always precarious.[67]

The model steam-power factory of Josep Bonaplata, known as *'El Vapor'*, came into production in 1833; the first steamship came off the slipways of the Nuevo Vulcán works in Barceloneta in 1836; demand for modern machinery for the textile industry stimulated the creation of a number of firms in the early 1840s, followed, in the middle of the next decade, by big new enterprises intended to supply modern industrial machinery and transport of all types. The most renowned and enduring of these was La Maquinària Terrestre, founded in 1855. Subscribed by large numbers of small investors, the firm was launched with the biggest initial capital yet seen in Barcelona: this was a remarkable expression of the collective confidence of the Barcelonese bourgeoisie at what – as we shall see in the next chapter – was a time of serious political and economic uncertainty, redeemed for optimism only by large textile orders from the armies of the Crimea. By 1862 there were thirteen big metallurgical firms in Barcelona, but most collapsed in the slump of the second half of the decade. Even La Maquinària came near to closure, surviving a virtual shutdown in 1867. Barcelonese engineering remained a proud endeavour, producing the first Spanish locomotives in 1882 from the workshops of Maquinària; but it was a flagship without a fleet. The steel industry remained limited by high costs and crises of supply, justifying Francesc Cambó's dismissal of his fellow-citizens as 'table-fork folk'.[68] In steel and heavy engineering, Barcelona was never able in the second half of the century to rival the Basque country, which had the raw materials to hand.

As with fuel, so with communications. Barcelona did not get the kind of infrastructure which fundamental industrialisation required until well into the nineteenth century. In 1834, the anonymous of the *Succesos de Barcelona* was delighted with the pace of the paving of the city streets 'so that within two years Barcelona will be one of the most magnificent cities of Europe' but this was not matched by road-building in the province, where between 1814 and 1848 only 148 kilometres of new roads were built. In that year, the Junta de Carreteres de Catalunya was formed, initiating a modest revolution. The efforts of the Junta, however, failed to satisfy the demands of Barcelonese manufacturers who eventually financed a programme of their own through the provincial authority, the Diputació; this aimed to extend the first-class road network from Barcelona by fifty kilometres a year, but did not start till 1877. The year of the formation of the Junta de Carreteres was also that of the opening of Spain's first railway line from Barcelona to Mataró. By 1855, Mataró, Granollers, Molins de Rei and Sabadell had been transformed by rail-commuting into 'suburbs of Barcelona'. But the Spanish railways came too late, on too small a scale and at too high a cost to meet the needs of Barcelona's industry. The opening of the Mataró line gave Spain thirty kilometres of track at a time when France had 1,900 kilometres. Spanish rail freight charges were so high that at the end of the century it was cheaper to bring corn to Barcelona from Charleston than from Saragossa, and wool from Buenos Aires than Leon. The problem was inseparable from that of fuel supply: Catalan steamships had the same trouble; their freight charges were, on average, four times those of British competitors. Still, by making the coal they consumed cheap, steamships and trains helped industry concentrate in Barcelona, where the railway network of Catalonia was centred and where her international shipping congregated.[69]

Even when protection was conceded in principle, bureaucratic habits could inhibit trade. Madrid was still making discriminatory regulations for New World trade in 1828, when the American Empire was in ruins. The toll-court of the port of Barcelona in the 1840s dispensed 'the most expensive justice in the world'. In a novel of 1844 Milá de la Roca depicted the fly-swarm of official boats that clung to every ship entering the harbour: the pilot, boat, the customs, the coastguards, the health authority, all expecting their cut. The law-abiding importer of a box of cigars had to make 'more stops than the stations of the cross', bearing a chit that needed fourteen or fifteen counter-signatures. Contraband, corruption and slave-patrol dodging became big business while Barcelona's industrial revolution dragged its feet.[70]

Yet in this unpropitious place, out of adverse circumstances, a great industrial city gradually emerged, breathing, according to the poet Zorrilla, 'fire and smoke like the volcanoes'. The leap from a pre-industrial or proto-industrial society happened quite suddenly, in the mid-nineteenth century. Even in textiles, Barcelona's most advanced sector, only three per cent of yarn production was mechanised in 1835, compared with 99.04 in 1861; steam-power in the industry as a whole generated only 289 watts in 1841, 9,500 in 1870 – while in the same period the number of businesses in the field fell from 4,470 to 827, a clear sign of reorganisation for mass production.[71]

Since Barcelona's industrial revolution seems impossible to explain by virtue of geography or economics, it is tempting to fall back on contemporaries' own favourite explanation, the appeal to 'spirit'. Duran i Bas thought the Barcelonese exemplified 'virility and enterprising vigour' – the old Catalan attributes of hard work and acquisitiveness particularised. Since nowadays one of the major problems for the survival of minority languages in Europe generally is their lack of a modern industrial and technological vocabulary, Josep Pau Ballot's praise of Catalan as an industrial tongue is a strong testimony in favour of some link between Barcelona's economy and the presumed national characteristics of the Catalans: 'what sciences,' he asked, 'what arts are there in our society, which the Catalan language lacks the means to express? Machines? Equipment? Production methods? Manufactures? The more industrious a nation is, the richer its vocabulary and the more varied its means of expression.'[72]

Since this sort of perception of the Catalans had been around for so long, it is not surprising that they should have come to believe it and, believing it, to act on it and so turn it into the truth. The Catalan industrialising 'spirit' also owed a lot, to judge from the way it was characterised by one of its greatest living representatives, to self-differentiation from Castile; Joan Güell i Ferrer, indignant at Castilian resentment of Catalonia's industrial 'monopoly', contrasted the fruits of honest labour by the sweat of the brow with the rentier-empire of the idle. 'People who rely,' he declared, 'on hard work, intelligently managed, and on thrift, create capital and increase with wealth. Indolent, lazy people, who put their faith only in what others' work produces, or in liquid wealth or in the gold of other nations, such people get their just deserts in the form of poverty, decline and ruin.' No contemporary could have failed to recognise this as a characterisation of Castile: it was inserted into a long protectionist harangue in which the corrupting effects of alien bullion were likened to those of imported manufacturers.[73]

Perhaps Barcelona's industrialising spirit was simply capitalism – not far removed from another self-accepted element in the Catalan stereotype, love of money, 'the country's other blood' as Francesc de Gilabert called it. When industrialisation began in the eighteenth century, it was fed by savings from a remarkably broad segment of society. M. Andreu Vidiella's research into investment in shipbuilding in eighteenth-century Barcelona shows, to be sure, that merchants were the biggest single category of investors by occupation, especially in the larger contracts, but in the period 1745–60, twenty-two per cent of the capital came from the artisanate and nineteen from mariners, with seven per cent supplied by the official and professional classes.[74] Industrial development may have absorbed some investments diverted from the parasitical capitalism so detested by Güell. The Bensi family, for instance, came from Genoa in the late sixteenth century, at a time when Barcelona was a transit point for American bullion on its way to Genoese banks; like a number of their fellow-countrymen, they set up in business as money-handlers, gradually diversifying into commerce and, from the late seventeenth century, into industry.[75]

If a capitalist 'spirit' was abroad in eighteenth- and nineteenth-century Barcelona, it was as reminiscent of greed as of parsimony and ultimately bred industries which were insecurely based and firms which were inadequately funded. The speculators' critics had plenty of material for satire. Narcis Oller's novel, *La febre d'or* (1890–3), depicts a brittle world of numerous companies each with large nominal capitals and a few, nervy subscribers. According to a pamphleteer of 1858, the newly opened Bourse was an 'Eldorado', a 'gambler's synagogue' in which speculators searched for 'the philosophers' stone' and 'everybody played and won' – briefly. The British consul reported home on 'the passion for speculation' by which 'capital has been diverted from proper investment'.[76]

There is, however, a body of evidence in which the spirit of Barcelonese industry can be seen, solidly realised: the factories, palaces and public buildings erected by the captains of industry. The factories are most revealing of the ethos of the industrialists. The notions that informed them were captured by a newspaper's praise of the factories of Sabadell in 1855: the nobility of work, the power-hunger of a meritocratic bourgeoisie, the puritanical morals of 'Victorian' paternalism. 'And these factories, grand and elegant . . . are sumptuous palaces which ought to inspire their owners and all the people with pride: for these palaces are not paid for by flattery or intrigue or the sweat of the common man; but by hope and unremitting work. These palaces house no pharaohs, no orgies, but are a means of life for hundreds of families. These palaces are not there to inspire vanity or arrogance, but love of work and respect for effort and for merit. These palaces, in short, are the wealth, the well-being and the proper pride of a civilised, free and independent nation.'[77] Descriptions of life in the textiles mills at the time (below, pp. 172–3) reeked, on the contrary, of 'the sweat of the common man'. But the praise offered here was not disingenuous. Factory builders sensed a genuine contrast between the common good served by their edifices and the vainglory of all that past ages had produced on a similar scale. Theirs were the first palaces of production in a history of palaces of consumption. An excursion from the centre of town to the police barracks housed in the Casaramona factory, designed by Puig i Cadafalch in 1911, reveals a building which expresses this ethos perfectly: two fairy-tale campaniles preside over a battlemented skyline, below which huge windows in ranks of slim bays flood the interior with light from large interior spaces. Churches, castles, palaces and artists' studios are all archly quoted or brazenly trumped.

THE SPANISH CITY

It took a long time for Barcelona to become economically 'integrated' with Spain. The travellers' guide of 1842 gave rules for the conversion of weights and measures which summed up a thousand years of sundered economic destinies: one Castilian pound weight was equivalent to one pound, one ounce and two and six-sevenths quarters in Catalonia. One Castilian rod equalled four palms and one and eleven-seventeenths of a quarter-palm in Catalonia. A Castilian *real* could be exchanged for one sou and tenpence-halfpenny in Catalonia. But the logic of Spain's geography, the growth of Barcelona and the limitations of Barcelona's industrial revolution, which needed a protective screen from the rest of the world and an open door to Spain, all combined to forge irrefrangible links of mutual dependence.

Geography, which has helped to make the Catalans a distinct nation, has also helped to make Barcelona a Spanish port. For all that has been said about the poverty of Barcelona's communications, she remains almost uniquely well placed, by the low standards of Spanish outlets to the Mediterranean, for access to the rest of Spain. When the independence movements of the New World destroyed the precarious relationship Barcelonese traders had so recently established, the *Diario de Barcelona* commended instead the interior of Spain – 'an alternative America at a lower risk'.[78] Barcelona's industrial revolution, which

made Catalonia more distinctive within Spain, also increased the ties
of dependence. The campaigns for protectionism show that Catalan
industrialists were always aware that they needed the Spanish market.
At the end of the century, Valentí Almirall professed to believe that
Barcelona could compete in Europe, but no one involved in the
manufacturing industry, not even the most fervent Catalanists, seem
to have believed it. The 'national' architecture founded by Domènech
i Muntaner is Spanish in inspiration, not specifically Catalan, although,
as we shall see, it became distinctively Barcelonese. The music of
Albéniz is a pan-Spanish pastiche – his *Iberia* the musical equivalent
of the 'Poble Espanyol' of Montjuic (see p.218).

The history that made Barcelona a Spanish port, the sounds and
images that make her a Spanish city, do not necessarily limit her
options for the future. The long history of Barcelona's relations with
the rest of Spain show, if they show anything, that neither a 'more
separate' Catalonia nor a more 'united' Spain is necessarily prefigured
in the past. Advocates of both courses – and of the many variants,
like a centralised, 'uniprovincial' Catalonia, or a 'greater Catalonia'
including neighbouring communities, or a Catalan state within a tiered,
federal Spain and Europe – will have to look elsewhere for their
arguments, and, preferably, to rational calculations of the future
interests of the inhabitants of the principality. Political debate in
Catalonia, as in the rest of Spain, tends to be saturated in historical
references and people need to be reminded of history's limited relevance. It would be unavailing as well as arrogant for an historian to
try to tell people what to do, but it is part of his job to show them how
they got to where they are. Barcelona's route to her present has lain
through Spain. If Spain is to be excluded from her future, the break
has to be made in awareness that she cannot be excluded from her
past.

IV

'The Crucible of Hope':

Barcelona and the Catalan World

Muira, muira l'ingrat qu'al sonar en sos llavis
Per estranya regió l'accent natiu, no plora
Que al pensar en sos llars, no es consum ni s'enyora,
Ni cull del mur les lires de les seus avis.

(Death to the ingrate, who hears upon his lip
In foreign land, his native tongue, yet does not weep,
Or, when he thinks of home, unmoved by deep desire,
Does not pluck from the wall his ancestor's own lyre.)

— B.C. Aribau, 'La pàtria'

Catalonia, with its Cleons in Calico, and Catalines in cotton, is the strength and weakness of Spain; and no province of the unamalgamating bundle which forms the conventional monarchy *'de las Españas'* hangs more loosely to the crown than this classical country of revolt, which is ever ready to fly off.

— Richard Ford, *A Handbook for Travellers in Spain*

Sin Barcelona habría faltado a los catalanes el crisol que haría la síntesis de sus esperanzas; el pedestal que elevaría su cultura al plano internacional, reduciendo la mentalidad de barretina a una definición ética y espiritual; yunque y martillo, en una palabra, la herramienta de un pueblo renaciente. Por encima de divisiones burocráticas y gracias a un acto de fe de todos los catalanes, Barcelona se convirtió a la sazón en la verdadera cabeza y en el verdadero corazón de Cataluña.

(Without Barcelona, the Catalans would have lacked a crucible in which to blend their hopes and a pedestal on which to raise their culture to a level at which it could be internationally acknowledged. Their market-place mentality would never have become the basis of a genuine system of values. They would never have had the hammer and the anvil, the forge – in short – of a renascent nation. In spite of divisions over methods of government, and thanks to an act of faith of all Catalans together, Barcelona became at last the real head and the real heart of Catalonia.)

— J. Vicèns Vives, *Los catalanes en el siglo XIX*

The Patchwork of Identity

Across the plaça de Sant Jaume, from the rival splendours of the palace of the Generalitat and the City Hall, the right-wing regional government and the left-wing city council emit hostile glares. In self-celebration they put out flags; in mutual recrimination they put out scandals; they strike adversarial postures modified only by the fear that the vagaries of the electoral system may one day force the parties that form them into coalition. The reasons for their rivalry are many and various. Among them is the fact that though the inhabitants of the city hall are all good Catalanists, they were put there by the votes of non-Catalan immigrant workers, mostly Andalusians, whose loyalty to Catalonian identity, traditions and language is, at best, slight and secondary. The paradox of modern Barcelona is that it has become less and less a Catalan city, while investing more and more in its image as the capital of Catalan culture. With difficulty – in most respects, against the odds – Catalanism has conquered the Catalan masses; that has been a great achievement of its intellectual inventors and their heirs. In Barcelona, however, the movement is still faced with a large section of the proletariat who seem almost ineducable in Catalanism. One of the greatest problems for the administration today is how to complete the process which has converted Catalan consciousness from a hieratic to a demotic phenomenon.

This is not a peculiarly Catalonian problem. All over peripheral Spain, mass awareness of 'ethnicity' or ethnic identity has been slow to emerge or re-emerge in modern times; it has been limited not so much by statist and centralist repression – though that may have been effective – as by popular resistance to intellectual pabulum, or by the imperfections of communication between the erudite originators of Spain's ethnic myths, on the one hand, and ordinary people on the other. Ethnic self-perceptions among the peoples of modern Spain originated among intellectual élites and have been communicated only gradually, and with great difficulty, to people at lower educational and social levels. The first Catalanist mayor of Barcelona, Bartolomeu Robert (1842–1902), wrote in 1901, 'The ideas' – he is referring to Catalanism – 'begin by taking root within the cohort of intellectuals. It is only later that they descend to the masses.'[1]

These 'ideas' in search of an ethnicity in nineteenth-century Spain were not racialist, except in some Basque thought, but in every case – Basque, Catalonian, Galician, Aragonese, Valencian, Andalusian, Canarian – were historicist: they justified the claim to distinctive

institutions for these various peoples on the grounds of a particular
reading of history, in which the identity of each community was the
inevitable outcome of its historical experience. Historicism is a learned
vice and modern traditions of the nationalisms of all these peoples can
be traced back to the works of academics and *littérateurs*. Of course,
this may be merely a trick of the evidence. Eloquent apologists naturally
out-talk the silent majority, even when they profess to speak on their
behalf.

To deny the popular roots of movements that have asserted the
identities of peripheral communities in Spain is not to ignore other
forms of popular particularism. Local, regional and provincial diversity
of identity, laws and customs has always characterised Spanish life.
Indeed, this particularism, it can be argued, is so ubiquitous, so
variegated, so tenacious and so narrowly focused that it militates
as strongly against intellectual constructs like 'Greater Catalonia' or
'Euzkadi' as against submission to a centralising Spanish state or a
single peninsula-wide sense of identity. Catalonia, for instance, as
was pointed out by one of the great popular historians of Catalan
nationalism, Antoni Rovira i Virgili (1892–1949), is itself a product of
slow and uneven symbiosis among much smaller historic communities
which have retained their own identities along with their own distinctive traditional baggage: customary, dialectal, devotional, institutional.
That is why in 1898 – a crucial year in the political progress of
regionalist and devolutionary movements in Spain and especially in
Catalonia – the major organ of Catalanist opinion denounced 'the
localism of the areas or provinces, 'reacting against the preponderance
of Barcelona, because they fail to recognise the greatness of Catalonia'.[2]
There is much truth in Richard Fletcher's remark that all the troubles
of Spain in the last 500 years have stemmed from the pretence that
she is one country. But it would be idle to suppose that Euzkadi, say,
or Catalonia could, with any greater success, become the homes of
unitary states.

Particularism is built into Spain's geography. It is not surprising
that the most mountainous country in Europe after Switzerland should
be characterised by the same 'diversity within diversity' as distinguishes the Swiss conundrum. Only on the central plateau can one
contemplate the horizon without interruption and it is perhaps no
coincidence that it was here, in Castile, that the notion of a unitary
Spanish state was conceived and adopted as a political programme.
Elsewhere, most landward vistas are severely limited. Cultural habits
and historical experience have reinforced geography. It is hard for

anyone who has not been to Spain, or read the works of Julian Pitt-Rivers, Gerald Brenan, William Christian or Julio Caro Baroja, to realise how endogamous, how hidebound and how autarchic the communities of rural Spain are or have been, even today and in the very recent past. Catalonia, in particular, has always been riven into introspective valleys and isolated hamlets. In the early seventeenth century, José de Patiño (1666–1736) who knew Catalonia as well as any Castilian could, complained of the consequent ungovernability of the principality, as if it were a moral defect: 'Catalonia is thickly populated, not in the sense of having a large number of towns, but in the multitude of tiny hamlets, barely amenable to the orders of the courts or the instruction of educators, deprived of learning and social order, raised up without peaceable habits and with few of the benefits of religion.'[3]

Above all, it seems to me that Spain is divided by what I call a devotional particularism. It is worth pausing on this point, since it is unfamiliar and sometimes barely intelligible to people from cultures where rationalism or the Reformation had greater impact than in Spain. The wonderful books of William A. Christian Jr provide a great deal of evidence about the history of what is usually called 'popular religion' in parts of the country, from which it is possible to infer that it has been in worship, perhaps more than in the course of any other activity except, perhaps, war, that Spaniards have forged their awareness of collective identities. A Spaniard's sense of being Spanish, for instance, could formerly be measured – in some cases, can still be measured – by the intensity of his devotion to national cults like those of the Virgen del Pilar or Santiago de Compostela or Santa Teresa de Jésus. Certain ethnicities can be identified to some extent with particular cults – like San Fermín for the Navarrese, the Candelaria for Canarians, the Virgin of Montserrat (though she has become more and more the focus of a pan-Hispanic cult) or Santa Eulàlia for Catalonia. But the most remarkable fact is that in the Spanish valley studied by William Christian in the 1960s, most devotion was directed to shrines within twenty-five kilometres' distance and little was attracted by cults whose centres were more than 100 kilometres away.[4]

Nearly half a millennium of unification and evangelisation has failed to prise Spaniards from their adherence to local religion. To William Christian's valley, the post-Tridentine clerical élite brought the universalist cults, popular with the more sophisticated congregations of the late medieval and early modern church, of the Virgin Mary and the suffering Christ. The villagers had responded, as had their ancestors,

to the first missionaries' message, by adapting the proffered symbols
to their local need for tutelary deities. Christ and His Mother were
stripped of their universal significance and were relocalised, as it were,
under advocations drawn from comforting local toponyms. They
became the Virgin of this place, the Christ of that. In short, they
displaced the patron saints only in the same limited way as once the
saints had replaced pagan gods. Something similar, I think, happened
in seventeenth-century Catalonia during the episcopate of Bishop
Ramon de Sentmenat (d. 1664), who declared war on forms of popular
observance which he regarded as pagan survivals. Whenever regional-
ism in the nineteenth century stood aside from the intellectuals'
priorities to speak with a convincingly popular voice – in the work of
the jurist Manuel Duran i Bas (1823–1907), for instance, in the 1850s
or some of the writings of the evangelist Josep Torras i Bagès (see
below, p.158) in the 1890s – it talked about religion and advocated
solutions to Spain's problems more in terms of concessions to popular
religious feeling than political devolution. When Duran i Bas cried,
'Leave the provinces their local cults, their beliefs and their laws, their
truths and their household gods!', he was consciously abjuring the
language of intellectual Catalanism, which shunned the word 'province'
and demanded political, educational and fiscal institutions for Catalonia, not freedom to venerate local saints. It is not surprising that
secular intellectuals, with their historicist myths, should have fared
little better in this sort of world than the priest with their universalist
cults.[5]

In Barcelona, the Counter-Reformation made surprisingly little
impact. Pre-Tridentine religion was left largely intact. Although in
1546 the city had only seven parishes and fifteen religious communities
– perhaps about a third of what one might expect, by Spanish standards
generally – the houses of religion were populous and the parishes well
served with resident clergy. According to the census of 1553, six per
cent of the population were in orders of some sort. Although the figure
includes claimants to clerical status and legal privileges who were, at
best, in very minor orders or humble positions of service to the church,
this suggests a relatively high level of pastoral ministry in the city. New
foundations were few: the university, the Magdalens' reformatory, the
Monasteri dels Angels, the Jesuits, who opened their house by Santa
Maria del Pi in 1545, the discalced Carmelites, the Minims. The cults
we hear of sound old-fashioned, more concerned with the promotion
of local deities than with the promotion of the universal theological
verities of the Council of Trent: still, they had a strongly penitential

flavour and there is some evidence of an overall intensification of devotion and a growing emphasis on the sacraments. Plagues called forth great acts of public devotion: processions of flagellants wielding the 'scourge of the anger of God', accompanied by relics, around the Marian churches and chapels of the city; if that failed to work, the flagellants proceeded round five more shrines spaced in an arc round the vanished perimeter of the thirteenth-century walls. Finally, ceaseless prayer would be ordered on a rota basis throughout the city's churches. The council frequently sponsored pilgrimages to Montserrat or even Santiago de Compostela in expiation of vows made in times of plague and on one occasion built a chapel as a thank-offering to St Sebastian, where, after another plague, the local cult of Sant Magí became centred.

The impression that Barcelonese religion was more concerned with survival in this world than salvation in the next is corrected only by the assurances of Joan Gestí, the rector of the city's Jesuits in 1558, that confessions and restitutions made in penance were increasing. The Jesuits themselves were instrumental in propagating a more active form of Christian life and a keener doctrinal awareness. They preached in schools and in the houses of other orders, encouraging their listeners to reflection on the sacraments as means of salvation. As in other Spanish towns in the second half of the century, the printing history of catechisms – which took off in Barcelona in 1563, perhaps about a decade later than in Spain generally – was an index of a growing evangelical vocation among the clergy and, it is tempting to suppose, a growing public response.[6]

The local divinities who survived the Counter-Reformation and whose cults best express Barcelonese identity, are Eulàlia and the Virgin of La Mercé. Eulàlia, whose banner blessed the great battles of Catalonia against the Spanish state, could easily have become the patroness of Spain. In the late eighth century, the custodian of her relics was King Alfonso 'the Chaste' of Asturias, whose victory over the usurper Mauregatus in 788 ensured the survival of the dynasty from which the kings of Spain descended. St James seems, at the time, to have been a partisan of Mauregatus, at whose court the first hymn of praise was written that identified James as the 'head' of Spain. It seems only to have been Alfonso's desire to conciliate his enemies that led him to adopt the future Santiago, whose rise from then onward left Eulàlia to be revered mainly in Oviedo and Barcelona. Though her splendid shrine is before every worshipper in the cathedral, brilliantly lit in the gaping undercroft below the high altar, her cult had been secondary in forging Barcelonese identity, in the last 300 years, to that of La Mercé, who is the focus of fervent devotion and, every September, of a fiesta which has been appropriated by the municipality as a celebration of civic spirit. No priest appears at the proclamation of the fiesta; at mass the following day socialist councillors, who never see the inside of a church for the rest of the year, file past the Gothic image in its glazed camera behind the captaincy-general and kiss the Virgin's stole. At the entertainments which fill the main squares on the following days, rock bands alternate with traditional tumblers before and after the great parade of giant dolls depicting monarchs, saints and clowns. The Virgin had claimed the affections of the Barcelonese at least since 1361, when the present image was sculpted, and perhaps for a hundred years before that, from the time of her apparition to Jaume I, whom she commanded to found the Merced-arian Order for the ransom of captives from the Moors. Her present dominance, however, dates from 1697, when her intervention to thwart a plague of locusts induced the city to endow the fiesta which has kept her cult alive. Today, whenever Barcelona football club, or another of the city's sporting teams, wins a major championship, the team comes to the shrine of La Mercé to sing a *salve* in her praise.

The Barcelona Football Club's main local rival is Español – the very name which, in Spanish and meaning 'Spanish', is an immigrant's riposte to Barcelonese Catalanism. Even without the differences be-tween the Catalan city-centre and the Spanish suburbs, Barcelona would be too big and too diverse for particularism to be eliminated in favour of common civic loyalties. In recent times, urban growth at a threatening pace, democracy and the promotion of 'community values' have favoured the development of strong neighbourhood feeling, based on *barris* or districts, or on individual streets. Discussion groups, a cyclostyled press, neighbourhood welfare schemes, conservation societies, political lobbying campaigns and local history clubs have proliferated in the small cells of a large hive. The late nineteenth-century effort to root out this sort of local feeling by numbering the districts and building uniform streets, has been outgrown. This makes the promotion of Catalanism more difficult in immigrant *barris*. The regional government's policy, which is to concentrate the campaign for Catalanism on the teaching of the Catalan language in schools, provides just the sort of issue which could excite 'neighbourhood' opposition, threatening to cleave family life with a generation gap and to sequester portions of the timetable which most customers of the education system want to be devoted to the teaching of non-Spanish languages, especially English. Historically, the problem of Catalanism has been that of coping with it inside the Spanish state, the most urgent future problem will be that of spreading it around Barcelona.

THE MIRROR OF CATALANISM

Most attempts to explain the problem of Catalanism have foundered on the prior difficulty of saying what Catalanism is. Catalan intellectuals, indeed, have been unable to agree even on the meaning of 'Catalonia'. Her two perhaps greatest spokesmen took diametrically opposed views. For Josep Torras i Bagès (1846–1916) Catalonia was a community defined by its faithfulness to certain traditional values proper to the country's rural and mountain hinterland – including Catholic piety, allegiance to the old customary laws and codes of privilege, and a language that had always been alive in the mouths of peasants. For Valentí Almirall i Llozer (1841–1904), Catalonia was the embodiment of progress, essentially urban and maritime, secular without being impious, with a duty to drag the benighted countryside behind it. Catalanism is, in a sense, what the two thinkers had in common – the desire to conceptualise Catalonia, to make it more than a geographical expression. In these pages, the term is used to cover the full range of its possible meanings, from the sense of being Catalan, to the desire to conserve and promote Catalan culture; from sentiments of kinship with other self-professed Catalans, to resentment or hostility towards non-Catalans and, in particular, the Spanish state; from political programmes embracing devolution, autonomy, federalism or separation for Catalonia, to 'pan-Catalan' or 'greater Catalan' imperialism which aims to create a Catalan state or quasi-state extending beyond the boundaries of historic Catalonia; finally the reductionist policy of 'putting Catalonia first' is included – which is as much as socialist or communist 'Catalanists' today, who reject overtly nationalistic language, will admit to.

The problem of Catalanism, like most problems, appears to change its nature according to the perspective from which one approaches it. French scholars, for instance, find the durability of Catalan identity, the strength of Catalan self-assertion, constantly surprising. From the perspective of France, where the small Catalan minority has felt at home in the French state for a long time, the reserve evinced by Spanish Catalans towards Spain has seemed to demand explanation. From within a federal system like that of the United States or a hodgepodge of historic communities like the United Kingdom, the uneasy interlocking of allegiances to the narrower community and the supra-national state seems less odd. The French, on the other hand, have forged one of the few relatively successful unitary nation-states in the world and treat other experiences as abnormal. In Britain it is known and understood that the Scots can take as much pride in a Scottish victory at Wembley as in a British victory at Waterloo: with this analogy for Spain's relationship with Catalonia, there is nothing comparable in France. Thus when Pierre Vilar, one of the greatest historians of modern Catalonia, first visited Barcelona as a young teacher from France in 1927, he found the intensity of the Catalanism he encountered both stirring and shocking.

This was during the dictatorship of General Primo de Rivera, who had come to power in 1923, overestimating the seriousness of secessionist gestures made by the Catalan authorities during a parliamentary crisis a few years before. The régime's over-reaction had included a ban on the public use of the Catalan language and on the display of symbols of Catalanist sentiment. The dictatorship's teeth were bare but rotten and, in an atmosphere of unenforceable repression, all forms of forbidden fruit, including Catalanism, were thriving. Vilar was living in the Students' Residence run by Miquel Ferrá, an ivory tower of professional intellectuals, including the lexicographer Pompeu Fabra – guardian of the endangered heritage – and Nicolau d'Olwer, a liberal politician and historian who wrote books on impeccable subjects. In this high-minded atmosphere, Vilar found some of the more bizarre manifestations of Catalanism to be strangely narrow and mean. He was delighted with Catalans' loyalty to their persecuted language and felt moved when theatre audiences rose with tears in their eyes to sing the banned Catalan anthem. He was disturbed, however, at a friend's insistence, in defiance of the facts, that such 'Spanish' intrusions as bullfights and flamenco could not be found in Barcelona; and upset at how, at the dinner-table, his fellow-residents pointedly declined to laugh at Eugeni d'Ors's jokes, because the great Catalan writer had deigned to accept the honour of a place in the Royal Academy in Madrid. Another feature which struck Vilar – the insistence of Catalan intellectuals on talking French or English to Spanish-speaking foreigners – was simply routine. When the leading Catalan historian, Jaume Vicèns Vives, came to Oxford to lecture a few years later, he insisted on using his unintelligible English in preference to the Castilian which his audience would at least have been able to understand. In every respect Vilar found his Catalan hosts

abounding in openness and generosity except in their attitude to
Castile.[7] The paradox inspired him to write the most exhaustive and,
for its length, inconclusive study of the origins of Catalanism ever
undertaken.

Yet that uncomfortable pettiness of Catalanism is part of its essence.
No truly satisfying sense of identity can be built up entirely from
within; it has to have an external point of reference, an excluded 'other'
outside it. Catalans and Castilians behold each other through a highly
polished glass which reflects back some suspiciously inverted self-
images. Catalans, for instance, like to think of themselves as common-
sensical, practical, industrious, provident, reasonable and scientific;
their stereotype of Castilian weaknesses includes lack of realism, addic-
tion to the useless, laziness, fatalism, uncompromising pride and
morbid concern with metaphysics. For their lack of the classic 'Spanish'
virtues of austerity, honour, spiritual priorities and altruism, Catalans
are caricatured in Castile as grasping, materialistic, blasé, pedantic
and mean-spirited. Those who like to think of themselves as Catalans
are bound to espouse their stereotype more strongly, because, while
Spanish identity can dispense with the image of the Catalan and
still survive, Catalanism would be unthinkable without conscious
self-differentiation from 'Spain'. Even in the atmosphere of freedom
and mutual respect cultivated among the historic communities of
democratic Spain today, echoes of the pettiness lamented by Vilar are
still discernible. The Barcelona papers have columns designed to help
their readers purge their Catalan of Castilian influences, usually by
forsaking what are said to be Castilian neologisms in favour of archaic
romance terms. Every traveller's bag of Barcelonese anecdotes includes
stories of replies received in Catalan to questions asked politely in
Castilian.

Catalanism would not be what it is without resentment of Castile.
That does not mean, however, that it is just a negatively charged
particle. It includes self-sufficient Catalan patriotism that comes from
within the history of the principality. And it is in Catalonian history,
as well as in the mutual perceptions of Catalans and other Spaniards,
that an understanding of its nature has to be sought. In most studies,
it has been seen either as the collective sentiment of a nation or the
political programme of an interest-group. In both guises, its origins
have been tracked down to the mid-nineteenth century. It found
historians almost as soon as it found utterance and some of its earliest
spokesmen were anxious to be its chroniclers. One of the most distinguished in both roles was Francesc Pi i Margall (1824–1901); he

was also, in a sense, the most politically successful of all Catalanists, for no other politician of that persuasion had ever risen to be head of the Spanish state. His mildly liberal historiography and his sympathy for socialism – he was an enthusiastic reader of Proudhon – attracted clerical censorship and sent him, briefly, into exile until the revolution of 1868 gave him an opening in political life which he was quick to exploit. His writings had identified him with the ill-understood but impressive ideals of 'democracy' and 'federalism', which, partly as a result of his own powerful recommendation, became key terms in the republican constitution of 1873. Part of the theoretical basis of his federalism was the conviction that his native Catalonia, like other communities inside the Spanish state, was a 'nation' in the senses current among nineteenth-century intellectuals: a linguistic entity, an autochthonous race, a community with a distinctive historical experience and unity. Catalanism – awareness of this and espousal of political aspirations to match – was simply the natural expression of inherent nationhood. In the next generation, the same explanation of the emergence of Catalanism was documented by Enric Prat de la Riba (1870–1917), who also wrote a Catalanist catechism and became president of the Catalan regional authority created in 1914. It was no cause of embarrassment that Catalans' awareness of their national destiny had matured only at about the same time as that of the Italians and Germans.

Other historians were soon demanding an 'historical' as well as a 'natural' explanation of Catalonia. Not until the 1960s, however, was a picture built up of the contexts to which the emergence of Catalanism in its various forms seemed to belong. These included, most importantly, the Catalan cultural 'renaissance' or *Renaixença*, which both salvaged Catalan pride in Catalonia's distinctive cultural heritage and demonstrated the unlimited potential of the language; the legal particularism and nostalgia for ancient liberties which had played a part in attracting Catalans to the romantic-reactionary banner of Carlism in the civil wars of 1833–75; the distinctive social profile of Catalonia with its relatively large bourgeoisie; the divergent economic interests of industrialised, protectionist Catalonia and agrarian, free-trader Castile; the failure of the Spanish state to deliver what Catalonia demanded – a strong, prosperous home market and imperial success – the failure of the Catalan élite to capture the Spanish state for 'modern' and 'progressive' goals; the boost federalism gave to devolutionist and separatist politics; the strength of sentiment nurtured by emigrants from Catalonia, heightened by the threat posed by the huge numbers

of nineteenth-century immigrants from non-Catalan Spain.[8] Outside
the range of these more or less useful analyses, there was no shortage
of silly explanations, such as incompatibility of spirit between Catalans
and other Spaniards – a notion which, expressed in the curious argot
of Spanish academic discourse, could be made to sound plausible –
and Masonic conspiracy against 'the sacred unity of Spain'.

Often cited as the first text in the modern Catalonian nationalist
tradition is Josep Pau Ballot's *Gramàtica i apologia de la llengua
catalana* of 1814, a largely ignored vindication of the literary status
and possibilities of Catalan. The nineteenth-century Catalan revival is
conveniently held to begin with Carles Aribau's poem, 'La pàtria', of
1833, but for a full exposition of political Catalanism one must turn
to the 1840s and the works of Antoni Ribot Fontseré (ob. 1873), Josep
Narcisi Milá de la Roca (ob. 1883) and Josep Ferrer Subirana (ob.
1844). These were all men of markedly different political and intellectual stamp: a liberal progressive, a rather mystical idealist and an
ultramontane Carlist respectively; but they established between them
the kernel of a mythic reading of the Catalan past which was passed
on to the great spokesmen of Catalanism in the late nineteenth century,
who again diverged in almost all their views. Pi i Margall was a
socialist sympathiser; his one-time collaborator, Almirall, was a liberal
rationalist; Prat de la Riba was a bourgeois conservative and Torras i
Bagès a clerical reactionary with a social conscience. But there was a
common core of Catalanist myth to their work.

The elements of this myth – I use the word in the technical sense
to mean a version of the past believed for its convenience, without
seeking to imply that it was all untrue – were:

I. *The Catalans are not an apodictic race but 'an historic nation'*,
or, in Rovira i Virgili's formula, 'not an anthropological, but an
historical race' – a product of historical, not biological evolution.
Almirall uses the word 'race' loosely but his historical model is
essentially the same as the other writers.

II. *The Spanish state is a Castilian state*, imposed by force of arms
on the victims of the Castilians' 'passion to command'. There
is some truth in this; but the common fate of the Spanish kingdoms
was the result of dynastic accidents; the Catalan élite was happy
enough, for the most part, to collaborate with centralising governments in the eighteenth century when economic conditions were
favourable; and there has always been room for Catalans in the

corridors of ministries in Madrid. The Catalanist version of history could be taken to absurd lengths, even to representing Joan II in the 1460s as the first of a series of Spanish tyrants – and this was more than a decade before the earliest alleged inception of the Spanish 'state'.

III. *The Catalan language was a victim of Castilian linguistic imperialism.* Again, this is only partly true. Until the Franco era, centralising governments tended to practise linguistic favouritism rather than oppression. The War of Independence against Napoleon produced a glut of popular Catalan poems in praise of Spain. Intellectuals abandoned the language for literary purposes readily enough in the eighteenth century and only rediscovered it on a wave of nineteenth-century romanticism, medievalism and sentimentalism. It was a long time before they were sure of themselves in the use of the tongue. In the 1920s, when everyone who was anyone in Barcelona made a point of avoiding Spanish, the Catalan leader Cambó still thought that Catalan was only 'proving itself' as a medium for 'every expression of the spirit'.

IV. *Catalonia's privileges were the just rewards of centuries of good service* to counts and kings from time immemorial, or else contractual obligations dating back to the origins of the state.

V. *Catalonia had always been loyal*, provoked to rebellion only *in extremis* by Castilian excesses, especially those of the bogeyman, the Count of Olivares, who had demanded unprecedented fiscal contributions from Catalonia before the revolt of 1640. Thus Ribot Fontseré could represent the military dictator Espartero (see pp.167 –9), who bombarded Barcelona in 1842, as another Olivares; there could hardly be a more potent spell with which to conjure up Catalans' hatred. The anonymous *Cataluña vindicada* of 1842, a dialogue between soldiers from different parts of Spain (of whom the Catalan and Aragonese interlocutors are suitably learned and intellectually nimble) rakes over the blame for the bloodshed of 1640 onwards with predictable results. It is worth noticing that the theme of Catalonian loyalty in the Catalanist tradition is intelligible only if one remembers that almost all Catalanists – even Almirall, who insisted on Catalonia's right to independence – regarded themselves as Spaniards as well as Catalans. Usually this included snide snipings at the allegedly imperfect Hispanicity of Castilians: '*Españoles; ¡sí! ¡Más que vosotros!*' as Maragall exclaimed. They advocated the

España de todos of Prat, the 'Spain with justice' of the later leader
of Catalonia Francesc Cambó. Though Almirall sometimes talked
the language of separatism, his published programme for the salvation of Catalonia did not even go so far as federalism.

VI. *The emasculation of Catalan liberties by Philip V in 1716 was
a disaster for the whole of Spain.* The curious feature of this part of
the myth is that Catalanists of left and right believed it for mutually
contradictory reasons. For Ferrer Subirana, for instance, the Nueva
Planta of 1716 was a break with tradition which undermined the old
hierarchy of church, town and nobles, and opened the way to
revolutionary and democratic influences. For Rovira i Virgili, it was
an authoritarian gesture that destroyed liberty. Both sides probably
exaggerated its importance. It was more resented by nineteenth-
than eighteenth-century Catalans.

In the early years of the Catalanist revival, there was surprisingly
little attempt to propagate this sixfold myth at a popular level. The
intellectual Catalanists devoted themselves to promoting Catalan
language and literature, founding educational institutions and funding
research into the history of the medieval Catalonian state. An early
critic of the limitations of academic Catalanism, Joan Sardá, pointed
out that a poem like Aribau's 'Pàtria' – generally considered the first
great work of the *Renaixença* – was 'too literary' to have any popular
appeal. The criticism would with equal aptness be made of most
Catalanist writings. Typical of the beginnings of Catalanism was the
great poetry contest of 1842, organised by Joan Castada after a Literary
Academy lecture on courtly love. The specified themes were medieval.
The winning poem was about the Catalan crusades, the runner-up –
in Castilian – about a Catalan knight. This keynote resounded throughout the early history of Catalanism. The Catalanists gathered every
year from 1859 at their revived 'Floral Games' (*Jocs Florals*) to declaim
the virtues of Catalonia and the message of Catalonian nationalism in
verses so archaic and arcane that none outside the literary élite would
read them. Even their newspapers, like Almirall's *Diari* or Prat's *Veu*
were late in the field – 1879 and 1890 respectively – and forbiddingly
upmarket. When at last they won a proper organ of government for
Catalonia, the Mancomunitat, in 1914, they almost bankrupted it by
the generosity of their educational budget. To people with strictly
political or – like most peasants and workers – economic priorities,
Catalanists were of dubious relevance. They appeared to put literary

culture above political rights, as when Torras i Bagès argued, 'In order to have Catalan poetry, we must have a Catalonia'. This was to invert most people's natural order of things.[9]

Although – for reasons we must turn to in a moment – Catalanist politicians could attract substantial votes in all free elections from 1898, there was little popular enthusiasm for the Catalanist message during the first great era of electoral progress for Catalanism between 1898 and the civil war. One of the apostles of Catalanism, Bartolemeu Robert, admitted as much to a reporter from Madrid in 1901. 'The most important section – indeed, the vast majority – would be satisfied with economic and other decentralising measures. But there is also another group, to which I belong, which hopes for more: the total triumph of a regional solution. That is, we demand for Catalonia her language, her laws, her customs, even her theatre.'[10] Again, the Catalanists appear as culture-vultures, staring hungrily at the well-stocked aviary of art and learning in Madrid.

Reference to the neighbouring and overlapping nationalisms of Valencia and Aragon can help to illustrate how Catalanism thrived in academic isolation from the masses. Valencianism originated as a kind of Catalanist heresy – a protest by the Valencian élite against the vision of a 'greater Catalonia' conceived in Barcelona. Valencia was to have its own revived identity, its own autonomy. Valencianists disliked calling their language 'Catalan'; Catalan and Valencian were both dialects of Limousin – *lemosín* was the preferred term. Teodor Llorente (1836–1911), first pontiff of Valencianism, invented a curious historical myth, according to which Valencian troubadors of the Middle Ages possessed a different culture from their Catalan counterparts, and had evinced greater awareness of the unity of 'Hispania'. Like most heresies, Valencianism was soon riven by schisms of its own, but it remained an esoteric creed, at least for the rest of the nineteenth century. In 1896, the republican federalist, Constantí Llombart, complained, 'The Valencian people has failed to respond with the enthusiasm and interest which the glorious cause that is their own ought to have awakened.' The Aragonese movement's history closely parallels that of Valencia, although of later origin: it is almost entirely confined to this century. In Aragon, Catalan speakers were only ever a tiny minority and Catalanism was regarded with even more suspicion than in Valencia. But it had to be emulated, as it could not be ignored. Many of the early advocates of an autonomous Aragon actually lived in Barcelona, exiled from their roots, attracted by the vibrant cultural life of the half-alien metropolis. They organised historical congresses and, from 1894, their own rival to Catalonia's Floral Games in Sara-gossa. They philosophised about the 'Aragonese soul' and 'Aragonese ideal', and Julián Calvo Alfaro dreamed of an 'Aragonese state', though most of them, like the Valencianists, professed a transcendent loyalty to Spain. Their justification of *Aragonesismo* was strictly antiquarian and evoked virtually no popular response.[11]

THE REVOLT OF THE PASTRYCOOKS

Despite its academic origins and fissile character, Catalanism came in the late nineteenth and early twentieth centuries to take the form of a mass movement, spreading from political cliques and artistic and antiquarian élites, to wield enormous muscle-power in a democratic age. In a sense, Catalanism had always been 'around' as a political issue: the small Catalan political nation was never without self-awareness; it always wanted the special treatment and the wider or greater power for which its ancestors fought in 1640–52 or 1705–14. After the experience of the eighteenth century, when Catalonia was forcibly integrated into the political system of the Spanish monarchy and willingly integrated into its economic system, and when – according to a common belief of historians – the chances of submerging Catalan identity within a Spanish 'super-state' were greatest, the Junta of Barcelona, formed to fight the war against Napoleon, still wanted to turn the clock back. The terms in which its members addressed Catalan deputies to the Cortes of Cadiz in 1812 were guarded but clear:

For although it must after all be admitted that political advantages would ensue from making uniform the laws and liberties of all the provinces of the monarchy, so that, when the present crisis is over, it does not emerge as a body riven into disparate pieces, nevertheless, when a plural solution is considered in other terms, or when insuperable obstacles appear to the realisation of such a salutory measure of uniformity, then it can be said that Catalonia must not only keep its present rights and privileges, but also recover those which it enjoyed at the time when the august house of Austria occupied the Spanish throne; since the incalculable sacrifices it is making in defence of the Nation render it fully worthy to recover its prerogatives; and its extraordinary efforts in loyalty and love for its sovereign must be strong enough to blot out from the account and appraisal every last shadow of those events long past.[12]

At a time when another war of succession threatened the Bourbon dynasty, it was daring of the notables of Barcelona to recall the last such conflict and to refer in glowing terms to the Habsburg era, which Barcelona had fought bitterly to prolong at Bourbon expense. Despite the tentative language, and the long qualificatory clauses which were made to postpone the real message of the sentence, the Junta's Catalanism seemed unambiguous. It had the same nostalgic references, the same archaic air, as would become familiar in Catalanist tradition over the next century – and the same insistence on special status for Catalonia compared with the rest of Spain.

The insistence on the 'specialness' of Catalonia has always been precisely the element of Catalanism which the rest of Spain has been reluctant to concede. The centralisation of administration, and uniformity of fiscal and military obligation, were policies of almost every nineteenth-century Spanish government, except during the First Republic of 1873–75. This ensured a long gestation for Catalanism as a movement in the interests of the province. The incidents which marked the start of its continuous history, however, were limited to Barcelona and explain, if they do not justify, the taunt that Catalanism is a Barcelonese 'invention'.

The circumstances of the affair are complicated. In 1840, together with all the self-proclaimed liberal and progressive centres in Spain, Barcelona had welcomed the seizure of power by the tough centralist general Espartero; this 'fellow with balls', the strong-man of the liberal cause, was a wagoner's son, judged too sickly in his youth to study for the Church. Launched by accident, through entanglement in the war against Napoleon, into a military career that began unexpectedly and continued startlingly, he was elevated by a classic *pronunciamiento*. He ruled in the liberal interest which professional soldiers – as followers of a career open to the talents – tended to espouse in that period. From subjects of the state, he expected the iron discipline of the parade-ground or front line. Later in life, he developed a certain *folie de grandeur*, proclaiming himself the Duque de la Victoria, erecting statues of himself in public places and continuing to crush dissent, before retiring – like a Sulla or a Cincinnatus – to the comforts of provincial citizenship in Logroño. At first, however, he was hailed in Barcelona as Spain's deliverer from the corrupt and unskilful hands of the regent-Queen Mother, María Cristina.

Once in power, however, Espartero called down the curtain on the 'progress' he was said to represent. The workers' 'voice', Rámon Simó i Badia, accused the bourgeoisie of encouraging their employees onto the street in his support by paying them full wages.[13] His Catalan friends felt deceived. He accused Barcelona of attempted tax-dodging and draft-dodging – the inhabitants of Barcelona 'have no natural properties which exempt them'. He was undisguisedly a pro-English free-trader at a time when protectionism was becoming the focus of emergent workers' political organisations and unionism in Barcelona. Between October 1841 and December 1842 a series of municipal revolutionary Juntas, variously controlled by the artisanate and the big proprietors, all confronted Espartero's government.

Two affrays were particularly menacing: the first in October 1841 when the Junta demolished fortifications erected to overawe the city after the rebellion of 1715; the second just over a year later when a new, more 'respectable' Junta was blamed by the government for urban barricades and a 'pastrycooks' revolt'.

A service-industry proletariat was in rebellion against its bourgeois masters as much as against Madrid. The genie of this suddenly unbottled unrest was Josep Maria Carsy, an officer ignominiously discharged from the army who had devoted his considerable demagogic powers to a republican newspaper which he edited. Its normal readership was small, but the inflammatory circumstances of 1842 created a public for rabble-rousing. By appealing to the protectionist self-interest which united all classes in Barcelona he was able to fill the streets with a mob which representatives of every form of disaffection were disposed to join – Carlists, liberal 'moderates' opposed to Espartero, Catalanists. Though commonly called a 'republican' rising, this was an old-fashioned riot, converted into a political movement by an unholy alliance of which protectionism was the only shared policy. The decisive moment in its transformation occurred when a large part of the city militia joined the insurrection and began exchanging fire with the regular garrison. On 14 November the regulars in the old university barracks and the shipyard guardhouse raised the white flag. Carsy proclaimed a Junta with himself at its head. Blockaded by sea, surrounded on land, the movement had no chance of consolidating this deceptive early success. Intimidated by the strength of the besiegers, the militia returned to its lawful allegiance and Carsy fled aboard a French ship. Rioters remained in arms under a charismatic vagrant called Crispí Garcia, who had made his living before the revolt by selling matches. They were bombarded into submission, but not before the cannon had destroyed 400 buildings. The following year the pattern of violence was almost exactly repeated. First, in May, General Zurbano, who commanded the garrison, inflicted provocative reprisals when he 'imagined himself insulted'. The tensions of the summer which followed culminated in the reconvening of a 'people's Junta' which capitulated only after two months of terror and 'many days' of bombardment.[14]

This orgy of *enragé* violence represented the shape of things to come in a city that was not permanently to discipline its lumpenproletariat and 'anarchic classes' for another hundred years. In the immediate future, it provoked a tough reaction from the Espartero government. As it crawled back to control of the city, the old patriciate was brought to book and, to some extent, held to ransom. The demolished fortifications had to be rebuilt at the city's expense; heavy fines were levied with compensation for damage to government property and to the persons and property of the victims of the insurrection, including the regular soldiers killed and wounded. The tobacco factory and mint – which were thought to be nests of revolutionary violence but which in fact, by promoting prosperity, nurtured stability – were suppressed. Catalan political movements generally were tainted by association with an episode that was both a crime and a mistake. Catalanism's first blood was drawn in a struggle which was Barcelona's rather than Catalonia's.

The mood of the rest of the decade was well captured in a British consul's report of January 1847: 'gendarmes *à la française*, secret police, paid press, coffee-house politicians and much capital embarked in manufactures'.[15] It was a perfect environment for the germination of Catalanist sentiment. Catalonia's distinctive economy was again beginning, after a long interval, to give her interests which were divergent in some respects from those of the rest of Spain, together with the means to pay for lobbying and propaganda. The shock of the events of 1842 and 1843 had evoked from a few writers comparisons with events 200 years before. After more than a century of peace between Barcelona and Spain, Spanish armies had marched in to bludgeon the city in repression of a movement of defiance of the centre. A peace that had survived the years of reactionary rule in Madrid from 1814 to 1833 could not survive the triumph of liberalism, partly because hot-air liberalism – government-led and free-trader – in Madrid was incompatible with steam-liberalism in Barcelona. In its early years, political Catalanism grew in the craters of Espartero's bombshells.

The Speculator's Utopia

As the demolished walls of the citadel were painfully rebuilt, the city authorities became obsessed with the image of walls as chains of despotism and constrictors of progress. They seemed to encircle the city with bleakness and envelop it in shadow. They were an irksome legacy from an unenlightened age. The early nineteenth-century idea of progress in Spain was expressed in the language of movement and light (as well as of steam) and the walls were perceived as an impediment to both. Although space inside the city had been created by the abolition of houses of religion in 1836, that was a bonus about which the Barcelonese felt equivocal: it had been imposed by central dictation from Madrid, and although the Barcelonese élite prided themselves on their own liberalism, clericalist tradition and catholic habits remained strong among a minority of them. Only the demolition of the walls could satisfy the city's need to expand and match the people's environment to their ascribed 'spirit' of dynamism, energy and industriousness. In 1844, Felip Monlau's emotional philippic, 'Abajo las Murallas', was fêted by the city council.

The published version opened with the council's decree in favour of the industrialisation of Barcelona, not only on commercial but also patriotic grounds, for 'industry nowadays is one of the great objects of international rivalry'. The walls were militarily ineffective – a conclusion for which the successful French invasion of 1823 was cited as evidence; they led to overcrowding and enfeebled health. If the walls remained, Monlau suggested, the useful and active population could move outside, leaving the inert clients of central government behind. 'Let those who live off the public purse stay inside the walls. Let the officials of Barcelona stay there and suffocate. For those who live by their labour, profession or industry – the productive, the industrious elements of Barcelona – want to breathe the air of freedom and independence and have it in their power to do so. Into the country, then, and we shall found there, if we have to, a new Barcelona!'[16]

The cholera epidemic of 1854 was blamed on the walls: they were said to cram the inhabitants into insanitary warrens and inhibit the circulation of air. Although the memories of 1842 had been too strong for the central government to permit the destruction of any part of the fortifications, the question was being transformed from a political to an economic and aesthetic one by the sheer pressure of population, or unplanned extramural growth, of city traffic and of the growing fashion for planned urbanisation. In 1859 the city held an architectural

competition for a plan for an enlargement (*eixample*) of the city. On
27 October the plans were submitted to public exhibition and attracted
huge crowds. The most popular designs were those of the official
victor, Antoni Rovira i Trias, and Ildefons Cerdà, who had not entered
the competition but who had made a design which was included by
order of the Madrid government. On merit, the balance of the argument perhaps lay on Rovira's side: he had related the street-plan of
the projected Eixample to that of the old medieval city into which the
new streets had to feed by scattering a ring of piazzas around the old
town, from which the new roads would radiate. Cerdà's plan looked
more rigidly 'modern'. He made only minimal use of nodal piazzas
and masked the old town with a doctrinaire grid-plan of boulevards and
public gardens. He was accused of imposing a monotonous geometry
on Barcelona, of building the new without deference to or even
acknowledgement of the old and of surrounding the city with comfort-
less wind-tunnels. On the other hand, his conception was bolder and
more original, its classless uniformity inspired by social crusading, its
lack of historical references by revulsion against baroque display.[17]

Underlying opposition to the Cerdà model was political rather than
aesthetic. The protest movement was less against the Cerdà plan than
against government interference with the decision-making of the civic
authorities. The Eixample became an unbuilt battleground for the continuing struggle of Barcelona against Madrid, a Trojan plain on which a
pamphlet war was fought. Something had to be decided. Relentless
demographic growth made the form of the Eixample too urgent to be
left to the politicians. In 1863, for instance, the rate of growth of the
population of Barcelona was 27.42 per cent – three times the Spanish
national average.[18] The city could not afford the indulgence of prolonged bickering with the government, or an indefinitely postponed start
to the work. Yet only political change brought a respite from the conflict.

The revolution of 1868, which ejected the Bourbons from the
Spanish throne, introduced a brief era when centralisation ceased to be
an unremitting government priority; federalism and even 'cantonalism'
became respectable; at the very least, the idea that Spain was a
partnership between centre and periphery began to animate government policy. The remaining walls of Barcelona (left from the demo-
litions of 1854) came down in 1869, and the Eixample began to take
on the configurations of the Cerdà plan. Despite the delayed start and
the slow initial growth, Barcelona's boom in the late nineteenth century
was so rapid that the expectations of the plan were exceeded. In-filling
robbed the plan of its best feature, the expansive parks and garden

squares. The effect can best be observed by the visitor today in the
Passage Permanyer, one of the earliest modifications inserted into
Cerdà's grid, between the carrers de Pau Claris and Roger de Llòria.
It was highly fashionable among artists of the late nineteenth century
– the pianist Vidiella and the *uomo universale* Apel·les Mestre both
chose to live here – but it is hard to see why. The architect, Jeroni
Granell i Berrera, apparently thought that his low-built terrace of
one-storey, mews-like cottages with their fussy ornament were 'in
English taste'. One of Cerdà's intended spaces seems, instead, to have
been sacrificed to a development which is both mean and pretentious.

The Eixample was an extraordinary gesture of confidence in an
era disfigured by extremes of poverty and prosperity, urbanity and
violence. The railway and new opera house were opened in 1848, the
stock exchange in 1858. In 1854–6 Barcelona endured the worst mob
violence for nearly a century and a half. Factories were being erected
by industrialists and burned down by Luddites. The idealism of the
Cerdà plan was counterpointed by utopian socialism, advocated in the
slums by admirers of Cabet's *Icaria*. Catalanists founded the poetry
contests of the Jocs Florals and workers the early unions. The democratic grid of Cerdà's design contrasted with the hierarchy of the
tiered interior of the Teatre del Liceu.[19] These are, perhaps, the
characteristic contrasts of a culture in a hurry, a city transforming
itself in a borrowed image. The most directly comparable example of
the Eixample's sudden grafting of a criss-cross of nineteenth-century
branches onto the trunk of an ancient town is to be found in Madrid,
where the Marqués de Salamanca, the great wizard of deficit finance,
laid out the district that bears his name in the 1860s. The many stories
told about him were sparks struck from his flashy way of life: he had
a personalised railway carriage and a private dance-troupe; he stole
Napoleon III's chef with a promise of higher pay. The showy, caddish
profile, the shady deals – he bribed the Queen Mother in the course
of his railway speculations – and the rickety finances, which ended in
his ruin, all seemed to sum up the effects of the mid-century 'gold
fever' which also characterised Barcelona, and which was blamed
for diverting capital from industrial investment into unproductive
speculation. In fact, Barcelona's expansion was more sedate and better
grounded in local sources of wealth-creation than Madrid's, but its
effects were similar: agonising social problems and a similar look. Both
cities acquired the outer garments of a standard Euro-metropolis. In
Madrid's case, this clothing was worn as a disguise. In Barcelona, it
represented the way the inhabitants really saw themselves.

THE REALM OF ICARUS

Barcelona's industrialisation was poor, nasty and brutish. The very heroism of Barcelonese entrepreneurism – which accomplished so much so quickly with so few resources, in an unpromising place and adverse circumstances, meant that the accompanying crisis in the living standards of the workers may have been worse than in some other industrialising communities. It is hard to be sure, because Barcelona had no Engels or Chadwick on hand to report the conditions; but some remarkable testimony has survived: from Ramón Simó i Badia, a self-educated worker who left the factories of Sarria for the lobbies of Madrid, where he founded a workers' press; from Jaume Salarich, a fairly philanthropic physician whose work on working-class health was patronised by well-intentioned proprietors; and Ildefons Cerdà, the designer of the Eixample, who undertook a remarkable statistical survey of working-class life in Barcelona after the industrial disputes of 1854, in an attempt to explain the problems to himself and contribute to their future solution. All three were writing à parti pris, but from different standards: the horrific picture they collectively present is therefore probably reliable. It helps to explain the fearful pattern of life in the mid-century city, the fitful mass violence, the intermittent plague.[20]

Salarich's clinical picture of the effects of breathing in the atmosphere of the textile mills – profuse sweat, languor, gastric trouble, respiratory difficulties, laboured movements, poor circulation, mental torpor, nervous prostration, pulmonary corrosion and poisoning from noxious machine oils and dyes – are confirmed from personal experience by Simó i Badia. Reports of fourteen- and even sixteen-hour working days can be found, though Cerdà's figures and Simó's complaints suggest that in the mid-century twelve or thirteen hours was the norm. Cerdà investigated particularly the sort of diet workers could afford. A bachelor, at the time of his survey, could, by the expenditure of something over half his wages, secure adequate nourishment, including daily soup and a little meat. A married couple with two children, however, at the same relative level of expenditure, were condemned to a diet almost exclusively of bread and potatoes, with the odd sardine. Salarich was convinced that debilitating hunger was a major cause of workers' susceptibility to disease.

All writers, however, stressed the effects of an industrial environment on workers' morale more even than their material plight. Jaume Balmes, the great ethical critic of Barcelona's industrial revolution, thought them worse off than the slaves of antiquity, who had at least some means of protection from the economic lurches and fluctuations that could turn poverty into destitution overnight in the Barcelona of his day. 'How,' demanded Simó i Badia, 'can you expect human beings who have been converted into industrial machines, with no source of stimulation, no hope for the future, to take any pride in work which murders them body and soul?' The Catholic paper which urged workers to see their masters as divine instruments for their sustenance also warned owners that 'the mechanics in your factories are made of the same clay of which you are formed . . . and must not be confused with the machines you have in your workshops'.[21]

The slums of early industrial Barcelona were fearsome incubators of disease and disorder. Rapid growth attracted a rootless population of rural poor into an alien environment that was improvised out of ill-adapted city dwellings, already centuries old, in the Raval, or out of shanty towns cobbled together on the outskirts. There was one early purpose-built worker's suburb, Barceloneta, begun in 1753 between the site of the citadel and the docks; it was a remarkable example of eighteenth-century urban planning, with its rational grid of streets and uniform terraces, but was unsuitable for its purpose, cramped and bereft of open spaces; it conveyed the same feel of a military settlement as the almost contemporary experiments in urbanisation at St Louis and Georgetown in Minorca, which were intended to accommodate garrison families. Nor could it cope with the increase in population that followed its construction. The author of an inquiry into the cholera epidemic of 1854 claimed that some of its buildings enclosed thirty-two families – which he reckoned as 128 souls – in fifty-four by sixteen foot spaces. Yet this environment had been expressly designed to alleviate 'the many perils to which those who live in shanties of wood and other inflammable stuff are exposed'. A model estate had become an infernal warren. Death bred most intensely in the working-class colonies inside the old walled area, where – unlike Barceloneta – sanitation was primitive or non-existent. 5,657 deaths were blamed on cholera in 1856, 3,717 in 1865.[22]

Barceloneta was designed not only 'to provide breathing space' and 'for the adornment of the dockland and the convenience of its growing population' but also for an avowedly political purpose: 'to contain', according to the Gaceta de Barcelona, 'the breakdown of order that tends to occur when people are so densely mingled'. The real effect of the creation of 'suburbs' for industrial workers, as Barcelona's industrialisation progressed, was exactly the opposite. Class consciousness, accompanied in some cases by a sense of identity based on the 'neighbourhood' replaced the traditional loyalties. Radicals and trade unionists had a sea to swim in, though they often foundered: Barcelona's workers have always been hard to organise and, once organised, harder to control. There is no convincing evidence that Barcelona's masses were effectively radicalised until well into this century – they did not vote en masse until 1929, though enfranchised from 1861 and permanently from 1890. When they took to the streets, they had a habit of disappointing agitators by exposing some non-ideological cause. Still, in the slums and factories, conditions for their radicalisation existed and ideologues were already attempting to exploit them systematically in the 1830s, perhaps as early as the 1820s. The most vivid testimony is of the year 1852 when, as a young Carmelite, the future Bishop Lluch i Garriga visited a factory at lunchtime to find the workers all listening in silence while young children read aloud from 'highly coloured political journals which generally spread subversive doctrines, mocked holy things, ridiculed the practice of religion, insulted the priesthood, spoke ill of the proprietors and government and preached socialism and communism'. Salarich, the physician whose philanthropy was measured in doses from a position of convinced superiority, blamed the authorities for 'granting the masses rights which are not appropriate for them'. Looking back many years later on the formation of Barcelona's first workers' association, the Societat de Protecció Mutua de Teixidors de Barcelona, Joan Alsina, one of the founders, characterised it as a move in the 'desperate struggle of capital with labour . . . to correct the ever-growing abuses of the egoism of some manufacturers'. Of course, neither he nor anyone else would have ventured such an analysis at the time. And, on the whole, what little is known about the motivation of the working-class movement in nineteenth-century Barcelona – not the mob violence of successive hot summers, with which it is often confused – seems more pragmatic than ideological, more economic than political, more capricious than consistent.[23]

Luddism is usually the first manifestation of proletarian unrest in an era of industrialisation. A parliamentary commission of inquiry into machine-breaking in Alcoy in 1821 pronounced it 'an isolated incident caused by the desperation of men who pursued their interests blindly and understood them imperfectly'.[24] But incidents of a similar character recurred at Camprodon in 1823 and in Barcelona during the revolutionary outrages of 1835 (see above, p. 143). Revolutionary violence during the next major outbreaks in 1840, 1842 and 1843 was,

as we have seen, concentrated on political objectives which had no
particular virtue for the working class. Resentment against industrial
mechanisation, however, was a dormant force, reflecting the pace of
change. The industrial explosion of the mid-century revived Luddism
at a moment of acute political danger.

THE REBELLIONS OF VERMIN

A 'progressive' putsch in Madrid in 1854 brought to power the centralist general, Espartero, who had bombarded Barcelona during the
uprising of 1842. For Barcelona, therefore, the radical triumph was
equivocal. On the streets of the city, the response was one of ill-defined
radical enthusiasm. The sudden, unlawful seizure of power at the
centre seems to have stimulated hopes of further changes – of various
and incompatible kinds, of course – and to have encouraged the
methods of the mob. Workers' sense of grievance against the automated
plant which Catalans charmingly called *selfactines* had never been so
desperate or so menacing; in the previous five years the number of
machines in the city had reputedly doubled. On the night of 14–15
July a Luddite attack was launched. Eight factories were targeted. In
most, damage was superficial, except at the plant of Pere Arnau, where
the factory was burned down and the proprietor's family immolated
in the conflagration, and at Castells and Company, where the owner
was wounded by a pistol shot. The riots were quelled, or at least
abated, by the force of personality of the republican-democrat leader,
Josep Anselm Clavé, whose diffuse artistic gifts were never more
effective than in rhetorical forms and radical causes. 'Workers!' he
said. 'Do you think we have brought about this revolution so that you
can dishonour it with your crimes?'[25]

By 18 July, the workers' movement had been deflected into strike
action. Violence in other Catalonian towns continued, however, and
the atmosphere in Barcelona was full of menace and fright. The
captain-general left his house to sleep in the shipyards; the progressive
General La Concha, returning from exile in Paris, saw 'fear painted
on the faces of the city bosses'. The objectives of the strikers widened,
a ban on *selfactines* accomplished little as new targets were sought with
swivel-gun speed: the right of association, the adoption of collective
bargaining, higher wages, shorter hours, the exclusion of cheap female
and child labour. The Luddites had grown up with apparently magical
suddenness, with the experienced and disciplined leadership of the

weavers' union, now fourteen years old, waving the wand. But the utopia was invaded by apocalypse; on 20 July, the first rumours of cholera were reported. Within a few days the epidemic was verified. The city was under seige from within.[26]

The workers' leaders showed their maturity after the captain-general, who had shifted his hiding place to the British consulate, emerged, having made a show of dignified resignation, to escape by sea, on 5 August. Urged by La Concha, who took interim control of a now dangerously mutinous garrison, they issued an appeal for a return to work on the eighth: 'otherwise the working class will be committing suicide'. In a concurrent declaration, the owners expressed their faith in the success of a political revolution and a constituent national assembly 'in common with the workers'. Barcelona rallied to La Concha's slogan: 'confidence in the future'. The delinquents of the period of the riots and the strike were pardoned and the 'useful and active classes joined forces to tear down the walls. As the onset of winter brought the epidemic to an end, the retrospects of the press were astonishingly evasive; it was said to be the cholera that had closed the factories, abetted, according to the workers' propagandists in Madrid, by 'the flight of the capitalists'.[27]

A brief but remarkable winter of compromise and co-operation ensued. On the one hand, the new civil governor, Ciril Franquet, encouraged workers' associations and collective bargaining under the direction of an inter-trades Junta, although these things were still technically illegal. On the other hand, without a renewal of worker violence, the ban on *selfactines* was revoked in secret and ignored in practice, while the authorities advised owners to continue using them 'while appearing to prepare their substitution'. Franquet negotiated deals for peace in the silk and cloth industries, based on an average working week of seventy-two hours and the owners' promise to use their best efforts to increase production and safeguard jobs. The effects of these concessions, however, were to encourage the workers' demands and fortify the employers' obduracy. The workers' Junta, which Franquet had tried to wield as a tool of his conciliatory policy, proved to have a dangerous cutting edge; by April 1855, it was said to be plotting a general strike. When selective stoppages began towards the end of the month, the city's leading industrialist, Joan Güell i Ferrer, closed down his factory and went to Nice. If not quite a declaration of war, this was a sign that the cordiality of preceding months was over. On 30 April the government banned strikes and all further collective bargaining, adding a ban on lockouts as a token gesture of even-handedness.[28]

In May the repressive policy was confirmed by the publication of the decree revoking the ban on *selfactines* and the appointment as captain-general of General Juan Zapatero, an officer of iron discipline, limited imagination and monstrous egotism. He spoke of duty as if he had a monopoly over it. He was compulsively repressive. At moments of tension he spoke of 'exterminating rebels'; his reply to formulae of compromise was that 'there was no alternative to obedience'. In July 1856 he went to the lengths of having a corpse publicly garrotted, when an officer condemned for a crime of passion had killed himself to escape the humiliation of public execution. Earlier that year, he ended an interview with Josep Anselm Clavé by seizing his interlocutor by the throat and shaking him like a rat.

The cycles of repression and violence that accompanied his rule were not, of course, all Zapatero's fault. The hour had produced the man. Carlist insurgency was rife, filling the Barcelonese bourgeoisie with the fear of slaughter by an alliance of predatory peasants, hobéreau aristocrats, fanatical clericalists, vengeful absolutists and opportunistic bandits. For Zapatero, the Carlist threat was either a valid reason or a useful pretext for his hard line with the workers. He seems, moreover, to have believed that the malcontents were only a small minority of troublemakers; the attitudes of the French consul, Barradère, who thought 'fifty or sixty agitators' were the 'whole problem', which could be solved by their removal from Barcelona, were probably shared widely in the official and commercial circles in which the captain-general moved. The anonymous chronicler of the troubles of 1856 thought them the 'work of vermin', and that the genuine workers taking part were 'very few'. Even the philanthropist Salarich derided the idea that the masses had 'rights'. Zapatero's apparent conviction that he was engaged in a struggle in which weakness was unthinkable and compromise unpalatable has to be understood against the background of the Barcelona of his day: these were years of a precarious bonanza, an industrial gold-rush, which filled shanty towns with half-savage immigrants, cheapened life and bred danger and disease. His war against the mob was the encounter of brutality with barbarism. The workers' employers were men of civilised affectations, their leaders often men of education and ideals; but these refined layers were thin in the cauldron of society that was near-full with dregs and dross.

Public order was maintained more by luck than judgement during 1855. There were five elements in Zapatero's policy. First, he made 'examples'. The most notorious case was that of Josep Barceló, a notorious strike-leader put to death for his alleged part in a scandalous rural murder in which a peasant family had been exterminated by 'bandits' disguised in the uniforms of the popular provincial gendarmerie, the *mozos de escuadra*: Barceló was condemned largely on the evidence of witnesses who were dead by the time of his trial. Secondly, Zapatero used troops to break strikes. Thirdly, he tried to enforce the law against collective bargaining by outlawing even unimpeachably philanthropic associations on the 'terrible day' of 22 June. Fourthly, he deported alleged workers' ringleaders in droves; an exercise in official clemency commuted the sentence of exile to Cuba which he sought to impose and removed the troublemakers only as far as Andalusia. Finally, he 'reformed' the Catalan militias, after some Barcelona militiamen refused to go into action against strikers; this was a euphemism for a purge, which removed between a third and a half of the men in many units and almost the entire artillery corps. All these measures cut two ways: the examples gave the wrong sort of encouragement to others and offended the liberal bourgeoisie, for whom constitutional liberties were sacred. To break strikes with troops was to use a stopper where a safety-valve was needed. Despite the ban on associations, according to the French consul writing in October, *'ces sociétés, juntes et comités continuent à fonctionner, si ce n'est pas ostensiblement, comme ils l'avaient fait jusque là, tout au moins sans prendre la peine de se cacher'.*[29] The exiles created living martyrs. The purges of the militias added trained cadres of disaffected men to the potential ranks of revolution.

Still, the policies seemed to have been temporarily effective. A general strike called in late June of 1855 passed off without bloodshed. Barcelona had an unwonted summer of relative peace. But repression cannot both succeed and survive. Zapatero's methods were increasingly loathsome to the classes he needed on his side. Concentrating his fire on the unionised workforce, he overlooked the more dangerous enemies he was making among the 'respectable' and the untouchable. The first hint of a silent coalition of the bourgeoisie and the mob came in November, 1855, when the rumour of a relaxation of the protective tariff brought Barcelona to 'ebullition, if not revolution'.[30] Reports of a wage-cutting conspiracy of owners in Sabadell provoked letters to the workers' paper in Madrid with wild threats of bloodshed. The following month a strike in the Rosés factory over the reinstatement of a dismissed worker, who happened to be secretary of the weavers' union, was broken by scabs whom the workers pelted with rubble from the ruins of the burned-out Arnau factory. In January 1856 the national legislative assembly received a petition which warned that 'the proletarian class of Barcelona would rather die by the sword than by degrees'. The long period of economic dislocation and industrial turbulence had swelled the *Lumpenproletariat* – from whom the scabs and the revolutionary 'vermin' could be recruited – while the 'responsible' workers with a stake in stability had shrunk. Replying to liberal accusations that workers' associations were being manipulated by 'Carlist agents' and 'Russian gold', the *Cotton-thread Workers' Manifesto* declared, 'The hidden hand that agitates the workers is not the clergy's or the Carlists' but that of misery'.

The allegation of clerical influence was a curious canard. There were individual clergy, inspired by simple humanity or callow notions of 'Christian socialism', who encouraged the workers' movement; these tried to make something of Balmés's doctrine, 'the fate of the impoverished cannot be left to the chance circulation of wealth'. Others were passionately engaged in the strictly evangelical mission launched in the diocese of Barcelona from 1850: they shared St Antoni Maria Claret's approach, careful 'not to utter a single word of politics – and, thank God, no one ever caught me out'. Most, however, subscribed to the views on social disorder expressed by Bishop Costa i Borràs in 1851, 'seeing no remedy save religion and repression'.[31]

In the first six months of 1856, the coalition Zapatero was creating against himself began to coagulate. In May, employers' demand for an extra half-hour's work a day in the mills was debated with the workers without violence. There seemed to be some truth in Franquet's belief that workers and owners alike were looking together for political solutions – the liberalisation of everything except trade. Zapatero was spreading his fire to include bourgeois republicans and democrats. After the purge of the militias, he seems to have felt convinced of his strength in the event of a shoot-out. In July, always the most dangerous time of the year, the news that the progressive ministers in Madrid had been arbitrarily dismissed was received at first in Barcelona with restrained expectancy; for once, revolutionary violence seemed to be monopolised by Castilian towns. But a slow fuse can start a big fire. The conflict that began on 18 July was to be the bloodiest Barcelona had known since 1715.

The insurgents were not workers, or not workers alone, but the mob in alliance with bourgeois radicals. The motives were not economic, or not primarily economic, but political. The rising began after the militia commander called on Zapatero to warn that his men were loyal to the progressive cause and to propose the formation of a Junta – the traditional revolutionary mechanism – to run Barcelona's affairs while the central government was in 'crisis'. Zapatero's reply was that he 'saw no other course than to preserve this Principality in obedience to Her Majesty'. Troops occupied strategic points as popular demonstrations gathered. The militia's arms, and many of its men, appeared on the popular side. Shots began as night fell. In fighting on the 19th, Zapatero's second-in command fell wounded. The fire was hotter still on the 20th. As Zapatero threatened 'extermination', his troops conquered the street redoubts – *'très fortes'*, according to the anonymous commentator, *'et remplies d'insurgents'* – dismantling the barricades to cries of 'Long live the Queen!' The rebels' 'home quarters' in Sants and Barceloneta were bombarded from Montjuic.

On the 21st an assault party under General Villalonga drove the defenders out of the Casa de la Ciutat. A general attack was launched at two in the afternoon and by nightfall only Gràcia and some isolated pockets in the central area remained in rebel hands. The rebels were 'massacred as they [were] captured'. The anonymous commentator hid behind a gun emplacement of sacks of earth to watch 'an enormous massacre' in the carrer de l'Unió. *'Il y a beaucoup de victimes innocents, ce qui arrive toujours . . . Le spectacle a été magnifique.'*

THE VIEW FROM THE SOUTH-WEST CEMETERY

Officials' conviction that the bourgeoisie would soon get over the shock, and evince pleasure initially concealed, was justified in the event. Like Barcelona's other disasters, that of 1856 was succeeded by a wave of optimism. In 1860, Barcelona's habitual anti-militarism was forgotten in the celebrations of victory in Morocco. Reconciliation with the regime was celebrated in a royal visit, greeted by one of the city's biggest textile manufacturers with lilac banners, bordered with portraits of heroes of Morocco, emblazoned with the figures of the royal family and adorned, over a background of a factory roof-scape, with the legend 'To her majesty from *La España Industrial*'. This should be understood as evidence of canny collaboration with the regime, rather than unbridled enthusiasm; the images were equivocal – the queen looked grotesquely fat, her boy demented and her husband daft – and when the Bourbons fell to a putsch in 1868 Barcelona was variously delighted or indifferent. In the meantime, however, the new-found security was there to be enjoyed. Bourgeois life moved out of the cafés onto pavement terraces and out of the house into the gas-lit streets that dazzled Hans Christian Andersen when he visited in 1862.

The slack money and new money of what one novelist called the 'gold-fever years' created a market for art and architecture that impressed Barcelona with the showy, experimental look that has characterised *le style barcelonais* ever since.

Conventional wisdom was that great fortunes could only come from stock-market speculations – 'the Bourse that has conquered the world'.[32] In fact, however, the most conspicuous fortunes can be traced back to manufacturing – often in a pre-industrial, craft-like line of business – or to colonial exploitation or to the marriage of both. Some industrial capital was self-regenerating – like that of the richest man in mid-century Barcelona, Ignasi Girona, who started as a watch-maker and diversified into banking and the metallurgical industry. Much of it, however, came from the New World, sometimes from emigrés-in-reverse who eluded the 'liberators', more often from Cuba, which remained part of the Spanish monarchy and provided Catalans with means to wealth, in slaving, tobacco planting and the sugar trade. The history of the Güell family, who became dominant voices in Barcelonese politics and, through their patronage of Gaudí, influential moulders of Barcelona's modern appearance, perfectly illustrates the interplay of these two types of wealth. Joan Güell i Ferrer (1800–72) was the founding patriarch of the dynasty, the son of a failed Cuban nabob. He returned to Cuba in adolescence and made a fortune of his own, big enough to establish him in business in Barcelona, where he bought a textile mill in 1836. In 1841 he founded what was to be the most admired factory of nineteenth-century Barcelona, El Vapor Vell, on a new site in Sants. He diversified by investing in the fledgling metallurgical industry, subscribing substantial capital to the seminal business of Pablo Llobera and Company in 1841, and in 1855, to the gigantic firm of La Maquinària Terrestre, which became the symbol, for the rest of the century, of Barcelonese determination to keep a local steel industry alive. In the 1860s he developed a new interest in agriculture; in part, this was the typical recessive syndrome of the nineteenth-century nouveaux-riches, turning from industry and finance to the traditional sources of aristocratic wealth. In part, too, it was the result of a genuine reformer's interest in promoting rural prosperity. Above all, it was a calculated business move, taking advantage of the new opportunities for Catalonian viticulture as a result of phylloxera in France.

The family fortune was grossly enlarged by the consequences of the marriage of his son, Eusebi (1846–1918) to Isabel López Bru; her brother, Claudi, was a saint *manqué*, whose canonisation would be proposed by the Jesuits, on whom he conferred lavish patronage; her father, Antonio López López, had been a poor emigrant from Comillas in Santander to Cuba, but, aided by the auriferous effects of that island, and a good marriage of his own, he rose to become Marqués de Comillas and a grandee of Spain. Eusebi and Isabel were able to hand both fortunes on to the next generation. Though the grandson of two self-made men, Eusebi cultivated airs of gentility to match the titles of count, viscount and baron which he acquired for himself and divided among his sons. To his official biographer, he was the epitome of 'the aristocratic sense' with 'the attributes of a gentleman and the manners of a prince'. It seems to have been easier to characterise his qualifications than to itemise them: a resonant voice was often mentioned, 'optimistic in a melancholy manner', an 'imposing counten-ance' and 'distinction, elevation and elegance'.[33] He continued the Güell role of wine-estate châtelains, concentrating – perhaps in con-scious imitation of the Rothschilds – on the creation of superior wines by uncompromising application of the highest standards of scientific and traditional viticulture. His Garraf estate was adorned with wine vaults by a pupil of Gaudí, who designed in person the crypt-chapel of his industrial estate at Santa Coloma, marking the entrepreneurial complex with reminders of the style of a rural seigneur, in the rough-hewn columns that lean over the nave like huge tree-trunks, the curly pews scattered beneath them like fallen leaves.

The tone of the *haut-bourgeois* life of the late nineteenth-century survives in the pages of Narcis Oller's three-volume novel of 1890–3, *La febre d'or*; in the grandiose stones of the new cemetery opened in 1883, fashioned into vast family pantheons where space to stack the dynastic successors of the nouveaux-riches could be provided at conspicuous cost; and in the larger-scale but similar edifices, the urban palaces, that housed them while they lived. The carrer de Milans of 1850, a street of romantic town-houses on the site of a demolished royal palace, represents an early phase of a tradition of upper-middle-class domestic architecture that was to scale the heights of the sublime and the bizarre in private commissions in the eighties and nineties to Josep Puig i Cadafalch (1867–1957) and Antoni Gaudí (1852–1926). Puig's efforts have very much the look of tombs transposed onto the sites of dwellings, particularly thanks to the pinnacled porches and oriel windows that reproduce the forms of the most favoured Gothic pan-theons. Gaudí's compositions were even more ostentatious and con-siderably livelier. The first in the great tradition of manufacturer's palaces was his Casa Vicèns on the carrer de les Carolines of 1883,

built for a tile manufacturer and clad in spectacular external tiling.
His next, far costlier commission, came from Eusebi Güell for a palace
in the heart of town, on the carrer Nou de la Rambla, on the edge of
the red-light district, but handy for the centre of social life – the
Rambla, theatreland, the cafés of the plaça Reial.

Here, between excursions to the obligatory social meeting places,
the Güell family could lead an inward-looking life. The entrance hall,
with the feel of an Assyrian temple, spreads the dull gleam of stone
around a tunnel-like central stone staircase which winds to the core of
the house: a towering salon, surrounded by galleries and internal
balconies, that is wholly isolated from the street and runs the entire
height of the building, under a tapering, paraboloid dome. The
disturbing paraboloid shapes that Gaudí loved are a unifying theme.
At floor level, the salon is decorated with murals on the theme of
charity and a baluster that reproduces in miniature the city's monument
to Joan Güell. To increase the recessive feeling of the journey through
the house, the outer reception rooms are divided by richly wrought
Mauresque hardwood screens and delicate marble colonnades of para-
bolic arches. Many visitors find the eccentricity disquieting, especially
in the baron's vast bathroom, where gilded art nouveau ironwork
climbs like creepers over the elliptical arcs that define the principal
spaces. To the family, however, the effect – sumptuous and secretive
but sober and solid – was just what they wanted; and Gaudí remained
their adopted architect for domestic, business and civic projects alike.

Puig devised interiors that had much in common with Gaudí's,
suggesting that secretive inner spaces, pillared rooms with inventive
columns and capitals, distrust of sidelighting and eschewal of the street
were all aspects of taste dictated by the social needs of the patrons.
The external forms the two architects favoured in maturity, however,
could not have been more sharply contrasted. The contrast can be
comprehended in a single glance in the passeig de Gràcia, where the
Casa Amatller, built by Puig in 1898–1900, adjoins the Casa Batlló,
inimitably remodelled by Gaudí from an existing conventional building
in 1904–5. Both houses are externalisations of fantasies, but Puig's,
with its angularity, its regular severity, and its explicit references to
other times and other places – to the Low Countries and the fifteenth
century in particular – seems restrained by comparison with Gaudí's
façade. The Casa Batlló has a bulbous skyline, swirling balconies and
a scintillating front encrusted with fragments of coloured glass. These
are palaces in visual effect, but not in functional intent; they were
built to be divided into apartments, including one for the family,

where the bourgeoisie of the middle rank could imitate on a smaller scale the style of the hoplites of industry and finance. It is one of the miracles of late nineteenth- and early twentieth-century Barcelona that such a distinctive and expensive culture could be so widely shared.

The symbol of this era of self-assurance was the 'Universal' exhibition of 1888. The idea originated with a Galician entrepreneur who had seen the Paris, London and Vienna exhibitions and realised that Barcelonese anxiety to be noticed was exploitable. It was taken up by the opportunistic mayor, Francesc Rius i Taulat, who came to office in 1885. Staid elements in the city, led by Valentí Almirall, denounced the project as a speculator's adventure. When the mayor summoned the world to Barcelona on 13 June 1887, for a date only eleven months away, everything had still to be extemporised. Yet not only did the citizens build on time the exhibition ground that sarcasts had deemed impossible, but also planted the plaça de Colón with palms and drove the Rambla de Catalunya and the Paral·lel through suburbs where they had previously got stymied. The frenetic creativity, the meretricious glitz, was exemplified by Domènech i Montaner's Gran Hotel Internacional, designed to be demolished. It was built in only fifty-three days and its five floors, with accommodation for 2,000 guests, proved unequal to the demand. The exhibition opened ten days late, drew exhibitors from twenty countries and attracted nearly 2¼ million visitors. The young Puig i Cadafalch was inspired with a vision of a 'great Barcelona'. The idea of Barcelona as a 'Spanish Milan', a centre of technical proficiency and economic efficiency, spread worldwide, and lasted.[34]

The City of Bombs

Rapid growth never happens painlessly. In 1860, Barcelona had less than 200,000 inhabitants. By 1897, when the city limits were redefined to incorporate the towns of the immediate hinterland, the official figure was 383,908. The conurbation contained over 500,000 people, for whom the streets of Barcelona were runnels for overheated passions. Social conflict could hardly be avoided. What is remarkable is how long its most serious manifestations were delayed. At times, particularly in the period between the extrusion and restoration of the Bourbons, from 1868–1875, disorder in Barcelona responded to the rhythms of metropolitan politics. Over the period until the 1890s as a whole, however, the dominant issues were traditional: military service quotas, food prices and, until late in the 1870s, the Carlist threat. And these were all, to some extent, socially unifying issues which directed popular agitation against governments, with the approval of the local bourgeoisie. High food prices, which dampened demand and threatened wage stability, were as unpopular with employers as with workers; military service – the 'tribute in the blood of the poor', as it was called in a popular Catalan tag, diminished the pool of industrial workers and, from the employers' point of view, wasted the workforce on irrelevant imperialist adventures. Wars, they felt, could usefully be waged in defence of protected markets, like that of Cuba, but not in order to acquire unexploitable desert in Morocco.

The Carlists – the romantic, reactionary party of clericalism, particularism and pedantic dynastic legitimism – were a useful bogey. They defended the status and wealth of the clergy against liberal despoilers; they upheld local diversity of custom and law against a centralising state; they advocated the cause of the line of the dispossessed absolutist pretender, 'King' Carlos V. They fought against all comers for lost causes and for the perpetuation of an almost vanished past. The incursions of their guerrilla armies awakened Catalonia's fiscal potential as never before since the war against Napoleon. In 1873, under the republican regime, the Diputació of Barcelona was able to put four battalions into the field against the Carlists and to distribute arms to reliable villagers. In 1874 a new monarchist Diputació imposed by the restorationist general Martínez Campos was able to levy the biggest-ever quota of recruits, 6,700 men, in the same cause. The fear and hatred city dwellers of all classes felt for Carlism filled the Barcelona press. The most eloquent characterisations could be found in a paper called *El Cañon Krup*, which called itself 'a shrapnel-sheet of the civil war'. A typical editorial of 1874 called for the Carlist 'terrorists' to be 'exterminated like moles', myopically undermining the cultivated garden. Papers like *Lo Somatent* kept before the public eye the image the Barcelonese most feared: a rabble armed with pitchforks and arquebuses attacking a classical cityscape.[35] The imminence of the Carlist menace is nicely captured in the memoirs of Josep Pla, whose childhood was dominated by the pressure exerted on a family caught up in a guerrilla war, and whose father, a rural mayor, saw himself philosophically as 'a collector of taxes for the Carlists today and for the republic tomorrow'.[36]

As the Carlist threat receded, the alliance of classes broke up. Bourgeois politics during the Restoration came to focus on Catalanist issues. The working class, ignoring its own enfranchisement, remained largely inert, while its leaders, distracted by the theological squabbles of the international socialist movements, found communication with their own natural constituency difficult. The main Spanish socialist trades union – the Unión General de Trabajadores – and the main socialist party – the Partido Socialista del Obrero Español – were both founded in Barcelona in the 1880s but rapidly became centred in Madrid. The participation rate in the first universal male suffrage election – for the provincial Diputació in 1871 – was only a little over twenty-five per cent: no election, provincial, municipal or national, produced a significantly higher figure until 1907. Of the votes that were cast, many belonged to 'ghosts' and 'frequent voters'. A purge ordered by Bartolomeu Robert in 1899 eliminated 27,000 bogus names from the electoral roll. Though universal suffrage applied continuously to all elections from 1890, it made little impact on the statistics or the results. In 1903, for instance, there were only 91,000 registered electors and less than 25,000 votes cast. For the allegiance of the politically-abstaining working class, the main competitors were revolutionary anarchists who wanted to bring down the system by *coups de foudre* and the advocates of 'economic' objectives: the socialists, anarcho-syndicalists and pragmatic trades unionists. They put as much effort into internecine strife as into the contest with capitalism.

When the rail link was completed, young French revolutionaries took the Barcelona Express and were frightened by the prostitutes on arrival; this was the character of the revolutionary anarchism that became the most potent force of Barcelona's political underworld: naive and puritanical. Secretive by nature, anarchist cells grew unseen in a period of relative social peace and emerged in the 1890s to take the city and the mainstream workers' movement – still resolved to collaborate with the bourgeoisie – by surprise. The first bomb exploded at the headquarters of the employers' organisation during the otherwise orderly May Day strike of 1890. In 1892, when the most powerful union in the textile industry, the Tres Clases de Vapor, was trying to establish a non-anarchist, 'possiblist' line, the missionary of violence, E. Malatesta, launched a subversive lecture tour from Italy among workers' organisations and anarchist coteries, urging on the growing enthusiasm for 'propaganda by deeds'. In February of that year, the opening bomb of a sustained campaign had brought death to the city's showpiece-square, the plaça Reial. In June the military authorities declared a state of seige; thus the terrorists had created their own cause. In 1893 there were fourteen incidents. In September, Paulí

Pallàs, a febrile reader of Kropotkin, used a bomb in an inefficient assassination attempt on General Martínez Campos. His execution provoked the worst outrage of the period: the bombing of the opera house, the sanctum of bourgeois values, where fourteen victims died. Instead of exploiting public revulsion, the authorities responded by scattering the buckshot of repression; among 415 'suspects' arrested by March 1894 was the solid anti-anarchist spokesman of the Tres Clases de Vapor, Josep Fontanals. Even so, terrorism began to decline. The bombing of a Corpus Christi procession in 1896 was an ill-calculated outrage; despite more than 400 arrests, the French culprit escaped, but the trial which followed does seem to have sapped anarchist strength: five deaths and sixty-eight sentences of between eight and twenty years were decreed, many of them commuted to exile in response to international pleas. Terrorism disappeared from Barcelona, except for the columns of clandestine flysheets, for ten years. Meanwhile, the truce was broken by provocations on the right: a tax strike sanctioned by the Catalanist mayor, Bartolomeu Robert, in 1899; a lockout to enforce lower wages in 1900.

Most workers' leaders probably regarded the terrorist interlude as an irrelevancy. However the chances of revolution were calculated, the campaign for workers' rights within the existing system had to be waged in the here-and-now by the formation of inter-trade organisations, the revaluation of labour and, as a means to the promotion of those ends, by strikes. Against the background of the defeat of terrorism, a tram strike in favour of a closed shop in May 1901 gave the anti-terrorist anarcho-syndicalists a chance to try their own revolutionary tactics of general strike. Shortly after, a steelworkers' stoppage for a nine-hour day provoked a declaration of martial law and sympathetic action on an unprecedented scale. For two months from late December, 12,000 men were out. In mid-February, the strikers declared a general strike; the call evoked a brief but impressive show of solidarity, with perhaps as many as 100,000 workers joining the action at its height. Antoni Estruch painted the strikers waving republican flags and the socialists accused the anarchists of allowing the strikers to be manipulated in futile political gestures. The most influential voices in the workers' movement – the anarcho-syndicalists, led or, at least, best represented by the peasant-turned-educationalist Francesc Ferrer – turned against the strike, perhaps because they felt unable to control it, perhaps merely because of their anxiety to stamp out the Bakhuninite heretics in their own ranks. With socialists and anarcho-syndicalists

apparently taking the side of the bourgeoisie, the strike seemed to fall
victim to an unholy alliance.

THE VICTORY BANQUET

Meanwhile, the scene outside the narrow cockpit of working-class
politics had changed. The experience of the Federal Republic of
1873–5 had shown that Catalanism was a potential avenue of power
for the Barcelona élite. Over about a generation's span, Catalanism
replaced anti-clericalism as the political religion of the radical bourgeoisie. The rapid rise of political Catalanism can be chronicled in a
series of conspicuous events: the start of a Catalanist daily press in
1879; the Catalanist Congresses of 1880 and 1883, which successfully
defended Catalonia's residual 'peculiar' laws and laid the foundations
for co-operative electoral strategies between Catalanist groups: the
Memorial de Greuges of 1885 – a petition for special constitutional
guarantees of Catalonian institutions and identity, presented by a
glittering alliance of industrialists and intellectuals, to King Alfonso
XII; the formation of the Lliga de Catalunya – in the long run, the
kernel of one of the most effective Catalanist parties – in 1888; the
formation of a sort of committee of grand strategy, the Unió Catalanista
in 1981 and its manifesto, the Bases de Manresa, proposing home rule
for Catalonia, in 1892; the Catalan speech by Angel Guimerà at the
Ateneu Barcelonès, the club that set the tone of intellectual and, to
some extent, political life in the city, in 1895. In the same period,
without yet turning Catalanism into a popular movement, the intellectuals intensified their efforts to address a mass audience, through an
increasingly popular press and organisations like Morera's workers'
choral society – attempts to find a popular cultural medium for
Catalanist utterance. Josep Torras i Bagès developed a type of evangel-
ism which combined Catalanism and Christianity in a single message,
which he summarised in the exceptionable slogan, 'Catalonia must be
Christian or nothing'.

It is conventional – but no less true for that – to attribute to the war
of 1898 a transforming effect on Spanish history. Until that time Spain
had defended the remains of her empire with a surprising degree of
success against slavers and secessionists; but the growth of respectable
independence movements in Cuba and the Philippines, and the intervention of the United States on their behalf, made defeat certain:
Spain's late political concessions did nothing to prevent war or avert

disaster. A naval strategy of 'honour without ships' left Spain with neither; only a sunken fleet, a sundered empire and a national humiliation. Catalonia was, in a sense, to blame for the war; other than for reasons of prestige, the empire was there to support her industries. The defeat, however, was a catalyst for the Catalanist and workers' movements alike, a vindication of their cases against the existing political and social systems. 'Home rule' was, briefly, before American pressure forced Spain to grant independence, a solution proposed for Cuba; in partial consequence, autonomy for Catalonia suddenly became a more realistic prospect. The profundity of the disaster was interpreted as a 'national' crisis requiring a 'national' solution; thus for the first time Catalanists became ministers in Madrid, despite the self-denying ordinance they had operated since 1881. The crisis of Catalan industry meant that the search for new markets was an urgent task that gave workers and employers common ground; in the over-optimistic opinion of some Catalanists, most notably Almirall, these new outlets could be found outside Spain.

As a result of all this, political Catalanism made its great leap forward between 1900 and 1907. In 1901, a new Catalanist grouping, Lliga Regionalista, won four of the seven parliamentary seats for Barcelona, with a fifth going to the non-Lliga Catalanist Republican, Pi i Margall. The active electorate was tiny, middle class and volatile, turning away from the Lliga in the 1903 and 1905 elections; but this apparent check concealed four important trends. First, the old politics, which made Barcelona a fief of the pan-Spanish liberals, were gone forever. Secondly, the Lliga, always more popular in the Catalan backwoods, was building its strength within the city of Barcelona; in 1905, for instance, the Radical Republicans – who at that time included non-Lliga Catalanists – won five of the seven parliamentary seats, but the Lliga captured the city council. Thirdly, the Lliga's share of the vote in Barcelona never dropped significantly below a quarter, while that of Catalanists generally was much higher, albeit incomputably so. Finally, Barcelona was on the brink of acquiring something like a mass electorate, and Catalanist electability would survive the change.

The circumstances were a confrontation with a curiously antiquated flavour. The interests of the 'Spanish state', narrowly conceived as a matter of pan-Spanish military effectiveness, clashed with Catalonian 'privileges': Catalans' rights to sources of justice within the principality. Without distortion, this could be represented as an issue of principle essentially similar to what was at stake in the revolt of 1640. The occasion of the clash was an unlawful raid by officers of the Barcelona garrison on the offices of a satirical magazine. Ever since the wars against Napoleon, the army had sanctified itself as a kind of guardian-angel of 'national' – that is, pan-Spanish – independence, identity and integrity: the distinctions between those three abstractions were confounded by an unquestionable trinitarian theology. Jokes about it were blasphemy; criticisms were attacks upon the state. On 23 November 1905, Barcelona's funniest periodical, *¡Cu-cut!*, published a cartoon alluding to the Lliga's victory in the municipal elections. Before a crowd receding into a sports hall for a celebratory banquet, a fat man and an ornately-draped hussar officer appeared in conversation. 'What are they celebrating here,' asks the fat man, 'with such a big crowd?' 'The Victory Banquet,' replies the officer. 'Victory?' says the other. 'In that case, I suppose they're civilians.' Except in Barcelona, there was more sympathy at large with the officers who responded by raiding the Catalanist press than with the injudicious satirists.

The incident awakened some elements in the Madrid government and national legislature to the menace of Catalanism; those already aware were confirmed in their suspicions and presented with a pretext for action. In 1902 the government had struck one blow against Catalanism by banning the use of Catalan in schools; this had the reverse of its intended effect, stimulating the proliferation of independent Catalan cultural organisations and educational institutions. But it had evoked no serious political reaction and may have encouraged Madrid to underestimate Catalanist feeling. The measure Madrid adopted in 1906 challenged Catalan sentiment even more directly by reserving to military courts the trial of any crime against the honour of the armed forces and the 'unity of the nation'. This could be stretched to apply to any strong Catalanist utterance. What was perhaps worse, it deprived Catalonia of jurisdiction, which was to be alienated to an intrusive and hostile tribunal.

Inside Catalonia there were two main consequences: a transformation of political awareness which took the turn-out in the 1907 elections to the dazzling heights of fifty per cent; and a coalition of virtually all Catalanist groups, in an umbrella-party called Solidaritat Catalana, won an impressive victory – forty-one out of forty-four seats in the Spanish legislature and nine of the ten contested seats for the provincial Diputació. These figures conceal the abiding strength of the main non-Catalanist bourgeois party (at that time called the Republican Union) who got nearly a third of the votes overall and rather more than that within the city of Barcelona; Solidaritat was, moreover, a frail coalition which could not survive its own success.

Nevertheless, an irreversible breakthrough had been attained; from now on there was always an official Catalanist voice, in the form of a majority in one or other of the main representative groups in Catalonia: the city council of Barcelona, the Diputació and the Catalan deputies in the Spanish assembly. The role of working-class votes in this achievement was demonstrated by the emergence of *soi-disant* candidates of the 'Catalan Left', who fought elections as a party in their own right from 1910 with fitful but sometimes notable success. Catalanism's permanent status was given institutional form from 1912, when, with government 'approval' – or, at least, recognition of the inevitable – the four provincial Diputacions of the principality were authorised to form a Mancomunitat or inter-provincial organisation, with budgets for culture and education, health and social services, agriculture and transport. This was not the 'home rule' with an internal legislature which most Catalanists wanted; but it was a proposal of their own for an institution they could control. Embracing the whole of Spanish Catalonia and functioning in Catalan, it was a Catalan government of a sort, embodying Catalan identity as no institution had done since 1716.

The political and cultural allegiances of this period cut across class divisions: just as there were working-class Catalanists, so a substantial portion of the Barcelonese middle class supported the anti-Catalanist Radical Republicans (as they came to be known). Class war remained, however, probably the biggest threat to Catalonia's economic and political progress alike. The recrudescence of bomb-toting terrorism in 1904, and the emergence in the years after 1907 of a genuinely popular and enduring trades union with an anarcho-syndicalist ideology (to be known, from 1911, as the Confederación Nacional del Trabajo or CNT), showed that both traditional revolutionary tendencies were still alive. Barcelona's continuing potential for mass violence was displayed in the 'Tragic Week' of July 1909. In some ways, it was the last of Barcelona's nineteenth-century riots, in which a self-motivated mob, intractable to the control of any known group, vented its rage on traditional targets; its effect, however, was to consolidate anarcho-syndicalism as the basis for the organisation of mainstream working-class politics in Barcelona for the foreseeable future.

It started when crowds gathered, urged by the papers of the Catalanist, republican and workers' left, to demonstrate against the embarkation of troops for Morocco; this was a respectable and rational protest. As most of the troops were Barcelonese, it was in the tradition of popular resistance to military service; as the huge contingent of

40,000 men augured a serious escalation of the war against the Moroc-
can tribesmen, it was also in the tradition of liberal anti-militarism,
which, since the Cuban defeat, had been uninhibited in Barcelona.
As usual, the military authorities over-reacted, banning meetings,
detaining protesters and on 22 July silencing communications with
Madrid. Working-class leaders tried to exploit the consequently tense
atmosphere. On 24 July, the socialist Fabra Ribas, the anarchist
Francesc Miranda and anarcho-syndicalist Miquel Villalobos Moreno
– an unreliable henchman of Francesc Ferrer – formed a strike committee. The strike that began on 26 July was intended to be a short, sharp
shock but got out of hand when police opened fire on a crowd in the
Rambla heading for the captaincy-general, after troops had refused to
shoot. The rioters got weapons from feebly defended armouries but
the anarchist intellectuals who thought the revolution had arrived were
to be disappointed. The only serious excesses committed during the
four or five days of mob rule were acts of arson. The incendiarists
seem to have been directed and, in some cases, actually paid by a
small and marginal group who limited their targets, with fanatical
single-mindedness and surgical precision, to premises owned by evangelical and, to a lesser extent, contemplative orders. Of eighty buildings
fired, thirty-one were schools or educational organisations, all run by
the church and all but four by religious orders, all but two of which
were for the children of the poor; fourteen were parish churches,
almost all of which belonged to religious communities; there were six
friaries and a seminary, two mission clubhouses for working men, six
centres of the Catholic working-men's circle and nine centres belonging
to religious welfare associations. Ten contemplative communities were
destroyed, including eight of nuns. No other consistent programme,
apart from this inscrutable anti-clericalism, could be foisted on the
mob.[37]

The police, however, chose to interpret the affair as the fruit of an
anarchist plot, partly in order to make an example of Francesc Ferrer.
Neither his career nor his writings made him a plausible suspect. He
was a peasant born who had started work in a factory at the age of
fourteen, showed prodigious intellectual gifts, became a republican
and freemason and, as if by a natural progression in this radical career,
espoused exile in Paris and the profession of a pedagogue. It was not,
however, his skill as a tutor but his talents as a gigolo that brought
him a fortune – most of it the donation of a single female 'pupil' –
which he used on his return to Barcelona to endow a string of
progressive, secular, co-educational schools for working-class children

and to subsidise an anarchist (and briefly a socialist) press. This well-spent wealth made him a major source of subversion. He was, however, an orthodox anarcho-syndicalist – indeed, he was the main voice of that tendency in Barcelona – who espoused industrial action as a revolutionary force and rejected terrorism. To their enemies, however, all anarchists were bomb-slingers and arsonists, and Ferrer's reputation had suffered by contagion when a pupil of one of his schools attempted to bomb the king in a Barcelona street. The outcome of his show trial, which shocked the world, was swayed more by his accuser's conviction of his guilt than by the quality of the evidence. On 13 October, he became a most convincing martyr for anarcho-syndicalism, helping that cause to conquer the working class in Barcelona and, ultimately to threaten the rest.

The Crowd on the Empty Balconies

The industrialist Gual Villalbí remembered the First World War as a time when it 'rained orders' in the factories and the streets were strewn with *fleurs du mal* – spies, deserters and refugees. The fictional not-quite nouveaux-riches of Carles Soldevila, 'Robert' and 'Lluisa', were representative characters of the time, 'excited by the accumulation of war-time profits into a febrile state that might, at a casual glance, be mistaken for renewed mutual passion'.[38] It was a frivolous period – the Teatre Principal was enlarged with an American Bar and a casino – and a time of suspense, lived under the threat of an end to the boom: cotton exports, which doubled during the war, were to plunge to little more than half their pre-war levels in the early 'twenties. Wartime full employment, followed by post-war layoffs, created ideal conditions for unions to breed. The CNT had 15,000 members in Catalonia in 1915, 73,860 in July 1918, 205,000 by the end of the year and 350,000 – so it was claimed – by the end of 1919. This new demand also threw up rival unions and inter-union gang warfare. A violent general strike in Barcelona in August 1917 left thirty-two dead and was followed by repression and 2,000 arrests. Combative strikes were at their height in 1919 and 1920, when 7.76 per cent and 8.4 per cent respectively of the working year were lost; the figure had never been more than two per cent before 1916. The focus of the unrest was the La Canadença power station, occupied by workers demanding union recognition on 5 February 1919. Textile workers came out on the 17th: on the 21st, the CNT made the strike officially general. Its history was notable for the power wielded by 'red censorship': the *Diario de Barcelona* was fined by the unions for publishing the official decree of a state of emergency. The union leaders, however, revealed their tactical immaturity when they came to an agreement with the employers and authorities on 17 March, conceding the main demands of the power-workers – union recognition, increased wages and an eight-hour day, and guaranteeing the strikers' jobs. This looked like a redoubtable victory, but, though the proposal was carried with difficulty at a mass meeting, it foundered on the issue of indemnity for strikers accused of other crimes.[39] The strike was renewed on 24 March and this time crumbled ignominiously until its official end on 17 April. The emergency regulations were not lifted for another six months; so far, Barcelona had spent most of the twentieth century under the suspension of constitutional liberties. Most of the street violence which followed was internecine; 128 of the 152 victims of the period 1921–3 were workers, including the CNT demagogue, Salvador Seguí, gunned down by an assassin from a rival union.

Though the romantic revolutionary, Francesc Macià, and some other Catalanist leaders tried to appeal to the masses to support the cause, the campaign for Catalan autonomy which dominated politics in Barcelona during these years left most workers cold. A small 'Catalan socialist' party started in 1923, but, in general, the socialists and republicans continued to hold aloof from Catalanist electoral politics. Trade unions remained indifferent. One short-lived organisation of 1881 was called Federació de Treballadors de la Regió Espanyola – implying that 'Spain' was just a geographical expression, but this was an uncharacteristic flash of wit. The words with which Salvador Seguí raised cheers in the streets of Barcelona in 1920 were thoroughly representative of popular sentiments. 'A problem of independence,' he said, 'or of autonomy: such a thing doesn't exist in Catalonia because we, the workers from there, don't want any such problem and don't feel it!' The attitude to Catalanism of Seguí and his friends in the CNT was one of healthy contempt for a Mandarin creed.

Workers' issues lost prominence under the 'iron surgery' of General Primo de Rivera's dictatorship, which began in September 1923. Primo's rule was 'born in Barcelona', where, as captain-general from March 1922, he was emboldened to seize control in part, at least, by bourgeois Barcelonese fears of the 'demagogic avalanche'.[40] Unemployment was conquered by 'tariff patriotism' and the dictator's massive public works programme. While the workers' movement subsided, Catalanism seemed an urgent cause, ham-fistedly repressed. These

were the main ingredients of the atmosphere Pierre Vilar found when
he arrived in Barcelona as a young researcher, surprised, during a
cinema performance of Abel Gance's 'Napoléon', to hear the audience
sing 'La Marseillaise' in Catalan. Under a regime which was both
rightist and centralist, Catalanism acquired a new, wide appeal. Its
progress is illustrated by an anecdote of Alfonso XIII's visit to the
Eixample in 1924. Sensing the subdued nature of his reception, the
king is said to have turned to General Primo de Rivera and said,
'Didn't you tell me that there were no Catalanists left in Barcelona?'
'That is so, Sire,' replied Primo. 'Well,' said the King, 'I can see that
there are plenty.' 'Where, Sire?' 'Behind those windows and balconies.'
Every bare balcony, said Alfonso, wore an invisible Catalan flag.[41]

V

'The Asylum of Modern Times':

Barcelona and Europe

*Veig allà el Pirineu amb ses neus somrosades
i al davant Catalunya tota estesa als seus peus,
i m'en vaig.*

(I see the Pyrenees, the gilded peaks of snow,
and all of Catalonia, stretched out at their feet,
And I feel drawn.)

> Joan Maragall, 'Oda Nova a Barcelona'

Africa begins at the Pyrenees.

> Attributed to
> Pascal

EUROPE AND SPAIN

'Y ou could say that Barcelona does not belong to Spain,' wrote Jaume Balmés, 'but is more like something imported from Belgium or England.'[1] Balmes was an arch-conservative who distrusted northern Liberalism and his remark was not entirely complimentary, but it reflected a perception of Barcelona as a 'European city' which almost every citizen would have shared by the mid-nineteenth century, when the remark was made. It remains an almost universal assumption about Barcelona – practically a badge of Barcelonese identity – to the present day. Yet the notion of a 'European Barcelona' is a truism redeemed by a mistake: it relies for its force on a presumed distinction between Barcelona and the rest of Spain – or, at least, the rest of Spain, less Catalonia. Barcelona is deemed to be European because Spain is thought of as an extra-European culture. If 'Africa begins at the Pyrenees', or if Spain is 'Europe's Tibet' – if, in short, in the words of the old tourist-board slogan, 'Spain is different' – then Barcelona's assumption of a European identity gives the city a peculiar status and a special role. Events in our own time, however, seem to be exposing the notion of the 'differentness' of Spain as a historical myth.

The conviction that Spain does not 'belong' to European culture began – though like any similar thesis about another European country it can be justified by reference to earlier texts – in the nineteenth century. It may originally have been a foreign conceit. The cult of the picturesque peddled abroad the vision of romantic engravers, in which Spain was an exotic and archaic land, peopled by swart gypsies inhabiting Moorish ruins. Spanish intellectuals peered with delight into the supposed cultural cleft. For those on the political right a 'different' Spain was a vindication of distinctively Spanish virtues, which the materialists and heretics beyond the Pyrenees threatened to pollute. For those on the left, the image was equally welcome as an explanation of Spain's 'backwardness' and hostility to progress. The world of Spanish intellectual debate became divided between *europeiz-adores*, who clamoured for more European influence, and *hispanizad-ores*, who defended Spain's impoverished chastity. Adored by one party, abhorred by the other, the myth was believed by both. It became entrenched in Spanish historiography as historians confronted the most conspicuous problem of the Spanish past: that of why the makers of the world's first great maritime empire – a captive market of unparalleled dimensions as well as an achievement of breathtaking prowess – should largely have failed to share in the commercial and industrial revolutions that accompanied 'the expansion of Europe'. This problem – called or confused with 'the decline of Spain' – could be 'solved' by a nice bit of semantic magic; if commerce and industry were classified as European activities, and Spain were docketed as a non-European land, the demonstration could be regarded as neatly complete. As Barcelona rapidly became Spain's major industrial centre, the same reasoning fed Barcelonese convictions and political claims, culminating in Almirall's exasperated cry for Catalonia to leave Spain in the interests of progress.

What made Spain different was a matter of debate, but three elements of her historical experience have commonly been alleged in explanation. The first two rely on the effects of the Moorish presence, which has often been represented as so pervasive and so enduring as to make Spain an honorary oriental land which has somehow got washed up on the wrong shore of the Mediterranean. Moorish settlement is commonly envisaged as carpeting Spain, at least to the Duero and the Ebro, like the dense pile of an oriental rug. Moorish culture is thought of as 'superior' to anything the Christians could produce;

and Spain's beauties, as well as her vices, are frequently attributed to
oriental influence. I have encountered scholarship which attributes
almost every innovation in Spanish art, from romanesque sculpture to
hispano-flemish architecture, to Moorish inspiration or craftsmanship.
The learned editor of a 1909 edition of Richard Ford's *Gatherings from
Spain* found evidence of the exotic strain in the Spanish character in
the fact that the trains failed to run on time. For a long time, it
was foreigners, not Spaniards themselves, who detected this eastern
flavour. It probably originated in early-modern Italian abuse, re-
proaching Spaniards' alleged impurities of blood. In the last century,
it was popular with travellers who judged Spain on the basis of
an acquaintance with Andalusia, where most Moorish survivals are
concentrated. Since 1942, however, when Américo Castro published
an impressive version of the fabric of Spanish history, woven, as it
were from three equal strands – Christian, Moorish and Jewish – a
veritable school of Spanish historians, supported from America, France and Britain, has devoted itself to the search for the Moors' cultural
legacy.[2]

There was a time when I was of their persuasion. As a young
researcher working in the Archivo General de Indias in Seville in 1972,
I lived in a piece of folded corrugated tin on top of a pension in the
old Jewish quarter. From there I could look out at night over the
tangled street plan of the old *aljama* to the Almohad minaret, below
the cathedral belfry, and the flying buttresses of the vast cathedral that
aggressively proclaims the success of the Christian Reconquest. I could
feel that these three ingredients of Spanish culture – Jewish, Moorish
and Christian – were spread before me: the three strands of Spanish
history, woven into the texture of a city. Long study and experience
have now convinced me that the Moorish contribution is conspicuous
only by its paucity. The magic carpet of Moorish settlement was patchy
and threadbare. Moorish Spain clung to the eastern and southern
coasts, to the Ebro and Guadalquivir valleys and to a few inland towns
and uplands. The Moors were a disparate crowd whose numbers
have never been convincingly calculated nor their composition clearly
analysed. They included Islamised natives and the assimilated descendants of east European slaves. The Berbers may have been a
smaller category than either of these. Pure Arabs were a tiny group –
perhaps 50,000 strong – whose immigration was confined to the eighth
century and who disappeared thereafter into the mélange of natives
and migrants. There was never a census of the Moors until the
expulsion of their last identifiable descendants in the early seventeenth

century; this yielded an unreliable tally of about 275,000, which cannot
be projected back because of the checkered demographic history of
communities which seem to have declined from the mid-thirteenth
century onwards, then to have surged ahead in the sixteenth. It would
be rash to suppose that the Moorish population of Spain was ever very
numerous – perhaps as little as five per cent, probably no more than
ten per cent at its height, though all assumptions are risky.

The enduring Moorish presence was, moreover, narrowly circumscribed. In most parts of the peninsula Moorish communities lasted no
longer than in Sicily or Apulia. Only Granada and Valencia remained in
any sense Moorish lands for longer, and they were important but
peripheral kingdoms, whose places in Spain suggest comparison with
those of Turkmenia, say, or Khazakstan in Russia. Until 1578, when
Morisco communities were resettled all over Spain, most Spaniards
probably never saw a Moor, except in the romantic versions offered
by novelists and poets. Demographic importance can be ascribed to
the Moors only by an act of imagination, and cultural superiority only
by a subjective judgement. Caliphal art was cannibalistic and that of
the Nasrids – from some points of view – decadent. Until the rather
phoney Mauresque revival of the last century, which was as strong in
Barcelona as anywhere, most patrons of art in Christian Spain avoided
Moorish taste – except in the form of some decorative arts where the
Moorish legacy is not peculiar to Spain but common to much of
the Mediterranean. Spanish languages – especially their poetic and
technical vocabularies – have inherited a lot of Arabic terms, which
are evidence of the scale of Moorish contributions in particular fields
but are not on their own enough to justify the traditional generalis-
ations.

The second explanation of Spain's 'differentness' treats the Moor as
other, rather than brother, but still exaggerates his importance. In this
traditional Spanish reading of the Spanish past, Spain's distinctive
historical experience was the Reconquest and Spanish identity was
forged in the white heat of a long crusade, begun almost at the
moment of Moorish invasion in 711 and sustained, with checks and
interruptions, of course, but without essential mutation or substitution
of 'spirit', until the fall of Granada in 1492.[3] In reality, conquests
from the Moors were the work of widely interspersed bouts of phrenesis
in the tenth, eleventh, thirteenth and fifteenth centuries. No ideological
continuity underlay these fitful and hesitant encounters, though the
idea of 'reconquest' of unjustly usurped lands can be found as a source
of legitimation in some texts. Nor did the occasional violence normally

depend on awareness of differences of religion, though at a late stage
the example of the crusades may have spawned some real odium. In
most encounters, there were Muslims and Christians on both sides.
The conventional hero of the Reconquest myth, El Cid, spent as much
time, after his exile from Castile, fighting for Muslims as for Christian
masters. It would be no more convincing to portray Spain as the
product of conflict between Christians and Moors than, for instance,
to see Britain as the result of the struggle between Saxons and Celts,
or Germany of that between Teutons and Slavs. The conflictive model
of the Spanish Middle Ages was invented in modern times, when the
Moor became the epitype of the enemy. He was never the prototype.

The third explanation of the supposed distinctiveness of Spain
attributes it not to any historical experience but to autochthonous
national 'character' inherited from a pre-Celtic 'Iberian' population.[4]
This theory seems to belong to the context of nineteenth-century
nationalism, animated by a desire to emphasise distinctions, which
were often feeble and usually invidious, between racial or linguistic
groups. Apart from its inherent improbability, it suffers from two
main defects: lack of evidence that the 'Iberians' ever existed, and lack
of means by which their legacy, if any, might be supposed to have
been transmitted. The evidence in favour of the Iberians consists of
mentions of the name in Roman texts and some cultural peculiarities,
mainly detectable in art forms, at some pre-Roman peninsular sites.
But the Romans were glib taxonomists and it is not clear what meaning
they attached to the term or whether, in Roman times, 'Iberians' were
thought of as belonging to a different classification from 'Celts'.
Evidence of a distinctive 'Iberian' room of the Archaeological Museum
of Madrid leaves the visitor dazzled by the splendours of a lost
civilisation, which produced the elaborately coiffured and attired
female stone figures of Baza and Elche, the lions and tapering 'pyramid'
of Pozo Moro, the delicately wrought gold candlesticks of Lebrija. But
these effects could have been produced by the interplay of eastern
Mediterranean influences on indigenous culture. They are all very
late, of the sixth to the third centuries BC. No evidence has yet been
found that Spanish cultures developed any features that distinguish
them from others of Celtic peoples of western Europe before the first
millennium BC.

However the 'differentness' of Spain is characterised, it looks like
an increasingly unhelpful description today, when the syncopations
that made Spanish history seem out of step with that of other western
European countries in the last century are over and done with. All the

big historic communities of which western Europe is composed now seem to have gone through similar historical experiences, though without perfect synchronisation. In as much as one can talk about a 'typical' western European past, Spain has had it: a pre-Roman Celtic culture; a Roman conquest; an impressively thorough Romanisation; barbarian invasions which led to the creation of sub-Roman states by relatively small migrant élites, who included the Moors; medieval *Staatsbildung* by means of the dynamic expansion of initially small political centres; the 'unification' of what was to become 'national' territory within frontiers which were determined by a combination of geography and dynastic accident with the limitations imposed by the formation of other strong states nearby; the creation of what was in effect a single and unitary state in tension with separatist or devolution-ist tendencies at the periphery; colonial expansion overseas, followed by the traumatic severance of empire; the conflict of 'constitutionalist' and 'absolutist' politics, ending at last in the triumph of the former; industrialisation; and the rise of parliamentary democracy.

These experiences have not necessarily happened in the same order or at the same times all over western Europe: Spain's imperial experi-ence came relatively early; her industrialisation took relatively long. But all the other states in the area have had their own departures from the same general pattern: England's constitutional conflicts were resolved relatively early; Germany and Italy took a relatively long time to develop unitary states. Spain looked odd in the last century because of her banana politics and backward economy; progressive consti-tutional development was frequently sent out of line by violent inter-ventions and coups; periods of stability were dominated by cliques and bosses. In the present century Spain continued for a long time to appear out of step, because of her neutrality in the world wars, her exclusion from the post-war democratic clubs and her late seduction by consumerism. Now, however, it is hard to detect any 'differentness' greater than that which distinguishes other member-states of the European Community from one another. What one might call the 'normalisation' of Spain has not been suddenly contrived, but was anticipated by much of previous Spanish history. General Franco, the self-proclaimed guardian of 'Hispanic' values, probably did as much to perfect it as any individual in his lifetime, by hectically promoting industrial activity and consumer habits while committing Spain to a future of partnership with western democracies. In partial conse-quence, Spain's democratic institutions today are not only abreast of those of other member-states of the European Community, but actually ahead: Spain's devolved system of regional government could become a model for the constitutional development of states, like the United Kingdom, which enclose a number of historic ethnicities or regions with divergent interests; it could even be the blueprint for a European super-state of the future.

Where does this 'European' Spain leave Barcelona? In the past, Catalans have seemed to see themselves as happy observers on a European shore, while the rest of Spain drifted off, perhaps to some Atlantic destiny as part of an imagined Hispanic identity, perhaps back to supposed African or oriental origins. That is no longer a convincing perception. Most Barcelonese intellectuals, however, could never be satisfied with the knowledge that they are European only or chiefly by virtue of being Spanish. They can take some comfort from the prospect that in a future 'Europe of regions', Catalonia's distinct identity could be enhanced as a result of Spain's assimilation by a super-state. For the loss of her claim to a uniquely European heritage in Spain, Barcelona could be compensated with the status of a European regional capital. If that proves insufficient, the Barcelonese can refor-mulate their historic claim; Barcelona can be seen as unique, not in having a European character – for that is common to the whole of Spain – but in always having embraced European identity with enthusiasm and conviction.

THE GOTHIC TRADITION

Barcelona certainly has a convincingly European look. Part of this comes from the grandeur of scale and geometrical precision of the urbanisations of the late nineteenth and early twentieth centuries, which remind the reader of the rationalisations and extensions of the streetplans of Paris and Vienna. A further contribution to the same impression is made by the copious surviving modernist ornament that clothes the streets in the first great international style of the twentieth century. Anyone who has entered a Parisian Metro station under Horta ironwork or sat in Glasgow on a Mackintosh chair, or taken coffee in an art nouveau café in Brussels or a Secessionist Konditorei in Vienna, would have been able to feel at home in Barcelona before the First World War. Few other Spanish cities have much of this sort of finery, and Barcelona's 'European' character must therefore be explored through her architectural traditions and her decorative arts.

Of the various international styles that have captivated Barcelonese architects and adorned the streets, Gothic has contributed most, perhaps, to the look and reputation of the city and has done as much as any other, until the present century, to give Barcelona a European air. For though it is commonly asserted – with the architect Gaudí it was virtually a faith – that Barcelona's Gothic is of a special 'Mediter-ranean' kind which contrives dim interiors and dramatic external shadows, the fact is that Gothic is a trans-Pyrenean style, transmitted to Spain from France. It never took root in Italy, except in the consciously 'European' Milan, and in Spain the great high-Gothic cathedrals of Burgos, León and Toledo were all created by the imagin-ations of patrons who had studied in Paris. Barcelona is known in Spain as the Gothic city par excellence and is uniquely Gothic in two respects: nowhere, in so concentrated a space, are high-Gothic buildings so numerous; nowhere did the Gothic tradition last so long or undergo so many faithful revivals. The survival and revival of Gothic in Barcelona is particularly conspicuous in the Catalan setting, because Catalonia's greatest medieval buildings, in the rest of the principality, are Romanesque.

The durability of Barcelona's Gothic look was accompanied by resistance to periods of neo-classicism. No writer of eighteenth-century Barcelona was a more loyal to the Enlightenment than Antoni de Capmany; yet none was more eloquent in the defence of Gothic architecture. His aesthetics were projected directly from the streets and shapes of his native city. Gothic was superior to 'Greek' for height and sense of space. It created spaces suited to meditation and 'secret reverence'. Neo-classical buildings, however mature, always seemed brash; by Gothic alone a sense of the past could be conveyed – 'a sort of delicious sorrow . . . best for the noble seriousness of a place of worship'.[5] Like Capmany, the Valencian Antoni Ponz (1725–92) made his career in Madrid, where he was secretary of the painters' academy. When he visited Barcelona in maturity to inventory the property of the expelled Jesuits, he was disgusted by the intrusion of Baroque altars into the aisle-chapels of Barcelona Cathedral. 'It would have been better not to have made them, since, as far as artistic criteria are concerned, the money spent on them was wasted and the church uglified.'[6] His dislike of the altars was in part a neo-classical reaction in favour of stylistic chastity and restraint, but his main concern was for the unity of the Gothic building. Barcelonese fidelity to Gothic is more remarkable when one recalls how it went on in defiance of prevailing taste. Within a few years of the publications of Ponz's description, Milan Cathedral, which had survived the Renaissance

with its Gothic character not just preserved but enhanced, was defaced
with neo-classical architraves on the west front for Napoleon's coron-
ation as King of Italy.

Loyalty to Gothic tradition was threatened with suspension in the
early nineteenth-century, when Barcelona's enthusiastic espousal of a
struggle for constitutional liberties seemed to demand 'enlightened'
townscaping. In 1823, when the French invaded in support of absolutism, it was an act of political defiance to drive the carrer de Ferran
through the old town to link up with one of Barcelona's three other
straight streets. To name the new street after the King, whom constitutionalists had temporarily adopted, willy-nilly, as the figurehead of
'national' resistance, seemed ironic when he abolished the constitution
for the second time. From the Rambla, the street led to the civic
centre, the plaça de Sant Jaume, where the façade of the townhall
looks down at a neo-classical enclave in the Gothic empire of the old
town. At the time the façade was built between 1830 and 1855,
Barcelona was fighting Carlism – Spain's Jacobite-like movement of
romantic reaction – as well as centralisation; liberalism was too strong,
for the moment, for traditional taste to prevail. A church and a
cemetery made way to improve the view. Even here, however, antiqu-
arianism triumphed over progress and the Gothic over the neo-
classical. A lobby led by Piferrer and Pi i Margall saved the Gothic
interiors and north-side façade from destruction; the niches intended
for Hercules and Minerva were occupied instead by statues of Jaume
I – a reminder of the imperial power of medieval Barcelona – and Joan
Fiveller, a semi-legendary town councillor of the fifteenth century
whose intransigence had supposedly compelled a king of Castilian
origin to pay a municipal tax on fish consumed by his retinue.[7]

The reaction against classicism began as soon as the new city hall
was built. In 1845, the most promising young talent among the
architects of Barcelona, Elies Rogent, burned his copy of Vignola's
classical manual of instruction. Influenced by the wider European
romantic movement, inspired with the idealisation of the Catalan past
by the *Renaixença* writers and the poets of the Jocs Florals, he
immersed himself in the study of medieval architecture. Out of his
work on the restoration of the monastery of Ripoll emerged the
idea for his neo-Romanesque university building of 1860, where the
harmony of the inspiration of tradition with the ideal of progress
was symbolised by the exposed cast-iron columns of the library.
In Barcelona, though Romanesque and Mauresque styles were also
cultivated, medieval models necessarily meant Gothic ones. When, for

example, a competition was held for a design for the west front of the cathedral in 1882, a Gothic design was decided on in advance. Tortosa and Girona had classical façades, but Barcelona was to remain true to its Gothic tradition and self-perception. Conservatism was the chapter's only criterion in selecting the successful design. Josep Oriol Mestres and August Font won the competition because their project most closely resembled the unexecuted fifteenth-century designs of a French master, though the public seems to have preferred Joan Martorell's florid conception, which was very high and omitted the rose window.[8] When Gaudí was invited to take over the church of the Sagrada Familia in 1884, a Gothic design had already been decided on.

A Gothic idiom therefore dominated the language of Barcelonese architecture when Elies Rogent began to gather a team of young architects to design the buildings for the great exhibition of 1888. The most influential member of the team was Lluís Domènech i Muntaner (1850–1923), a major figure in Catalanist politics – he became President of the Lliga and was twice elected to parliament – as well as the designer of some of the most original buildings of his day in Barcelona. His contribution to the designs for the exhibition was inspired by the 'search for a national architecture' which he had announced some years before; his formula for achieving this involved mixing Gothic structures and Romanesque details with fairly bold Mauresque decoration. The grandest of the temporary edifices of 1888, the Hotel Internacional, had florid castellations, square corner-towers with tall clerestories and, on the ground floor, a glazed arcade of arches of Mughal flavour. The only permanent building was the café known as the Castell dels Tres Dragons, to which Domènech gave a strongly Mauresque appeal in the splayed battlements and romantic minaret: the bleak façades probably owe less to 'functionalism' than to lack of time and money for Domènech's usual reckless use of ornament; its future as a home for a collective workshop of art and crafts ensured that the building would be something of a cynosure for artists into the new century. It now houses part of the zoo.

The effect of the work for Rogent and Domènech was to open Barcelonese architecture, in a period of prolific building, to a comprehensive range of medieval influences. The Gothic tradition remained strongest, however; Puig i Cadafalch (see above, pp.183–4) was a faithful successor to Rogent and Domènech – the historian of Catalonian Romanesque, the presiding genius of the Catalan movement. In the years when art nouveau and Expressionism were bending the forms of Barcelonese building out of the Gothic line, he punctured the Barcelona skyline with spikes and angles, spires and pinnacles and battlements. In the period after the First World War, a fashion for Mediterranean traditions interrupted the era of Gothic predominance, but Gaudí's perseverance with the Sagrada Familia ensured that the most conspicuous monument of the period – with the cluster of fantastically elongated, slightly concave spires that became the indelible symbol of Barcelona – would fix a Gothic image of the city in the minds of all educated people. Gaudí's pupil, Joan Rubió i Bellver, who built the Gothic bridge of sighs over the carrer del Bisbe in 1926, actually proposed a remodelling of the city centre to enhance its Gothic flavour.

CREATIVE BAD TASTE

Rubió was a Gothic purist, but most of the other leading figures in Barcelona's Gothic revivals were interested in other historic vocabularies that had elements in common with Gothic: Romanesque, because it was a style of enormous regional importance represented by the most admired monuments of rural Catalonia; Mauresque because it was a Spanish form, legitimised in Barcelona by Domènech i Muntaner and Gaudí. Gothic also had a further property as an international style characteristic of northern Europe rather than the Mediterranean: a link between the Spanish 'national' architecture proclaimed by Domènech and the 'European' look which the patrons and architects wanted their city to wear. To the northern heartlands of Gothic, Barcelonese architects now looked for new influences that would enrich their traditions. In the 1880s, the most influential imported models came from the Arts and Crafts Movement: the collaborative studio of decorative arts Domènech established in the Castell dels Tres Dragons had the feel of an urban Kelmscott; enthusiasm for 'total' design and for the revival of medieval crafts was probably owed to the same source. Barcelonese followers never adopted the anti-industrial commitment of Morris and his friends; Gaudí left some exposed steel girders even amid the luxury of the Palau Güell and designed the first block of flats with an underground carpark. Although he hated material values, he relied, until his late, reclusive years, on enterprising patrons and joined in the collective enterprise of the Barcelonese architects of the era: to produce an architecture that grew, out of tradition, into the ways of the modern world. In the 1890s art nouveau seemed to offer a suitable vocabulary: it was another international style, whose heartlands over-lapped with those of Gothic, whose main schools were in centres of European tradition; its forms had the subversive boldness of 'superbly creative bad taste'; and it was unashamedly 'modern'. Its influence helped to produce the art and architecture of the movement known in Barcelona as 'Modernism'.

The term is unsatisfactory because its secular connotations were rejected by some of the greatest practitioners, especially Gaudí himself, who anticipated the movement, or produced what might be considered its first building, in the Palau Güell of 1885–8. One way of dating the much-debated inception of Modernism could be to trace it to the moment when Gaudí rejected his first, rigidly angular design for the palace and introduced the parabola as its defining and unifying shape. Gaudí was also the author of the two buildings in Barcelona in which aversion from the straight line is taken to its wildest extremes: the Casa Batlló, where interior ceilings swirl like ridged whipped cream, and the notorious Casa Milá of 1906–1910, where there is no straight line in the entire composition. The intended effect of the Casa Milá was to give an impression of organic growth, of symbiosis between building technology and nature. Decoratively, it is barnacled and seaweed-draped, as if submerged in primal lifeforces – a *cathédrale engloutie*, eroded into curves. In the middle of the city, it provides an impact similar to that of a mighty ruin overgrown, say, by the jungles of Yucatán. Its critics found it unstable and grotesque. A typical caricature published in *¡Cu-cut!* showed a podgy boy in bolero and gaiters saying to his elegantly dressed mother as they hurried past the exterior, 'Mummy, do they have earthquakes here, too?'[9] These asperities, by acknowledging the building's 'unbuilt' look, testified to its success.

The Casa Milá came, if not at the cusp of Gaudí's career, certainly at a turning point, when the dandyism of his early work and early appearance was buried under an avalanche – slowly gathering, sud-denly falling – of religious sensibility. By all accounts, the young Gaudí, who arrived in Barcelona in 1869 as a seventeen-year-old provincial *ingénue,* had no very strong religious feelings; his sympath-ies were with liberal politics and, therefore, secular values. Much of the impact of his work, until well into middle age, derived less from depth of feeling than from technical brilliance, capricious invention and, above all, love of display, which made him the perfect architect for his showy bourgeois patrons. The façade of the Casa Batlló expres-ses this best, perhaps, clad in the shimmer of iridescent spangles, like a pop waistcoat, and topped with a conceit so outrageous as to threaten reverence with mockery: a scaly dragon's hump of a roof, pierced by the lance of the patron saint of Catalonia. The conquest of dandyism by Catholicism is a fairly well-established theme of the history of the last hundred years. An attraction based, perhaps, on some form of affinity – the panoply of the sanctuary, the drama of the liturgy, the 'superbly creative bad taste' of traditional Catholicism – has won thousands of such souls from Wilde to Waugh. The conversion of Gaudí had begun by 3 November 1883. On that day he had a spiritual experience which, as far as we know, he never precisely described but which convinced him that a miracle of St Joseph had brought him the commission to complete the church of the Sagrada Familia. This was intended to be a sort of Catalan equivalent of a tractarian church, a vessel to gather in the godless and a monument to the doctrine of salvation by grace through works. It was to be offered as an expiatory sacrifice for the sins of the city and to be built entirely on the proceeds of alms. 'Come with me and build something for God,' said Gaudí to an assistant whom he took to view the site. The intensity of his conversion was made ferociously apparent in 1894, when his Lenten fast imperilled his life. But religion did not come to monopolise his values or exclusively inform his art until the events of 1909 caused a crisis in his work on the Casa Milá.

The rioters who burned houses of religion in the disturbances of the Tragic Week (see p.192) unnerved the proprietor of the Casa Milá, who decided to dispense with the great statue of the Virgin that was to have dominated the façade, in case she proved a provocation to future secularist violence. Gaudí, disgusted by the pusillanimous evasion, virtually withdrew from the project. At the same time, the sacrilege of the Tragic Week seemed to make the expiatory purpose of the Sagrada Familia all the more urgent. Gaudí made an anchorite's cell of his studio in the crypt of the church and worked on little else after 1911. When the former dandy was killed by a tram, in 1926, he died barefoot in his shoes, with his jacket held together by safety-pins and a gospel book in his hand. During his long, reclusive afterlife in this world, he had continued to attract adulation and to entertain the great amid the rising bones of his church or under the dangling baroque busts and primitive casts that decorated his cell. His funeral procession was half a mile long and mourners lined every inch of the two-and-a-half mile route. But people forgot that he had once been not just in the mainstream but in the forefront of Modernism, and the myth of a

Gaudí who had always been withdrawn and isolated came to dominate even his fellow-artists' image of him.

Nor was the uniqueness of the Sagrada Familia produced by hermetically sealing the architect's genius. Gaudí had always affected to find fault with Gothic, which was 'incompletely evolved' and 'industrial'. Yet the classical and Baroque architecture, which he claimed to admire more, was never an informative influence in his own work in the way that Gothic was; and although a Gothic conception was imposed on the plan for the Sagrada Familia before he assumed responsibility for the project, it was typical of the work Gaudí was doing on other commissions at about the same time – like the pavilions of the Compañía Transatlántica in the early years of the project, or later, the Teresian College and the chapel of the Güell estate. Almost from the first, Gaudí's Gothic had two distinctive features: he modified its straight lines and acute angles with paraboloid shapes; and he interpreted it as a source of 'natural' rather than 'rational' patterns. This made his Gothic buildings inside Barcelona – he applied rather different rules when he built beyond the city – look strikingly different from, say, the historically accurate and angular work of Puig or the functionally austere frameworks erected by Domènech. For example, he always dispensed with flying buttresses, substituting bowed, angled struts which wrenched the buildings into curvilinear forms: in the interior of the chapel of the Colonia Güell, the supporting pillars are like vast tree-trunks, recalling the origins of Gothic in Abbot Suger's search for suitably shaped trees in the forests round Saint-Denis. The corridors of the Teresian College are formed of recessive paraboloid arcades, like fluttering ranks of angels' wings. In both cases, the effect is eerie, terrible and beautiful.

The Sagrada Familia was produced by the same cross-fertilisation between Gothic and Modernist ideas. The building's symbolism is densely, even ludicrously, complex, but the basic conception is simple. The dominant clusters of long, concave spires rise like giant tubers from the grotto-shrine which encloses the crypt and floor; from them the multi-coloured, ceramic-smothered sunburst finials which crown the composition sprout like flowers. It makes a deeper impression than other Gaudí buildings because of its intense passion, its utter solemnity – though even this is muted, to some onlookers' taste, by the bland naturalism of the sculptures of the finished façade. But it is not of a different kind from the rest of Gaudi's *oeuvre*, nor unrepresentative of its time. It seemed old-fashioned, by the time of Gaudí's death, or

soon after, because it had been so long a-building and had little in
common with the severities of rationalist thinking which were then
becoming fashionable. Yet it captivated Barcelona's leading rationalist,
Josep Lluís Sert, not least because, like all Gaudí's work, it was not
merely dazzlingly imagined but also carefully planned to suit its
function. Today, when it is still far from completion, it seems in every
way a more far-sighted building than anything created by rationalism.
'Post-modernism' – which is, in some ways, a return to architectural
dandyism and a celebration of frenziedly ludic values – has re-habilit-
ated the early Gaudí, too.

All the leading architects of the city borrowed from art nouveau and
Secessionism, and acknowledged the cult of natural form, in buildings
of the first and second decades of the twentieth century. Even Puig i
Cadafalch, whose angles and spikes made rather unsuitable settings,
introduced art nouveau stained glass into the Casa Amatller. Domènech i Muntaner blended Modernism with Mauresque and Byzantine elements in the Casa Lleó Morena, only a few doors from the
Casa Amatller in the passeig de Gràcia; it won him the city's prize for
the best building of 1905 and seems to have emboldened him to embark
on his most imaginative building ever, the effusive Palau de la Música
Catalana, of 1905–8. Structurally, this lavish concert hall in the carrer
de Sant Pere més alt, looks ahead to functionalism, even rationalism,
with its steel diaphragm, structural glazing and acoustic efficiency. Its
underlying forms remain in the Gothic tradition. But the big, pointed
arches are almost totally submerged by riotous décor which makes the
building a sort of lexicon of Modernist vocabulary. Outside, tumescent
turrets smothered in livid mosaics surmount a deep entablature decorated in mosaic with scenes of song and dance, appropriate to the society
which commissioned the work, the Orfeó Català. Below that, palm-like
arcades, supported on colourful pillars in floral motifs, with deeply
carved capitals adorned with leaves and flowers, enclose bulging,
sinuous balconies. The arcades continue inside the auditorium, giving
the upper circle the feel of the deep triforium of a pilgrim cathedral.
The proscenium is swirled in curves, the defining lines smothered by
gigantic mouldings of horsemen and trees emerging from the living
rock and of Orpheus, Eurydice and Pegasus; the effect suggests an
urbane grotto, like that of Horace's Pyrrha. Every pillar and every
recess seem to be splattered by the bright pallettes of two brilliant men
whom Domènech employed as mosaicist and stained-glazier, Lluís
Bru i Salelles and Antoni Rigalt. With his next great building, the
Hospital de Sant Pau in the neighbourhood of the Sagrada Familia,

Domènech returned to austerely Gothic principles, but still used selectively the rich, even riotous effects of his Modernist period.

Domestic interiors of this period, as well as shop fronts and fittings, were executed with the same lack of inhibition as the Orfeó Català. The minor arts, where turnover was quick, were more easily and quickly conquered by fashion than architecture. The leading figure in interior decoration was Gaspar Homar i Mezquida (1870–1953), who worked with Domènech on the Casa Lleó Morera and produced influential marquetry furniture, inlaid with willowy geishas. Eusebi Arnau i Mascort (1863–1963), another protégé of Domènech, was a versatile sculptor who made a speciality of sculptural contributions to decorative schemes; his grandest work was done for the Palau de Música, but he also carved capitals and fireplaces for houses built by Domènech and Puig i Cadafalch, treating the fireplaces with the same bulging arcs, like distended bubbles or half-lily pads, that *modernista* designers favoured for sofa- and mirror-backs and shop windows.

THE WORLD OF ELS QUATRE GATS

There were cafés which looked more aggressively Modernist. The Café Torino of 1902, for instance, in the Gran Via, was a riot of art nouveau extravagance, with hardly a straight line in the place. In the plaça de Catalunya, the Café de la Luna of 1907 dripped with stylised frondeur and a theatrical clientèle. These, however, were the resorts of high fashion and high prices. They had Modernist décor but little Bohemian ambience. For that, one went to the places the artists not only designed but also frequented – above all, to the café which, from its opening in 1897 to its demise in 1903, was the art-world's creation and club, housed in a building of Puig i Cadafalch, Els Quatre Gats.[10]

Here, in contrast to the swirling exoticism of the Torino and the Luna, the decoration was almost homely. Ascetic and eclectic, it evoked an artist's studio of the time, full of incoherent clutter. The main saloon had broad, low, Gothic windows, a ceiling of heavy, machined, dark beams, tile-hung lower walls and hard, sturdy furniture. From a presiding position hung one of the vast, erstaz-medieval chandeliers without which no Barcelona domestic interior of the time seems to have been considered complete: Ramon Casas once sketched Santiago Rusiñol sitting in one. The upper walls were bespattered with select kitsch bric-à-brac – all on a small scale but for the huge, dominant oil-sketch of the owner, Pere Romeu, with the painter,

Ramon Casas. They sat together on a tandem bicycle, good-naturedly straining for progress, with doubled backs and set teeth, in cycling socks and jodhpurs. The painting hung there until a car replaced the bicycle and a more up-to-date image went up.

Though Romeu and Rusiñol were the most creative forces in the world of Els Quatre Gats, Casas seems in retrospect its most distinguished member. Like Rusiñol, but more so, he was a child of privilege. His father was a nabob who had made a fortune in the Indies; on his mother's side, he was heir to a textile mill. His fortune thus combined two typical sources of the wealth of Barcelona in his day. Artists had formerly relied on grants from a city council that accepted unquestioningly an art patron's role for study-trips to Rome. Casas and Rusiñol, however, preferred – and could afford – to go to Paris instead. There, with Romeu and Miquel Utrillo, who was to become the fourth of the 'cats' of Els Quatre Gats, and other Barcelonese artists who were attracted by their example, they selectively absorbed the lessons of Impressionism and equipped themselves to challenge the realistic, historical and anecdotal conventions still dominant in the art schools of their native city. When they returned, they brought their spending-power with them, and used it to create and promote a self-consciously radical circle of artists. Outside that circle, they had more admirers than customers, except for their commercial graphics; so money of their own was necessary. It helped to pay for the indulgences of the life of Els Quatre Gats – the shaky finances of the café, the succession of ephemeral publications, the exhibitions and poetry readings.

No Barcelonese painter has ever excelled Ramon Casas in technical mastery or faithfulness to the idea of beauty. Yet he created a new and challenging style. He had every qualification to be an amateur dabbler – in his self-portraits, with a fat cigar always stuck into the bowl of a pipe, he is the image of the rich eccentric – and yet he dedicated himself to painting and the graphic arts with single mind and full heart. His finest works are genre-scenes which capture fleeting moments – usually of a story which is dramatic and tragic in varying degrees. Their subject matter covers a wide range of human experience from intimate secrets to public conflicts. In *Plein Air* – a work admired enough to be bought by the city council in 1891 in spite of its heavy Parisian flavour – a young woman seated alone in an open-air café observes a man in the distance, framed by an impressionistic townscape. In a portrait of the artist's sister and brother-in-law at coffee (1892), the charm and languor of the scene conceal pointed personal and social commentary; the man's attitude of spineless *ennui* inversely balances his wife's purposeful and upright pose. The most memorable canvases are those in which the social commentary is most overt. 'Barcelona 1902' is an extraordinarily dynamic composition, in which a mounted civil guard is about to trample a sprawling, dramatically foreshortened worker in the foreground, while the crowd is cleared by the cavalry from a space which seems to grow before the onlooker's eyes. It was in fact painted in 1899, apparently without any intention of documenting a specific incident, but renamed after a violent strike in the later year.[11] Patriotic scruples led the Spanish committee to reject it for the Paris Exhibition in 1899, but in 1902 it was acclaimed in Madrid. Casas's most famous – and, in his day, most popular – work was 'Garrote Vil' (1893), recording the public execution in that year of a nineteen year old who had cut the throats of his victim and accomplice for a gold watch. Some aspects seem ironic the clergy are a corpulent contingent under an enormous crucifix; the penitents' black conical caps prod towards the centre of the canvas like pitchfork-prongs. The main purpose of the painting, however, seems to be simply to document with fidelity a scene of extraordinary emotional power at which the painter was a witness. The public loved its engaging horror more than they feared its social import. It belongs to a well established genre of horror-paintings in Barcelona, always popular and frequently connected with the traditions of public scourging, common until the early nineteenth century, and public execution, which continued until 1908.

Casas's reputation as a rebel against his class seems exaggerated. He was a shrewd and critical observer rather than a rebel. He never forsook a bourgeois way of life or abandoned its comforts. He was more at home in his time, perhaps, than almost any other artist of his generation; while Gaudí, in the depths of his tortured soul, rejected the values of industrial society, Casas was one of the first men in Barcelona to own a motorcar. While Nonell found his models in the gutters and the suburbs, Casas got them from the cafés. He was invited to paint a portrait of the king. While Apel·les Mestres fled to the clericalist extreme right, Casas remained in the mainstream of Catalanist politics. He shared the concern of the Barcelonese middle class for practical applications of art, and produced a huge corpus as an illustrator and commercial artist. Most conspicuous among this output is a haunting poster for Dr Abreu's syphilis cure, in which a rather raffish prostitute extends a flower in one hand and holds a serpent behind her back; characteristically of Casas's ability to puzzle us, we are left uncertain which of these symbols denotes the curse, and which the cure.

Casas was the finest, Rusiñol the most effective talent of the world of Els Quatre Gats. Soon after his return from Paris Rusiñol erupted into the seaside village of Sitges, just outside Barcelona, and turned it into a theatre of his ideas and a playground of his friends. It was already a haunt of painters when Rusiñol discovered it, apparently by accident, in 1891. He bought property there and, from 1893 to 1899, was the impresario for a series of what he called 'Festivals of Modernism', at which he made speeches defining Modernism in imprecise but potent language. The highlight of the first – bafflingly called the Second Festival – was a performance of Maeterlinck's *L'Intruse*, of the next a parade through the streets of two canvases by El Greco which Rusiñol had bought in Paris and exhibited alongside his own. He cultivated the idea, and attempted the practice, of total art, illustrating his own books, criticising his own pictures, writing the publicity for his own plays and libretti, meticulously 'designing' his art and his life in detail. His influence and his energy helped to make Barcelonese art talkative, even declamatory, and self-justificatory, and to make a cult of novelty. If his showmanship was of the very highest order, his painting ran it close in quality. He was not quite such a consummate technician as Casas but he produced genre scenes and human studies of stark beauty and nicely judged restraint, which seemed to exemplify the 'sincerity' he extolled as the aim of art.

The name of Els Quatre Gats was coined in tribute to Le Chat Noir of Paris; but it was also a self-proclamation of the founding friends as a small band of outsiders. It is now a commonplace to point out that Modernism was a minority taste in Barcelona even in its heyday. Casas and Rusiñol sold little to private patrons; the brilliant but more avant-garde members of the circle, like Nonell, Picasso, and Joaquim Mir, even less. Within a few years of the turn of the century, Modernism was under attack from proponents of an anti-Parisian, anti-Impressionist reaction known as *Noucentisme*. By the time of the Great Exhibition of 1929, the decorative excesses of Modernism were regarded with horror in a world of functional aesthetics. A guide of that year bewailed the 'misfortune' that brought so much building to Barcelona during the Modernist supremacy.[12] The Café Torino, on which the leading Modernists had collaborated in design and decoration, was demolished to make room for the Joieria Roca of 1934 by Josep Lluís Sert, its curves raped by the incisive lines of rationalism. But despite the sacrifice of much Modernist art to revolutions of taste – especially the interior decorations and the shop fronts, two forms which are notoriously fragile and yet were modernist specialities –

Barcelona is still splashed with the motley of its own eccentric art nouveau. The bullring is sandwiched between a vast mosaic butterfly and a circus of ornamental flowerbeds in art nouveau patterns. The spires and stained glass of the Casa de los Punxes lead towards the sunflower ornaments that crown the spires of Sagrada Familia. Gawpers gather under the mosaic mushroom-forest of the Parc Güell. The jaws of the Casa Milá drip; the jowls of the Casa Batlló bulge; the dozens of shops – pharmacies, especially, but also bakeries, restaurants, bars, haberdasheries – still wear their *fin de siècle* finery, their gaudy curves, with pride. Images that identify Barcelona with that era are indelible. They are impressed on every visitor's mind. Barcelona would have no distinctive 'profile' as a city without them.

THE NEW CENTURIONS

In the early years of the new century artists began to gather in a new group, presided over by the columnist Eugeni d'Ors. He seems to have fancied himself as a sort of Spanish Oscar Wilde, photographed with long hair, a centre parting, an abstracted countenance, an expansive manner and a lavish buttonhole. In the time of his influence, however, he was an energetic reagent against *fin de siècle* decadence. Adopting his lead, the innovators called themselves *noucentistes*: the term was coined to distinguish them from 'Modernists' – a name which embarrassed or outraged the Modernists themselves. Noucentism was the product of a generation gap, devoted to a cult of youth, proclamatory – a little late, it must be said – of new values for a new century, and noisily rejecting the art of the academics of the Llotja and the Modernists of the cafés. D'Ors was its pontiff. The acolytes on whom he laid hands by naming them in his column, 'Glosari', from 1906 or publishing their names and work in the *Almanach dels noucentistes* in 1911 became its priests. Like all such brotherhoods, intellectually esoteric, personally exclusive, it was defined as much by who was left out as by what was admitted. Still, it was a genuine movement with positive, distinctive and coherent features. It continued or renewed the search for a peculiarly Catalan art. D'Ors' novel of 1912, *La ben plantada*, symbolised the indomitability of Catalanism. Nogués illustrated the subject as a tall, upright female; poor but pious; as indifferent as a statue to the rage of the mean, crabbed figures – plutocratic and militaristic – who dance around her frenziedly, stones in hand. Noucentism looked to the Mediterranean for the sources of a Catalan heritage, away from the Paris that had influenced or engendered Modernism, to 'these immortal daughters on the other side of our sea'. It responded to the call of the writer of the first personal artist's 'manifesto' of twentieth-century Barcelona, J. Torres García, 'to turn to the tradition of art which belongs to Mediterranean lands' instead of 'alien' Impressionism, pre-Raphaelitism and Symbolism. Finally, and in consequence, Noucentism was a classicising movement. The Roman excavations of Empùries influenced Barcelonese artists of the era of the *Almanach* as those of Italica had influenced the early Sevillian Baroque; they sought simple structural principles and, with contempt for the decorative, the recovery of form.

The most characteristic art of Noucentism was, perhaps, talk; but sculpture ran it a close second. Enric Casanovas sculpted solid Mediterranean women in granite-like stone: his Majorcan peasant woman was an Iberian goddess; his 'Youth' a rather *Männlich* Minoan. Josep Clará embodied everybody's idea of Noucentism in his muscular representations of Teresa, the heroine of *La ben plantada*. Any of these sculptures, dropped from even a moderate height, would have shattered the fragile, drooping, *modernista* nudes of a sculptor like Josep Llupinol, who, despite his avowed contempt for the style, found the over-studied and therefore rather uncommunicative eroticism of Rodin irresistible in his own work. For most of the painters who belonged to the movement, Noucentism was a haven, rather than a home, on their way to more radical and avant-garde styles, but it helped for a time to produce some of the more brilliant and luminous works of Torres García and Joaquim Mir, who, in Majorca and Tarragona, captured Mediterranean light as faithfully as any painter has ever done.

Architecture, always slower to respond to fashion than quicker, cheaper art forms, took a long time to absorb Noucentism. A few buildings of before the First World War seemed to anticipate or reflect Noucentism, but were perhaps only continuing the tradition of nineteenth-century neo-classicism. In the carrer Ample, for instance, the building of the Societat del Crèdit Mercantil, of 1896–1900, has a masonic feel, with its low pediment and the central bay of its third storey, formed by a tympanum-like eye enclosing a window. The architect, Joan Martorell i Montells, also built a Gaudiesque Modernist-Gothic pastiche, at about the same time, in the form of the Collegi Sant Ignasi de Loiola. In the carrer de Balmés J. Torres i Grau built the outstanding Foment d'Obres i Construcció in an early *noucentista* or pre-*noucentista* style, but the neighbouring numbers

81 and 169 in the same street, constructed at about the same time, between 1908 and 1910, are Modernist with historical references – Hispano-Flemish and Gothic-Mauresque respectively. Not until after 1913, when J. Torres García published *Notes sobre l'art* with a Greek portico on the cover, did Noucentism begin to take over the way Barcelona looked; today, though *noucentista* buildings are less identifiable and less conspicuous than those of Modernism, they are probably more numerous. J. Folch i Torres (1886–1963) built villas of a rustic Italian flavour with Palladian entrances, recessed and colonnaded. J. Goday (1882–1936) was responsible for slightly Baroque palazzi and the acclaimed school buildings, such as those of the carrer del Carme, which embodied Barcelona's commitment to public education in elegant form. Francesc Folguera (1891–1960) was influenced by the Florentine Renaissance, designing façades which strongly echoed Brunelleschi, as did Nicolau Rubió (1891–1981) and Raimon Duran Reynals (1895–1966) whose humanistic composition, the church of Maria Reina de Montserrat on Pedralbes, of 1922, could have been transplanted from the Tuscan countryside. Antoni Puig i Guiral (1887–1955) was an accomplished architect of the same generation who built Italianate tower-villas, like the Casa Guarto, and Mediterranean pastiche, like the Valencian- or Andalusian-looking carrer Ample number 46.

The apogee of the *noucentista* era was the International Exhibition of 1929, and in some ways the best memorial to the period is still the exhibition site on Montjuic. The event had been long planned and often deferred, first projected in 1901, scheduled for 1917 and almost scrapped because of the First World War, then held up by the political uncertainties of the twenties and competition from other international fairs. This long gestation meant that when the exhibition at last opened, it was clad in the finery of bygone hand-me-downs, housed in buildings which looked fusty by comparison with the effortless rationalism of some of the foreign pavilions – especially of the German pavilion of Mies van der Rohe. The characteristic new constructions by Barcelonese architects for the fair were: Goday's Pavelló de la Ciutat – by Herrera out of Helsinki Station; the Olympic Stadium by Pere Domènech i Roura, with its spiky tower with the look of an elongated Bramantesque tempietto; the loggia and gardens of the 'Greek temple' by R. Raventós (1892–1976); the Pavelló de les Arts Gràfiques by Pelai Martínez Paricio (1898–1978) and Raimon Duran (now the Archaeological Museum), which has the form of a Florentine Renaissance octagon with round windows, mathematically disposed, and a recessed entrance, pilastered and pedimented; and the former hotels which line the plaça de Espanya, gaunt, heavily clock-towered and monastic in appearance, by Nicolau Rubió. These relics, scattered down the slopes and at the foot of Montjuic, like the debris of a battle, testify to Barcelona's last bid to project the image of a Mediterranean *polis*. In the light of the exhibition, Noucentism seemed an ill judged architectural adventure, thrown into shadow by the rays of rationalism, which conquered Barcelona for a new style in the new decade.

THE BONDS OF THE FATHERLAND

When I first visited Barcelona as a little boy in the 1950s, the most durable sight of the 1929 exhibition was the Pueblo Español, a collection of buildings on Montjuic, modelled on examples of medium-scale regional and vernacular architecture from all over Spain. It is still a tourist attraction, under the Catalanised name of 'Poble Espanyol', as pointless as any such 'theme park'. It seemed bizarre when I first saw it, and seems tawdry now. When new, however, it was both hugely esteemed and highly significant. Variegated and archaic, it seemed to offer a town-planning model that was refreshingly different from the monotony of the Eixample.[13] Escape from the tightly woven net of the Cerdà plan had been the aim of Barcelona's town planners, ever since 1903, when a new competition for a further enlargement of the town produced a series of entries designed to link the Eixample to the outlying towns with a rich new texture of streets. The Pueblo Español seemed a harmless, even laudable *divertissement*, which would provide attraction for visitors and recreation for citizens. All the intellectuals interviewed by the press at its inauguration liked it. Ortega spoke for the lot when he said he thought it would give 'all foreigners a clear and representative idea of what Spain is'.[14]

The terms of that praise betrayed the deeper significance of the Pueblo Español in the Barcelona of 1929. It demonstrated that the exhibition was a Spanish event, not merely Barcelonese and not at all Catalan. By implication, Barcelona was stamped as a Spanish city. In the introduction to the official catalogue, the Duke of Berwick sketched a historical panorama of Spain, with emphasis on her links with European-wide movements, without mentioning Catalonia.[15] The evasion with which Catalonia was treated, the intrusion which the Pueblo Español represented, were politically determined. General Primo de Rivera had seized dictatorial power in 1923 partly because of the disgust with which, as military governor of Barcelona, he beheld the separatism of some Catalan extremists. He proclaimed that he had taken office 'without any proposals to shoot anybody' but with the warning that 'the bonds of the fatherland are not even to be questioned'. Hostility to the idea of Spanish unity was, he opined, 'sick, abandoned, criminal and abominable'.[16]

Primo's repression, always tempered by inefficiency, was directed against the Catalanism of the urban middle class. The workers were bought off with policies of cheap food and full employment, to which, in Barcelona, the preparations for the 1929 exhibition made a major contribution. Paternalism – the language of Primo's politics, which, like many forms of rhetoric, gradually influenced and therefore increasingly reflected the behaviour of the regime – also blunted the edge of repression, which was just effective enough to stimulate an indignant reaction in favour of Catalanism without succeeding in inhibiting its spread. The ban on the Catalan flag, the extrusion of the Catalan language from public life and education, the abolition of the Mancomunitat and the dissolution of the Catalanist political parties created grievances and garbed Catalanism with the romance of a fugitive creed, celebrated in catacombs and fed on exiles' bread. The most incurably romantic of all Catalanist spokesmen, Francesc Maciá, was transformed from a marginalised dreamer into an effective symbol of national resistance. In 1926, his attempt to launch a comic-opera 'invasion' of Catalonia in the cause of liberation was turned back at the frontier by French border-guards, with all the advantages of bloodless martyrdom for its leaders. Yet, while no anti-Catalanist regime could ever be entirely successful in Barcelona, much of the rest of Primo's language and ethos were close to Barcelonese sympathies. In the adulation of industry, the espousal of protectionism, the effort to combine full employment with cheap labour, the advocacy of values of high production and hard work, Primo echoed the economic and moral priorities of a community he knew well from his days in Barcelona as captain-general of the province. At the level of talk, the passion to 'galvanise' society could be indulged in to ludicrous extremes, as in the dictator's plan to abolish the siesta and introduce 'a fork lunch at 10.30 or 11.00' in the morning.[17] The emulation of Europe was seen by the regime, as by many of the Catalanists, as a matter of the abolition of Spanish traditions and the adoption of frantic 'foreign' habits of hustle and bustle.

In the Ruritanian world of Primo's Barcelona, where two types of unreality, represented by Primo and Maciá, were locked in a conflict both solemn and ludicrous, the most progressive spirit was, perhaps, that of Josep Lluís Sert i López. Born into comfortable circumstances in 1902, he grew up with a strong sense of the social obligations of his class. His gifts were constructive rather than creative; he was a great organiser, administrator and teacher, but as a practical architect he tended to need the shelter of collaborative projects; his designs were derivative and dependent on the example or inspiration of heroes like Le Corbusier. He was a genie rather than a genius, responding to needs rather than imposing his own vision; popping out of the context rather than defying his times. Yet, despite his limitations, he became one of this century's most influential Spaniards, marking the face of Spain through his work as a propagandist of rationalist architecture, and later, after the Civil War, when he fled to a chair at Harvard, helping to define and spread the notions on which the urban planning of the fifties was conceived worldwide. His solutions suffered from all the arrogance of the modern planning tradition, but were not dogmatically inspired. The unprecedented problems of rapid urban growth in an era of global economic instability impelled the sort of dramatic response which Sert articulated. Blended with the paternalistic traditions of the Barcelonese bourgeoisie, his genuine anxiety to ameliorate the conditions in which ordinary people lived produced the magnificent orthodoxies of his day, which have since come to seem abominable heresies: 'slum clearance' that swept away human-scale housing; intimidating 'leisure zones'; uniform, minimalist estates; tower-blocks; all the instant detritus of the 'functional city'. Until his exile, Sert was that rare type of intellectual: the prophet honoured in his own country.

THE 'AMPLE HORIZON'

Though the rationalist solutions advocated by Sert are now out of fashion, they represented at the time the most radical and promising approach to the problems of Barcelona's rapid growth: into a megalopolis of over a million registered inhabitants in 1930. Because they are architectural – and therefore, in a sense, apolitical – solutions, they could be allowed to incubate freely under the Primo regime. Because they were the work of Catalanist intellectuals, and because they had a utopian flavour, and because they seemed a means of redistributing happiness in favour of the underprivileged, they could flourish from 1931 when the regime was replaced by a republic in which leftist and

Catalanist tendencies were strong. Rationalist architecture had, in some measure, the power of re-uniting the workers' movement with the Catalanist movement after Primo had wedged them apart. The rationalists' plan for the development of the city was, for sentimental reasons, called the 'Maciá Plan'.

Just as, in the 1890s, the last reception in Barcelona of the major international style of architecture had been anticipated by indigenous experiments, so the reception of rationalism in the thirties was preceded by a surprisingly long tradition. The basic ingredients of rationalist thinking in architecture – the aesthetics of function, the determination to exploit technology to the full – had animated the work of Domènech i Muntaner and even Gaudí. Under the functional simplicity of Gaudí's school buildings for the Sagrada Familia or the wine vaults designed at Garraf by his pupil Berenguer was a beacon for 'modern architecture' and, perhaps, a direct source of inspiration for Le Corbusier. A feature of rationalism as advocated by Sert and practised in Spain was its concern with the environment of mass housing, in which every outlook would be sunlit towards an 'ample horizon'; this recalls Gaudí's concern that his dwellings should enjoy access to the sun and be surrounded by a pallette of light.

In Barcelona modern architecture, as the term is now understood, began just when Noucentism was at its height and the buildings of the 1929 exhibition were going up. This was not only because of the impact of the foreign pavilions – German, Swedish and Yugoslav – designed on rationalist principles. Barcelonese architects had already begun new departures from Modernism and Noucentism in the direction of functional, rational buildings. In 1928 – while Le Corbusier was being diverted to lecture in Barcelona by a telegram from Sert on his way to Madrid – the Myrurgas factory by Antoni Puig i Gairalt (1887–1935) was begun, starkly innovative, as was a coldly functional block of flats by Ramon Raventós (1892–1959) on the corner of the carrer de Lleida. These examples seemed to show that rational simplicity and decorative austerity were natural developments within Noucentism, on which these architects had been nurtured. The same possibilities were even more strikingly manifest in Francesc Folguera's Casa de Sant Jordi on the corner of the carrer de Casp and via Laietana, begun in 1929, a building so maturely representative of modern architecture that it would be ascribed to the fifties or sixties by an impartial observer.[18] In the same year Sixt Yllescas built what might be called a pre-rationalist house in Gràcia, the Casa Vilaró. In 1930 in collaboration with Yllescas put up a revolutionary block of duplex flats in the carrer de Muntaner in which the visual relief on the outside derived from the eccentric (but functionally determined) geometry of the disposition of the windows, the boldness of the ship's-railing balconies and the delicacy of the pale green render.

Modern architecture was formally incorporated into a 'movement' or, at least, a club in Barcelona in March 1931, when Sert and Torres i Clavé organised their friends in GATCPAC. Decoded, the elaborate acronym signified 'Group of Catalan Artists and Technicians for the Progress of Contemporary Architecture'. The group's interest in rationalism was confirmed in October of the same year when, at a meeting in Saragossa, it was altered to GATEPAC – the *Spanish* Group for the same purpose – under the presidency of García Mercadal, the Aragonese architect normally credited with the first rationalist buildings in Spain. Most of the group's collective energy went into publicising the ideas of Sert and Torres, closely based on those of Le Corbusier, on town planning. Planning was a form of gospel which would save the urban masses from eternal immolation in the rubble of pandemonium or under its detritus. The demons' breeding grounds in tenements, gloomy courtyards and narrow streets would be abolished; new housing would be of modest dimensions, low cost and limited variety, but it would be open to light, space, 'pure air' and the 'ample horizon'. Work would benefit from planned amenities for leisure and health; efficiency would be improved by planned communications with the city; the needs of progress and civilisation would be paired. The solutions to the problems of the developing city were attainable by study and thought. Planning would deliver the just polity almost as a by-product of the civilised city, supplying the 'vital elements that every human being needs and which society has no right to deny'.[19] Ironically the only purely rationalist building to survive from the Gatepac era is a jeweller's shop on the Gran Via; thus the utopian ideal is to be found beyond a threshold crossed only by the rich. The Gatepac vision can, however, be seen embodied in two entirely characteristic examples: the Casa Bloc, built to house workers in 1932–6, and the Dispensari Central Antitubercolós of 1934–8. Both show the depth of Sert's discipleship of Le Corbusier. The Casa Bloc lurches around a series of right angles through a green space, hoisted aloft on ground-floor stilts. The clinic is built around a lecture-room based on Le Corbusier's rejected design for the assembly hall of the League of Nations.

Fortunately, perhaps, the plan Maciá, except for a few experiments, remained on paper. Its destructive potential was terrible in a city whose charm arose largely from the picturesque decay of a slummy centre. Torres Clavé's mock-up is a futuristic nightmare, with the old town dominated by gaunt towers, flimsy and precarious, like cardboard pop-outs. All that the Prince of Wales abhors in London could have been realised, had the Republic had more time and the city more money, fifty years ago in Barcelona.

The Cockpit of a European Conflict

The Spanish Civil War, which began in July 1936, subverted the rationalists' plans and dispersed their personnel. Sert took refuge in Harvard; Torres i Clavé died on the battlefield. Within the plan of the existing streets, the workers of Barcelona created in the early days of the war a utopia of their own. The revolt of part of the regular army garrison was successfully countered by a rising of 'popular militias' organised by anarchists, anarcho-syndicalists and left-Marxists. Behind their barricades a social revolution was enforced by armed gangs. When George Orwell arrived to join the revolutionary militia in the hope of being sent to fight 'fascism' at the front, he found every wall scrawled with the hammer and sickle and with the acronyms of the revolutionary parties. He got a lecture from a hotel manager for trying to tip a lift-boy. The barbers' shops had signs 'solemnly explaining that barbers were no longer slaves', and posters recommended the same metamorphosis to prostitutes. Revolutionary posters, 'flaming from the walls . . . made the few remaining adverts look like daubs of mud'. Loudspeakers in the Ramblas blared revolutionary music. Apart from an elderly lady with a poodle, the middle class seemed to have vanished. Everyone in the streets wore rough clothes or blue overalls 'or some variant of the militia uniform'.[20]

Orwell was exhilarated by the sight of a city that had succumbed to a workers' revolution. For the victims and bystanders, however, the revolution evoked successively terror and boredom. Joan Pujol Garcia – the future master-spy – was frightened not only by the armed mobs of amnestied convicts who supplemented the authentic revolutionaries, but also by the atmosphere of suspicion spread by denunciations between neighbours. It was a time of secret score-settling unparalleled since the days of the Inquisition. The renowned surgeon, Josep Trueta, who saved thousands of Republican lives during the battles of the Civil War, almost fell to 'revolutionary justice' in its earliest days, rescued from an anarchist kangaroo-court by a squadron of armed socialist street-fighters. Catalanists – whom the revolutionaries almost invariably classified as bourgeois – had particular reason to fear the triumphant workers' culture, which spoke in the same foreign tongue as Primo and Franco. The anarchist Durutti threatened to shoot the President of the Generalitat if he turned up for anti-fascist militia committee-meetings.[21]

The committees soon out-chattered the guns and fear gave way to milder forms of disenchantment. When false papers enabled him to come out of hiding, Joan Pujol was obliged to 'hang around attending endless meetings of the poultry-farmers' union'. The revolution was 'made', after the barricades, in individual work-places where, usually, local CNT chapels took over the management in defiance of the union leadership, the republican and Catalan governments, and most of the political parties. The economic success of the experiment lasted only as long as pre-war stocks. In 1937, Pujol and his companions-in-arms had to desert to the Nationalists in order to get a square meal.[22]

The initial success of the revolution in Barcelona, and the relative security of the city's position, remote from the front, made it the cockpit of the self-indulgent squabbles of the parties that formed the Republican side. The local political situation was of more concern to the native Barcelonese than the progress of the war; only intending fugitives like Pujol or uncomprehending idealists like Orwell were fretting for the front. The conditions were ideal for ideological in-fighting: the fervour induced by war, without any immediate apprehension of defeat; the presence of large numbers of mutually hostile gangs of gunmen; a deteriorating material and economic position which equipped the contenders with fuel for mutual accusations. The hatreds of anarchists and communists, Trotskyists and Stalinists were arcane and tribal, hardly understood by outsiders. Orwell's naive question to his fellow left-Marxists who disapprovingly pointed out members of the socialist militia was, 'Aren't we all Socialists?' This was like asking 'Aren't we all Christians?' at the massacre of St Bartholomew. Creeds have their theologies and no conflicts of heresy and orthodoxy have ever been so embittered as those of the left in modern times. The doctrinal differences were complicated by a contest for power between the collectives, the Catalan government and the government of the Republic. At the same time, the half-baked nature of the revolution of July 1936 raised a fundamental problem of strategy which divided the revolutionary parties and unions from the rest: whether the revolution should be prosecuted without compromise, regardless of the feelings of the bourgeois allies of the left and in defiance of the potential allies of the Republic among the western democracies; or whether it should be arrested or reversed in the interests of 'winning the war'. Apologists of the revolutionaries have always insisted that the revolutionary line was justifiable as a means to victory as well as an end in itself, but the anarchist outburst – 'as if the war has any meaning unless we can make the revolution at the same time'[23] – reveals a real difference of priorities. In these circumstances it is less surprising that internecine violence should have broken out among the Republicans in Barcelona than that it should have been delayed for so long.

The events of the blood-letting of the Barcelonese left are well known. On 3 May 1937 police units attempted to wrest the telephone exchange from the control of an anarcho-syndicalist collective. This may not have been intended to provoke a general confrontation. For several months, government-controlled units had been gradually replacing the popular militias in strategic positions, always with acrimony but usually without violence. The government policy was twofold: by rolling back the revolution they hoped to make the Republican cause more internationally acceptable; and by strengthening central authority at the expense of the uncontrollables they hoped to make the war effort more efficient. But the issue became a catalyst for the enmities of the communists and anarchists and their anti-Stalinist allies. The militia defending the telephone exchange resisted the police. Five days of generalised fighting claimed 500 dead. Orwell, unwillingly caught up in the shooting, was amazed at how the people of Barcelona, with the city's long history of civil commotion behind them, accepted the violence as 'a natural calamity' which generated a topography of its own, and patterns of participation and evasion which the locals knew and lived with: 'people take their places almost as in a fire-drill'. Most people were indifferent. 'Such a pity,' said Orwell's boot-maker, 'and so bad for business.'[24] The defeat of the anarchists was also a defeat for the Catalanist cause, which had seemed marginal to the conflict. The city was occupied on 7 May by a well-armed force of paramilitary guards loyal to the government of the Republic, which was now dedicated to centralising power, ostensibly in the interests of the war effort. Barcelona was thoroughly demoralised for the duration of the war; the alienated minorities no longer felt the Republican cause worth fighting for. After the days of May, communist strategy seemed to come straight out of a bunker, with as much energy – more perhaps – expended on the proscription of Trotskyists and the subordination of anarchists as on the prosecution of the war. Barcelona's self-proclaimed role as a European city was fulfilled when she became a theatre of pan-European conflict and a sacrifice for the international priorities of foreign powers.

The in-fighting would have been unthinkable had Barcelona been near the front line where optimism was enforced and camaraderie contagious. Now that the damage wrought by remoteness from the front was done, the war struck the city with devastating force. In March 1938, an Italian bombing campaign frayed nerves and clogged the hospitals day and night for three days. The motive of these raids seems to have been experimental: the Italians wanted to test the morale of a great city under a merciless bombardment, and perhaps to try out new high-explosive bombs. Franco's own ponderous strategy gave the city a respite almost until the end of the year. His final offensive was launched two days before Christmas. The Republican resistance dissolved more from desertion than from the blows of the enemy. The right-wing Catalanist Tomas Roig Llop took part in an unopposed and apparently unobserved walk-out by 400 new conscripts. Those compromised by loyalty to the Republic thought rather of escape than resistance.[25]

Orwell had realised, after some time in the city, that the working-class uniforms which impressed him so much on arrival were worn, in many cases, as a disguise. Tomas Roig Llop, for instance, found it useful to change headgear when he travelled between anarchist and left-Marxist headquarters, for one group considered a bare head evasive, while the other thought a cap was treasonable. Boilersuits and loose collars were forms of disguise most of the middle class was happy to discard. There was never much of a 'fifth column' in Barcelona but when Franco's troops marched in on 26 January 1939, a collaborationist bourgeoisie was waiting in the woodwork. The Francoist slogan, however – 'Spain Has Arrived' – could hardly be greeted with any enthusiasm by Catalanists. At best, they could praise the triumph of a lesser evil. The celebrations in the streets were caused, in most cases, perhaps, by one or both of two forms of reliefs: joy that the war was over, 'not that one side or the other had won'; and thankfulness again to be able to receive the sacraments of the church without fear. During the revolutionary supremacy, priests could only be sheltered in secret; when Joana Alier's daughter was baptised in 1937, there was no chrism for the anointing: the priest returned with some a year later.[26]

'SPAIN HAS ARRIVED'

The Franco troops were only the spearhead; in the next forty years, 'Spain' arrived in a more durable and insidious form, when hundreds of thousands of immigrants poured into the city to swell its official population to 1¾ million by 1981, and over three million in the metropolitan area. Catalanism, repressed by Primo, superannuated by the Civil War and crushed by Franco, might have been buried under this avalanche. Yet, when Franco died in 1975, and the President of the Catalan government-in-exile returned to the balcony of the Generalitat, he was acclaimed by natives and Spaniards alike. The words with which he triggered the cheers were an unconscious rebuke to 'Spain Has Arrived': '*Ja sóc aquí!*,' he cried: 'Here I am at last!' Since then, the Barcelonese working class has voted consistently for Catalan autonomy and broadly Catalanist cultural policies. There are differences of degree and of priorities between the programmes of the Socialist party and the Catalanists proper; but it remains true that in Barcelona's recent past a Spanish-speaking proletariat has been extraordinarily amenable to the sensibilities of a Catalan-speaking bourgeoisie. From the centre of Barcelona to the working-class suburbs, there are cultural differences but little real antagonism.

In 1982, a survey revealed some of the immigrants' reasons for respecting Catalan identity. The most eloquent respondent was an immigrant worker who professed to consider himself 'Catalan, although I am an Andalusian. It is here that I have developed the ability to sell my labour; here I have learned the little culture I possess and have created my home. This is my land. This is how I think of it, although my inner self is full of other tendencies.'[27] The majority view, however, was the product of less highly developed sensibilities. Most respondents favoured Catalan autonomy out of weariness with the rigid centralism of the Franco dictatorship, not out of Catalanist fellow feeling. In the working-class districts today, the atmosphere and speech remain Andalusian, not Catalan. In the relatively central district of Sants, cases have been observed of immigrants who have been 'absorbed' – that is, who have mastered correct Catalan, in ten or twelve years;[28] but, in the outer suburbs and townships, the context essential for this sort of 'absorption' cannot be found. Here, there is no evidence that a Catalan sense of identity has made any significant conquests among immigrants of the first generation; and Catalanisation of their children has to proceed delicately and by degrees if they are not to be alienated. The alliance of workers and Catalanists, which was a product of the Franco era, has survived, but uncemented, since the dictator's death.

The economics of immigration are illustrated by an interview recorded by Sebastian Balfour with an immigrant from Badajoz, who sold his house at home in 1950 for 7,000 pesetas, paid off his debts and bought a cave in Sabadell for 3,000.[29] Accommodated in caves or shacks or squalid blocks, the workers were exploited with longer hours and lower real incomes than in any other industrialised zone of western Europe; but the regime's policies of guaranteed work ensured that they were better off at home and gradually began to enjoy the comforts of consumerism and the economic benefits of a spectacular economic leap forward in the sixties. The traditionally combative masses of Barcelona no longer existed. The new hydra had drawn fangs. Political strikes were rare, even in the early seventies when anti-Francoist protest was at its boldest. The union elections of 1975 revealed a non-political majority among unionised workers.[30] Instead of being goaded by repression into the arms of the communists, they had drifted, from boredom and *embourgeoisement*, into entente with Catalanism.

'THE CITY OF PRODIGIES'

Hercules, the legendary founder of Barcelona, makes a suitable role-model for a city whose history has strangely paralleled his mythical career. Both have been poised between the love of Pleasure and Toil, with a strong inclination towards the latter, tempered by a good deal of dalliance with the former. Both were called on to perform prodigious feats, the most conspicuous difference being, perhaps, that Barcelona's Herculean tasks have been accomplished under Sisyphean burdens. Hemmed in by mountains on the landward side, restricted to seaward by unserviceable currents, Barcelona became the capital of a territorial state without conquering an inch of territory, and the heart of a maritime empire without possessing a decent natural harbour. When the empire was lost and the state dismantled, she became an industrial power, despite her dearth of natural resources. All her labours were responses to difficulties or disasters: her first boom followed al-Mansur's raid. Her seaborne empire was acquired to gain previously thwarted access to Mediterranean trade. Her challenge to Joan II occurred almost at the nadir of her late medieval decline. The construction of her artificial port began when her trade had collapsed, and was sustained through two centuries of more or less chronic adversity. She tackled successively the Habsburgs and Bourbons in times of mixed fortune and went on fighting when her cause seemed hopeless. The foundations of her manufacturing prosperity were laid when she was a conquered and occupied victim of a protracted era of war and defeat. Her industrial take-off in the mid-nineteenth century happened amid civil disorders that, in any other city, would have made long-term investment unthinkable. The struggle against Napoleon produced the first inklings of the modern Catalanist tradition. The tumults and bombardments of 1842–3 were followed by the flowering of the *Renaixença*. The bloodshed of 1854 was followed by the building of the Eixample. In the same period, the challenge of the steamship age was met by the construction of new artificial ports. The spirit shown by the merchants who had begun the first port in the fifteenth century was renewed in the manufacturers of the nineteenth who created a metallurgical industry out of nothing. After 1909 the song of Maragall's 'Oda Nova' and the spires of Gaudí's Sagrada Familia rose in defiance of the flames of the Tragic Week. The extinction of Catalan institutions in 1924 did nothing to interrupt a brilliant era in the arts or a dynamic period of growth for the city. After the double disaster of the Civil War – the revolution in 1936, the last 'Castilian' conquest in 1939 – growth was renewed at a faster rate than ever.

Today, Barcelona is a 'city of prodigies' – the glittering, even gaudy, marvels of modern arts with which the city is studded. Modern god-makers, her poets and artists, have begun work on an apotheosis to rival that of Hercules; the PR men of the 1992 Olympiad, who will bring Olympus to Montjuic, have stepped in with their meretricious help. Yet despite the admirable resilience with which the Barcelonese, for more than a thousand years, have made an adventure of every adversity and wrung an achievement from every disaster, none of the city's historic ambitions has been fulfilled.

There are few 'second cities' in the world to rival her, by any standard of judgement; but to be the best of the second is a frustrating fate and within Spain, in recent years, Madrid has drawn far ahead, especially in the one field – 'high' culture or 'the arts' – in which Barcelona has hitherto always excelled. The government of Catalonia has returned to Barcelona since the restoration of Catalan autonomy in 1978; but Catalan statehood is still truncated and, though the Catalans have abundantly proven their ineradicable durability as a distinct ethnicity, the precise nature of Catalonia's future as a political entity, within Spain and within Europe, remains a matter of debate. The period of mass immigration, which threatened to swamp Barcelona's Catalan identity, may be at an end, with the menace apparently contained, but the marginal parts of the Catalan world – in Valencia, the Balearic Islands and southern France – have regional interests, cultural identities and political directions of their own and seem determined, for the foreseeable future, to resist Barcelonese aspirations to any sort of pan-Catalan capitality. Meanwhile, the 'Europeanisation' of Spain – or rather, the accumulation of evidence of Spain's fully European identity – has deprived the Barcelonese of one of their favourite roles, as the most 'European' of Iberian cities. The year of the Olympiad will also bring the inauguration of the single European market, for which Barcelona's history of prosperity under protection-ism may seem a poor preparation; but to judge from Barcelona's record, a new 'era of difficulties' in the offing only betokens a new era of triumphs ahead. Today, when Barcelona is the heart of the biggest conurbation on the western Mediterranean seaboard, the essential character detected by a visiting Castilian humanist in the small and struggling city of 500 years ago can be seen to be amply confirmed: 'Oh, God of grace, I now behold a city, securely placed, very plenteous in the midst of a poor land. And I see her citizens, triumphant despite their dearth of natural resources, and her people possessed of all worldly prosperity, thanks to their own efforts alone.'[31]

NOTES

Chapter I

1. The image of the dog that failed to bark has been applied to seventeenth-century Barcelona by J. Amelang, 'Municipal Autonomy in Early Modern Spain: Two Recent Studies of Barcelona', *Actes del Primer Congrés d'Història Moderna de Catalunya* (Barcelona, 1985), pp. 23–4.

2. J.H. Elliott, *The Revolt of the Catalans* (Cambridge, 1963), p. 164.

3. A. de Capmany, *Memorias históricas sobre la marina, comercio y artes de la antigua ciudad de Barcelona*, two vols in three (Barcelona, 1961–3).

4. *Gesta Comitum Barcinonensium*, ed. L. Barrau Bihigo and J. Massó Torrents (Barcelona, 1961–3), p. 4.

5. F. Udina Martorell, 'En torno a la leyenda de las "Barras catalanas"', *Hispania*, ix (1949), pp. 531–65.

6. R. Collins, 'Charles the Bald and Wilfred the Hairy', in M. Gibson and J. Nelson (eds), *Charles the Bald* (Oxford, 1981), pp. 167–89. On the context of the legend see also P. Freedman, 'Cowardice, Heroism and the Legendary Origins of Catalonia', *Past and Present*, no. 121 (1988), pp. 3–28.

7. F. Soldevila, *Història de Catalunya*, i (Barcelona, 1934), 48–52; F. Valls Taberner, 'Estudi sobre els documents del comte Guifré I de Barcelona', *Obras selectas: estudios de historia medieval*, iv (Barcelona, 1961), 47–70.

8. Ausonius, *Epistulae*, ed. Peiper, Ep. 27, lines 68–9. I follow the interpretation of F.P. Verrié, 'Les activitats mercantils en el món antic' in F.P. Verrié *et al.*, eds, *El comerç en el marc econòmic de Catalunya* (Barcelona, 1983), p. 23, in preference to F. Giunta, *Punica Barcino* (Barcelona, 1988), pp. 9–13.

9. J.-O. Granados García, 'Los primeros pobladores del Pla' in *El Pla de Barcelona i la seva història: Actes del Primer Congrés d'Història del Pla de Barcelona* (Barcelona, 1984), pp. 67–82.

10. A. Duran i Sanpere, *Barcelona i la seva història*, i (Barcelona, 1973), pp. 97–119; similar conclusions have been drawn from the more modest Roman graves under Santa Maria del Mar by M. Ribas Bertrán, 'Descubrimiento de una necrópolis romana', in *Estudios*

dedicados a Agustín Durán y Sanpere, ii (Barcelona, 1968), pp. 5–32.

11. J.-O. Granados García, 'Notas d'arqueología romana de Barcelona', *Fonaments*, i (1979), pp. 107–10; F.P. Verrié et al., 'Excavaciones en la basilica paleocristiana de Barcelona', *Actas de la Reunión Nacional de Arqueología Paleocristiana* (Vitoria, 1987), pp. 7–38.

12. S. Mariner Bigorra, *Inscripciones romanas de Barcelona* (Barcelona, 1972), pp. 37–43; I. Roda de Mayer, 'La inscripción de Lucio Cecilio Optato', *Quaderns d'arqueologia i història de la cuitat*, xviii (1980), pp. 5–50.

13. *Obras de San Paciano*, ed. L. Rubio Fernández (Barcelona, 1958), pp. 7, 74; Duran i Sanpere, *op. cit.*, i, 120–3. Doubts of the existence of such classes of penitents are raised by E. Schwartz, 'Busstufen und Katechumenatclasse', *Schriften der Wissenschaftlichen Geselschaft in Strasburg*, vii (1911), cited by T.F. Matthews, *The Early Churches of Constantinople: Architecture and Liturgy* (Philadelphia, 1971), p. 126.

14. *Ibid.*, pp. 123–7; Ausonius Ep. 23; J.P. Migne, ed. *Patrologiae Latinae . . . cursus completus*, xix (Paris, 1846), col. 934; Paulinus, *Carmina*, ed. G. de Haitel (Prague, 1894), 10, line 231; Ausonius, *Carmina*, ed. A. Holder (1897), p. 163 (*Ora maritima*, line 520).

15. Jordanes, *De Getarum sive Gothorum Origine*, ch. 31. *Patrologia Latina*, lxix (Paris, 1869), col. 1274.

16. *Historiae adversos Paganos*, ed. C. Zaugemeister (Vienna, 1882), p. 561.

17. *Historia Gothorum*, ch. 120. *Patrologia Latina*, lxxxiii (Paris, 1862), cols. 1064, 1069.

18. J.-O. Granados García, *La transformación de la colonia Barcino* (Barcelona, reproduced photographically by the Servei d'Activitate Arqueològiques, n.d.), p. 357.

19. R. Collins, *The Arab Conquest of Spain* (Oxford, 1989), p. 274.

20. J.L. Shideler, *A Medieval Catalan Noble Family: the Montcadas* (Berkeley, 1983), pp. 50, 85.

21. P. Bonnassie, *La Catalogne du milieu du Xe siècle à la fin de l'XIe siècle*, two vols (Toulouse, 1975–6), i, 711–13.

22. Shideler, *op. cit.*, pp. 66–7; J. Sobrequés i Callicó, 'La cuitat mediterrànea de l'edat mitjana a la revolució industrial: el cas de Barcelona' in C. Miralles *et al.*, *Les cuitats catalanes en el marc de la Mediterrànea* (Barcelona, 1984), pp. 69–79; G. Feliu, 'L'evolució de les cuitats catalanes a l'alta edat mitjana' in M. Tarradell *et al.*, *Evolució urbana de Catalunya* (Barcelona, 1985), pp. 21–35; N. d'Olwer, 'Gerbert y la cultura catalana del s. X', *Estudis universitaris catalans*, iv (1910) 332–58.

23. For contemporary examples which justify this language see F. Udina Martorell, *El archivo condal de Barcelona en los siglos IX-X* (Barcelona, 1951); P. Català i Roca, *El día que Barcelona va morir* (Barcelona, 1989), pp. 32–3.

24. J. Mas, *Notes històriques del bisbat de Barcelona* (Barcelona, 1921), pp. 185–8; G. Feliu, 'Al-Mansur, Barcelona i Sant Cugat', *Acta historica et archaeolgica medievalia*, iii (1982), p. 53; F. Fita, 'Destrucción de Barcelona por Almanzor', *Boletín de la Real Academia de la Historia*, vii (1885), pp. 189–92.

25. J. Rius Serra, ed. *Cartulario de Sant Cugat*, three vols (Barcelona, 1946–7) iii, p. 449.

26. Bonnassie, *op. cit.*, ii, pp.833–6.

27. *Ibid.*, pp. 833, 849, 851–3, 855–6.

28. P. Bonnassie, 'Une famille de la campagne barcelonaise et les activités économiques aux alentours de l'an mil', *Annales du midi*, lxxvi (1964), 261–97; J. Ruiz Doménec, 'El origen del capital comercial en Barcelona', *Miscellanea Barcinonensia*, xii (1972), pp. 55–58.

29. *Cartulario de Sant Cugat*, iii, p. 76.

30. P. Català i Roca, *Extinció del vescomtat de Barcelona* (Barcelona, 1974), p. 12.

31. See J.M. Font Rius, *Jaume I i la municipalitat de Barcelona* (Barcelona, 1977); *Colección de documentos inéditos del Archivo de la Corona de Aragón* viii, pp. 120, 143; xiiii, pp. 4–6, 8–17.

32. Institut Municipal d'Història, Barcelona. Conseil de Cent: Fogatges XIX-5, f. 1.

33. See below, p. 70.

34. C. Batlle, *El municipio de Barcelona en el siglo XIV* (Madrid, 1977), pp. 206–7; J. Mutgé Vives, *La ciudad de Barcelona durante el reinado de Alfonso el Benigno* (Madrid, 1987), pp. 223–8.

35. C. Batlle, 'Aportació a la història d'una revolta popular', *Estudis d'història medieval*, ii (1970) 21–9.

36. J.N. Hillgarth and G. Silano, eds, *The Register Notule Communium 14 of the Diocese of Barcelona* (Toronto, 1983), p.210.

37. Mutgé, *op. cit.*, pp. 186–8.

38. *Notule Communium*, pp. 12, 31, 41, 87.

39. C. Batlle, 'El govern municipal a la baixa edat mitjana' in I. Roda et al., *El govern de les cuitats catalanes* (Barcelona, 1985), p. 72.

40. *Ibid.*, pp.74–7.

41. P. Molas Ribalta, *Los gremios barceloneses del siglo XVIII* (Madrid, 1970), pp. 48–9, 65.

42. *Dietari de la Deputació del General de Cathalunya*, ed. F. Udina Martorell *et al.*, two vols (Barcelona, 1974–77), i, p. 218.

43. Batlle, 'El govern municipal', p. 80.

44. J.M Torras i Ribe, 'El municipi català durant els s. XVI i XVII' in *El govern de les cuitats*, p. 88.

45. T.M. Vinyoles i Vidal, *La vida quotidiana a Barcelona vers 1400* (Barcelona, 1985), p. 32.

46. *Ibid.*, p. 119.

47. *Ibid.*, p. 81.

48. E.G. Bruniquer, *Ceremonial des magnífichs consellers y regiment de la cuitat de Barcelona*, ed. F. Carreras Candi and B. Gunyalous y Bou, five vols, (Barcelona, 1912), i. 19.

49. *Ibid.*, ii, pp. 69–100.

50. Vinyoles, *op. cit.*, p. 86.

51. P. Bonnassie, *La organización del trabajo en Barcelona a fines del siglo XV* (Barcelona, 1975), p. 57; Bruniquer, *op. cit.*, ii, pp. 70, 75.

52. Bonnassie, *La organización del trabajo*, p. 199.

53. J. Amelang, *Honoured Citizens of Barcelona* (Princeton, 1986), pp. 198–9.

Chapter II

1. J. Fabre, J.M Huertas, P. Bohigas, P. Encinas and P. Monés, *Monuments de Barcelona* (Barcelona, 1984), pp. 42–3.

2. A. Rumeu de Armas, 'La expedición mallorquina de 1366 a las Islas Canarias', *Anuario de estudios atlánticos*, xxvii (1981) pp. 15–23; F. Fernández-Armesto, *The Canary Islands after the Conquest* (Oxford, 1982), p. 156–8.

3. J.H. Elliott, *The Revolt of the Catalans* (Cambridge, 1963), p. 162; A. de Capmany y de Monpalau, *Memorias históricas sobre la marina, comercio y artes de la antigua ciudad de Barcelona*, two vols in three (Barcelona, 1961–3), i, 66–72; P. Vilar, *La Catalogne dans l'Espagne moderne*, three vols (Paris, 1962), iii, map 16. See below, p. 84–6.

4. 'Crònica del racional de la ciutat de Barcelona' (*Documents i estudis*, i, fasc. II), (Barcelona, 1921), pp. 117, 152.

5. R. Trías Fargas, ed., *Análisis económico del puerto de Barcelona* (Madrid, 1968), p. 50.

6. P. Banks, 'Montjuic, the Port and the City: a Reconstruction', in *El Pla de Barcelona i la seva història: actes del Primer Congrés d'Història del Pla de Barcelona* (Barcelona, 1984), pp. 113–28.

7. P. Bonnassie, *La Catalogne du milieu du Xe siècle à la fin du l'XIe siècle*, two vols (Toulouse, 1975–76), ii, pp. 841–2; *Liber Maiolichinus*, ed. C. Calisse (Rome, 1904).

8. J.H.Pryor, *Geography, Technology and War* (Cambridge, 1988), pp. 89–98.

9. *Colección de documentos inéditos del Archivo de la Corona de Aragón*, vi, p. 141, vii, p.122, xiiii, p.1.

10. F. Soldevila, ed., *Les quatre grans cròniques*, pp. 28, 33–4.

11. *Ibid.*, p. 577.

12. *Ibid.*, pp. 28–32; P. Bofarull y Moscaró, ed., *Colección de documentos inéditos del Archivo de la Corona de Aragón*, xi, (Barcelona, 1856) p. 4.

13. *Llibre dels feits*, p. 68.

14. J. Salva, 'Instituciones políticas y sociales', *Historia de Mallorca*, ed. J. Mascaró Pasarius, ii (Palma, 1970), pp. 387–8.

15. *Les quatre grans cròniques*, pp. 32–4.

16. F. Sevillano Colom, 'Mercáderes y navegantes mallorquines', *Historia de Mallorca*, iv (1971) pp. 467–70.

17. *Ibid.*, pp. 450–1; F. Sevillano Colom, 'Artesanía textil de la lana mallorquina', *Boletín de la Sociedad Arqueológica Luliana*, xxxiii (1970–71), pp. 157–78.

18. *Les quatres grans cròniques*, pp. 56, 673–4.

19. A. Santamaría Arandez, 'Mallorca en el siglo XIV', *Anuario de estudios medievales*, vii (1970), 165–238; B. Font Obrador, 'Mallorca en 1349', *Boletín de la Sociedad Arqueológica Luliana*, xxxiii (1964), pp. 245–60.

20. V. Salavert y Roca, *Cerdeña y la expansión mediterránea de la Corona de Aragón*, two vols (Madrid, 1956), i. pp. 126–7.

21. Ibn Jubair, *The Travels of Ibn Jubayr*, trans. R.J.C. Broadhurst (London, 1952), p. 336.

22. V. D'Alessandro, *Politica e società nella Sicilia aragonese* (Palermo, 1963), pp. 255–80.

23. J. Martínez Ferrando, *Tres siglos de disposiciones reales sobre Menorca* (Ciudadela, 1958), pp. 3, 10, 28.

24. J. Martínez Ferrando, *Jaume II de Aragón*, two vols (Barcelona, 1948), i, p. 132; *El fils de Jaume II*, (Barcelona, 1950), pp. 99–100.

25. Petrarch, *Africa*, VI, lines 31–4.

26. A.M. Cabañas, 'La repoblación de Sásser bajo Alfonso el Benigno', *VI Congreso de historia de la Corona de Aragón* (Madrid, 1959), pp. 539–49.

27. A. Boscolo, 'La feudalitá in Sicilia, in Sardegna e nel Napoletano nel basso medievo', *Saggi di storia mediterranea tra il XIV e il XVI secolo* (Rome, 1981), pp. 121, 126; *Documenti sull'economia e sulla società in Sardegna all'epoca di Alfonso il benigno* (Padua, 1973), p. 2; B.R. Motzo, 'Un progetto catalano per la conquesta definitiva della Sardegna', *Studi storici in onore di F. Loddo Canepa*, two vols (Florence, 1959), i, 165–80; J. Martinéz Ferrando, 'El exceso de población sarda en Menorca a fines del siglo XIV', *XV Congreso de historia de la Corona de Aragón*, pp. 319–31.

28. M. Mitja, 'Barcelona y el problema sardo en el siglo XIV', *VI Congreso de historia de la Corona de Aragón*, pp. 449–50; J. Mutgé Vives, *La ciudad de Barcelona durante el reinado de Alfonso el benigno* (Madrid, 1987), pp. 45, 315, 320–1.

29. P. Scanu, *Vincles entre Tarragona i l'Alguer* (Barcelona, 1979).

30. *Les quatre grans cròniques* (Barcelona, 1971), pp. 466–77, 704–15.

31. L. Mas Latrie, *Traités de paix et de commerce et documents divers concernant les relations des chrétiens avec les arabes de l'Afrique septentrionale au moyen âge*, three vols (Paris, 1868–72), i, p. 40; ii, pp. 108, 367.

32. *Ibid.*, ii, pp. 280–325; M.A. Alarcón y Santón and R. García de Linares, *Los documentos árabes diplomáticos del Archivo de la Corona de Aragón* (Madrid, 1940), pp. 289, 318, 397.

33. A. Huici Miranda and M.D. Cabanes Pecourt, *Documentos de Jaime I* (Valencia, 1976 – in progress), i, p. 187; M. Gual Camarena, *Vocabulario del comercio medieval* (Tarragona, 1968), p. 67; C.E. Dufourcq, *L'Espagne catalane et le Maghrib aux XIIIe et XIVe siècles* (Paris, 1966), pp. 68–9, 102.

34. D. Romano, *Los funcionarios judíos de Pedro el Grande de Aragón* (Barcelona, 1970), pp. 13–18, 26–30, 34, 39–41; Dufourcq, *op. cit.*, p. 142.

35. M. Gual Camarena, *El primer manual hispánico de mercadería* (Barcelona, 1981).

36. J.M. Madurell Marimón and A. García Sanz, *Comandas comerciales barcelonesas de la baja edad media* (Barcelona, 1973), pp. 152–208; J. Botet i Sisó, 'Notas sobre la encunyació de monedes aràbigues pêl rey Don Jaume', *Congrés d'història de la Corona d'Aragón, ii (1913), pp. 944–63.*

37. Dufourcq, *op. cit.*, p. 531; F. Udina Martorell, 'Un aspecto de la economía sarda en el siglo XIV: la acuñacion de moneda', *VI Congreso de historia de la Corona de Aragón*, pp. 647–61; V. Magalhães Godinho, *Os descobrimentos e a economia mundial*, four vols (Lisbon, 1981–4), i, p. 104.

38. J.N Hillgarth, *The Spanish Kingdoms*, two vols (Oxford, 1976–81), i. 263; A. Rubió i Lluch, *Documents per l'història de cultura catalana mig-eval* (Barcelona, 1908), i. 52–4; M. Menéndez y Pelayo, *Historia de los heterodoxos españoles*, vii (Madrid, 1948), 232ff; J. Carreras Artau, *Relaciones de Arnau de Vilanova con los reyes de la casa de Aragón* (Barcelona, 1955), pp. 43–50; P. Martí de Barcelona, 'Regesta de documents arnaldians coneguts', *Estudis Franciscans*, xlvii (1935), e.g. docs 28, 39, 58.

39. Mutgé, *op. cit.*, pp. 112–13.

40. *Les quatre grans cròniques*, p. 487.

41. *Comandas comerciales*, pp. 25–8, 199–204, 229, 238, 262, 294–5; J. Plana i Borràs, 'Els Benet, una familia de mercaders barcelonins', *La societat barcelonina a la baixaedat mitjana*, ed. C. Batlle (Barcelona, 1983), pp. 53–65; N. d'Olwer, *La expansió de Catalunya en la Mediterrània oriental* (Barcelona, 1926), p. 39; J.M. Madurell Marimón, 'Les activitats diplomàtiques i mercantils de Pere de Mitjalva', *VII Congreso de historia de la Corona de Aragón* (Valencia, 1967).

42. *Comandas comerciales*, pp. 29, 344.

43. *Regiment de la cosa publica*, ed. D. de Molins de Rei (1927), p. 168.

44. M. Riu, 'El redreç del comerç català a l'alta edat mitjana', in F.P. Verrié *et al.*, *El comerç en el marc econòmic de Catalunya* (Barcelona, 1983), pp. 39–40; C. Batlle, 'La mentalitat i les formes de vida dels mercaders catalans medievals', *ibid.*, p. 87.

45. T.M. Vinyoles i Vidal, 'El presupost familiar d'una mestresa de casa barcelonina per l'any 1401', in *La societat barcelonina*, pp. 105, 190; B. Metge, *Lo somni*, ed. A. Vilanova Andreu (Barcelona, 1946), pp. 80, 121; Eiximenis, *Terç de crestià*, ed. P. Martí de Barcelona and N. d'Ordal, three vols (Barcelona, 1929–32), i. p. 29.

46. J.M. Casas Homs, 'L'heretatge d'un mercader barceloní', *Cuadernos de historia económica de Cataluña*, iii (1970), pp. 9–112, especially pp. 18–19, 49, 57, 59; T.M. Vinyoles i Vidal, *La vida quotidiana a Barcelona vers 1400* (Barcelona, 1985), pp. 62–5.

47. J. Sobrequés i Callicó, 'La fortuna d'un mercader de Barcelona al siglo XV', *Cuadernos de historia económica de Cataluña*, i (1969), p. 163.

48. *Doctrina pueril*, ed. G. Schib (Barcelona, 1972), p. 187.

49. A. Sayous, *Les métodes commerciales* (Barcelona, 1982), pp. 146–7.

50. A. Garcia i Espuche and M. Guàrdia i Bassols, *Espai i societat a la Barcelona pre-industrial* (Barcelona, 1986), pp. 19–20; G. Feliu i

Montfort, 'La població del territori de Barcelona en el s. XV', *Estudis d'Història medieval*, i (1969) pp. 61–73.

51. Mutgé, *op. cit.*, pp. 153, 243, 273.

52. F. Carreras Candi, *La ciutat de Barcelona*, two vols (Barcelona, 1925), pp. 374–5; J.F. Cabestany i Fort, 'Una primera reforma urbana a Barcelona', *Cuadernos de arqueología e historia de la ciudad*, xvii (1977), pp. 141–54.

53. A. Duran i Sanpere, *Barcelona i la seva història*, i (Barcelona, 1973), p. 157.

54. J. Ferran, F. Viñas y Cusí and R. Grau, *Datos históricos sobre las epidemias de peste ocurridas en Barcelona* (Barcelona, 1907), pp. 371–82.

55. P. Bonnassie, *La organización del trabajo en Barcelona a fines del s. XV* (Barcelona, 1975), p. 20.

56. F. Guicciardini, *Viaje a España*, ed. J.M. Alonso Garno (Valencia, 1952) p. 41.

57. F. Fernández-Armesto, *The Canary Islands after the Conquest* (Oxford, 1982), pp. 29, 33–6, 81–2.

58. J.M. Delgado, 'Les activitats mercantils a l'època moderna', in F.P. Verrié *et al.*, *El comerç en el marc*, p. 107.

59. P. Vilar, *La Catalogne dans l'Espagne moderne*, three vols (Paris, 1962), iii, pp. 445–52.

60. *Ibid.*, iii, pp. 2, 4; E, Martín Corrales, 'El comercio de Barcelona con el mediterráneo musulmán, 1792–1808', *Pedralbes*, vi (1986), pp. 253–6; E. McDonald, 'Highlights in the History of the US Post at Barcelona', *Cuadernos de historia económica de Cataluña*, ii (1970), p. 25.

61. J. Carrera Pujal, *La economía de Cataluña en el s. XIX*, iii, pp. 115–16; J. Sala, 'Textos del *Diario de Barcelona* sobre la inauguración del Canal de Suez', *Cuadernos de historia económica de Cataluña*, ii (1970), pp. 173–81.

62. J. Carrera Pujal, *Historia política y económica de Cataluña*, four vols (Barcelona, 1946–7), ii, pp. 334–61; Trías Fargas, ed., *op. cit.*, pp.41–8.

Chapter III

1. *La Vanguardia*, 26 April 1881.

2. J.J. Trías Vejarano, *Almirall y los orígenes del catalanismo* (Madrid, 1975), pp. 156, 427–30.

3. A. de Capmany i de Monpalau, *Memorias históricas sobre la*

marina, comercio y artes de la antigua ciudad de Barcelona, two vols in three (Barcelona, 1961–3), i, p. 192.

4. J.N. Hillgarth, *The Spanish Kingdoms*, two vols (Oxford, 1976–81), ii. p. 271.

5. J. Sorequés Callicó, 'Aspectos económicos de la vida en Barcelona durante la guerra civil de 1462–72', *Cuadernos de historia económica de Cataluña*, ii (1970), pp. 215–86.

6. *Dietari de la Diputació del General de Cathalunya*, ed. F. Udina Martorell *et al.*, two vols (Barcelona, 1974–7), i, p. 250; ii, p. 119.

7. J. Sobrequés Callicó, 'La cuitat mediterrània de l'Edat mitjana a la revolució industrial: el cas de Barcelona', in C. Miralles *et al.*, *Les cuitats en el marc de la Mediterrània* (Barcelona, 1984), p. 89; J. Iglésies, 'El poblament de Catalunya durant els segles XIV i XV', *VI Congreso de historia de la Corona de Aragón* (Madrid, 1959), p. 270.

8. F. Soldevila, *Història de Catalunya*, ii (Barcelona, 1935), pp. 136, 156.

9. Soldevila, *op. cit.*, ii, pp. 145, 149–50.

10. J. Vicèns Vives, *Ferran II i la cuitat de Barcelona*, three vols (Barcelona, 1936).

11. C. Batlle, 'Una familia barcelonesa; les Deztorrent', *Anuario de estudios medievales*, i (1964), pp. 471–88; 'La oligarquía de Barcelona a fines del s. XV: el Partido de Deztorrent', *Acta historica et archaeologica medievalia*, vii-viii (1987), pp. 321–35.

12. M.R. Bultó Blajot, *Antologia de elegios y descripciones de Barcelona* (*Documentos y estudios*, xix) (Barcelona, 1968) collects these and other texts.

13. *Journal of a Younger Brother*, ed. S. Jennett (London, 1963), pp. 199–225.

14. A. Duran i Sanpere, *Barcelona i la seva història*, two vols (Barcelona, 1973), i, pp. 230, 296.

15. J. Amelang, *Honoured Citizens of Barcelona* (Princeton, 1986), pp. 112, 162, 175.

16. *Ibid.*, pp. 64, 77–80; J.H Elliott, *The Revolt of the Catalans* (Cambridge, 1963), p. 68.

17. Duran, *op. cit.*, ii, pp. 172–239.

18. Elliott, *op. cit.*, pp. 111–12.

19. M. Ribot i Iglesias, 'L'Aristocràcia barcelonina al regnat de Carles II', *Pedralbes*, v (1985), pp. 237–45; J.M Torras Ribé, *Els municipis catalans d'antic règim* (Barcelona, 1983), pp. 13–14

20. Elliott, *op. cit.*, p. 278.

21. *Ibid.*, epigraph, p. ii.

22. Elliott, *The Revolt*, p. 446.

23. *Ibid.*, pp. 460–1.

24. *Ibid.*, p. 498.

25. *Ibid.*, p. 504.

26. Duran, *op. cit.*, ii, p. 641.

27. Soldevila, *op. cit.*, ii, 313.

28. J. Sanabre, *La acción de Francia en Cataluña* (Barcelona, 1956), pp. 178, 183, 197, 281.

29. *Ibid.*, pp. 175, 183, 281, 330.

30. E. Giralt, 'La colonia mercantil francesa de Barcelona', *Estudios de historia moderna*, vi (1956), pp. 222–6.

31. Soldevila, *op. cit.*, ii, p. 333; Duran, *op. cit.*, ii, p. 644.

32. J. Amelang, 'Municipal Autonomy in Early Modern Spain', *Actes del primer Congrés d'història moderna de Catalunya* (Barcelona, 1985), p. 21; *Honoured Citizens of Barcelona*, pp. 34–41.

33. 'De La Neuville to Louis XVI, 26th June 1713'; S. Sanpere i Miguel, *Fin de la nación catalana* (Barcelona, 1905), p. 183.

34. *Ibid.*, p. 521.

35. V. Bacallar y Sanna, Marqués de San Felipe, *Comentarios*, ed. C. Seco Serrano (Madrid, 1957), p. 251.

36. Sanpere y Miguel, *op. cit.*, p. 622.

37. *Ibid.*, p. 629.

38. *Ibid.*, p. 671.

39. *Ibid.*, pp. 554–5; Soldevila, *op. cit.*, ii, pp. 19–20; J. Carrera Pujal, *La Lonja del Mar y los cuerpos de comercio de Barcelona* (Barcelona, 1953), p. 78.

40. Duran, *op. cit.*, i, p. 586.

41. A. Garcia i Espuche and M. Guàrdia i Bassols, *Espai i societat a la Barcelona pre-industrial* (Barcelona, 1986), pp. 68–9; R. Grau and M. López Guallar, v (1985), pp. 59–79; M. Tatjer Mir, *La Barceloneta del siglo XVIII al Plan de Ribera* (Barcelona, 1955), pp. 5–30.

42. P. Molas Ribalta, *Los gremios barcelonenses del s. XVIII* (Madrid, 1970), pp. 558–77; J. Carrera Pujal, *Historia política y económica de Cataluña*, four vols (Barcelona, 1946–7), iii, pp. 2–3.

43. F.J. Vicente Algueró, 'El motín contra Squillace en Cataluña', *Pedralbes*, vii (1987), p. 194; Molas, *op. cit.*, pp. 243–4; Amelang, *Honoured Citizens*, pp. 200–7.

44. Capmany, *op. cit.*, i. p. 467; Carrera, *Historia política*, ii, p. 240; Molas, op. cit., pp. 49–50.

45. *Ibid.*, pp. 127, 274.

46. Carrera, *Historia política*, ii, pp. 239, 245.

47. *Ibid.*, iii, pp. 47–8; Molas, *op. cit.*, pp. 311–12.

48. *Ibid.*, p. 126.

49. *Ibid.*, pp. 89–90.

50. *Ibid.*, pp. 18, 83, 122–4, 392, 408; Carrera, *Historia política*, iv, p. 74.

51. *Disertación histórico-político-legal por los colegios y gremios de la ciudad de Barcelona.*

52. Molas, *op. cit.*, pp. 108–9.

53. *Mémoires de Du Plessis-Besançon*, ed. Comte Horric de Beaucaire (Paris, 1892), pp. 192–3; Sanpere y Miquel, *op. cit.*, p. 671.

54. Trías Vejarano, *op. cit.*, p. 57.

55. *Guía satírica de Barcelona* (Barcelona, 1854), p. 10; J. Benet and C. Martí, *Barcelona a mitjan segle XIX*, two vols (Barcelona, 1976), i, p. 64.

56. Carrera, *Historia política*, i, 357.

57. F. Torrella Niubó, *El moderno resurgir textil de Barcelona* (Barcelona, 1961), p. 53; Carrera, *Historia política*, ii, p. 224; Molas, *op. cit.*, p. 349.

58. Carrera, *Historia política*, iv, pp. 77, 81, 138–41.

59. *Ibid.*, iii, p. 79; iv, p. 98; *Nouveau voyage d'Espagne fait en 1778 et 1779* i, 37–9; A. Ponz, *Viage de España*, xiv (Madrid, 1788), p. 88; J. Townsend, *A Journey through Spain*, i, p. 138.

60. Carrera, *Historia política*, iv, p. 99; P. Voltes Bou, *Estado estadística de la coyuntura económica barcelonesa durante el reinado de Carlos III* (*Documentos y estudios*, iv) (Barcelona, 1976), pp. 5–8; Garcia Espuche and Guàrdia Bassols, *op. cit.*, p. 61.

61. Carrera, *Lonja del mar*, p. 83; E. Moreu-Rey, *Revolució a Barcelona el 1789* (Barcelona, 1967), p. 76.

62. *Sucesos de Barcelona*, ed. J.M. Ollé Romeu (Barcelona, 1981), pp. 82, 100; Carrera, *La economía*, iii, pp. 36–9, 46.

63. *Sucesos de Barcelona*, pp. 23, 52, 67–77, 147.

64. *Ibid.*, pp. 170–1; Carrera, *La economía*, ii, 244–7.

65. *Sucesos de Barcelona*, pp. 148, 155.

66. Vilar, *La Catalogne*, ii, p. 327; Voltes Bou, *op. cit.*, p. 8; García Espuche and Guàrdia Bassols, *op. cit.*, p. 75.

67. Carrera, *Historia política*, iv, pp. 182–3; J. Vicèns Vives, *Los catalanes en el s. XIX* (Barcelona, 1986), p. 58.

68. *Ibid.*, p. 67.

69. B. de Riquer, *Història de la Diputació de Barcelona*, three vols (Barcelona, 1987), i, p. 25; *Sucesos de Barcelona*, p. 121; Benet and

Martí, *op. cit.*, i. p. 25; M. Izard, 'El comerç català contemporani', in Verrié *et al.*, *El comerç*, p. 136.

70. *La economía*, iii, pp. 61, 93–6, 127–8; M de la Roca, *Misterios de Barcelona* (Barcelona, 1844).

71. J. Nadal and E. Ribas, 'Una empresa cotonera catalana', *Reçerques*, iii (1974), pp. 47–52; M. Izard, *Revolució industrial i obrerisme* (Barcelona, 1970), p. 21.

72. Carrera, *La economía*, iii, p. 118; J.P. Ballot i Terres, *Gramàtica i apologia de la llengua Cathalana* (Barcelona, n.d.), unnumbered pp., pp. 264–5, quoted F. Soldevila, *Historia de Catalunya*, three vols (Barcelona, 1934–6), iii, p. 113.

73. Benet and Martí, *op. cit.*, i, p. 64.

74. Carrera, *Historia política*, i, p. 367; M. Andreu Vidiella, 'La financiación de la industria naval en Barcelona, 1745–60', *Pedralbes*, ix (1981), p. 269.

75. J.C. Maixé Altés, 'Aproximación a la colonia genovesa, un sector de la burguesía barcelonés en el s. XVIII', *Pedralbes*, vi (1986), pp. 237–40.

76. Carrera, *La economía*, iii, pp. 305–7, 313; J. Cortada, 'British Consular Reports on Economic and Political Developments in Cataluña, 1842–75', *Cuadernos de historia económica de Cataluña*, x (1973), pp. 181–2.

77. *La Corona de Aragón*, 7 February 1855; Benet and Martí, *op. cit.*, i, p. 67.

78. Carrera, *La economía*, ii, p. 68.

Chapter IV

1. B. Robert, *Legislatura de 1901: discursos del Dr Robert* (Barcelona, 1902), p. 55.

2. Carrera Pujal, *Historia política de Cataluña en el s. XIX*, seven vols (Barcelona, 1957–8) vi, p. 239.

3. S. Sanpere y Miquel, *Fin de la nación catalana* (Barcelona, 1905), p. 671.

4. *Person and God in a Spanish Valley* (New York, 1972), pp. 44–78.

5. M. Duran i Bas, *Discursos pronunciados en el Senado y en el Congreso en defensa del derecho catalán y de los demás forales* (Barcelona, 1883); J. Torras i Bagès, 'La tradició catalana', in *Obres completes* (Barcelona, 1948), pp. 242–6.

6. J. Bada, *Situació religiosa de Barcelona en el s. XVI* (Barcelona, 1970), pp. 45, 49, 55, 67–75, 124–6.

7. P. Vilar, *La Catalogne dans l'Espagne moderne*, three vols (Paris, 1962), i, pp. 132–3.

8. J. Pabón, *Cambó, 1876–1918*, three vols (Madrid, 1959–62), i, p. 99; J. Vicèns Vives, *Los catalanes en el siglo XIX* (Barcelona, 1986), pp. 259–65. I am indebted to J. Trías Vejarano, *Almirall y los orígenes del catalanismo* (Madrid, 1975), pp. 9–18.

9. Rovira i Virgili, *Historia de los movimientos nacionales*, p. 481.

10. Carrera, *Cataluña*, vi, p. 292.

11. E. Fernández Clemente and C. Forcadell, *Estudios de historia contemporánea de Aragón* (Saragossa, 1978), pp. 141–90.

12. Trías Vejarano, *op. cit.*, p. 31; M. García Venero, *Historia del nacionalismo catalán* (Madrid, 1970), Appendix.

13. J. Benet and C. Martí, *Barcelona a mitjan segle XIX*, two vols (Barcelona, 1976), i, p. 216.

14. J. Cortada, 'British Consular Reports on Economic and Political Developments in Cataluña, 1842–75', *Cuadernos de historia económica de Cataluña*, x (1973), pp. 156–63.

15. *Ibid.*, p. 163.

16. F. Monlau, *Abajo las murallas* (Barcelona, 1844), pp. 9, 12, 21.

17. A. Duran y Sanpere, *Barcelona i la seva història*, two vols (Barcelona, 1973), i, pp. 163–70; D. Mackay, *Modern Architecture in Barcelona* (London, 1985), pp. 3–5.

18. A. Saez Buesa, *La población de Barcelona en 1863 y 1960* (Madrid, 1968), pp. 62–3.

19. G.W. McDonagh, *Good Families of Barcelona* (Princeton, 1986), pp. 185–201.

20. R. Simó i Bada, *Memorial sobre los descuerdos entre dueños de taller y jornaleros* (Madrid, 1855); J. Salarich, *Higiene del tejedor* (Barcelona, 1857); I. Cerdà, *Teoría general de la urbanización* (Madrid, 1855), Appendix.

21. *Op. cit.*, p. 7; Benet and Martí, *op. cit.*, p. 133; C. Martí, *L'esglesia de Barcelona, 1850–7* (Barcelona, 1984), pp. 235–6.

22. M. Tatjer Mir, *La Barceloneta del siglo XVIII al Plan de Ribera* (Barcelona, 1985), pp. 39, 98; *Gaceta de Barcelona*, 12 May 1853; Cerdà, *Teoría general*, p. 487.

23. Benet and Martí, *op. cit.*, i, pp. 175, 181.

24. *Ibid.*, i, p. 349.

25. *Ibid.*, i, p. 353–7.

26. *Ibid.*, i, pp. 386, 424.

27. *Ibid.*, i, 451–2.

28. *Ibid.*, i, pp. 585, 617.

29. *Ibid.*, i, p. 336.

30. *Journal de Madrid*, 30 November 1855.

31. Martí, *L'esglesia*, pp. 301, 335.

32. N. Oller, *La Febre d'or* (Barcelona, 1927), p. 26.

33. McDonagh, *op. cit.*, pp. 71, 86, 113.

34. J. Rohrer, 'The Universal Exhibition of 1888', in *Homage to Barcelona* (Arts Council Exhibition Catalogue, London, 1985), p. 98.

35. B. de Riquer, *Història de la Diputació de Barcelona*, three vols (Barcelona, 1987), i, pp. 213, 224.

36. *Un senyor de Barcelona* (Barcelona, 1981), pp. 20–60.

37. J.C. Ullmann, *The Tragic Week* (Cambridge, Mass, 1968), pp. 283–97, 326–8 (with the table on p. 326 modified by data at pp. 182–275).

38. C. Soldevila, *Històries barcelonines* (Barcelona, 1970), p. 163.

39. Cf. C. Boyd, *Praetorian Politics in Liberal Spain* (Chapel Hill, 1979), pp. 121–35, who takes a different view, blaming the army for the failure of the settlement. See also J. Peirats, *La CNT en la revolución española*, i (Madrid, 1971), pp. 25–36.

40. F. Cambó, *Las dictaduras* (Barcelona, 1929), pp. 144–5, quoted S. Ben-Ami, *Fascism from Above* (Oxford, 1983), p. 34. The unpublished thesis of S.P. Carr, 'Industry and Society: Barcelona, 1914–23' (Oxford D.Phil, 1983), while emphasising the diversity of employers' views, amply documents resentment of the workers' movement.

41. Riquer, *op. cit.*, ii, p. 194.

Chapter V

1. *Obras*, eight vols (Madrid, 1948–50), v, pp. 972–3.

2. A. Castro, *La realidad histórica de España* (Mexico, 1954); J.L. Gómez-Martínez, *Américo Castro y el origen de los españoles* (Madrid, 1975).

3. C. Sánchez-Albornoz, *España: un enigma histórico*, two vols (Buenos Aires, 1956).

4. *Ibid.*, i, pp. 131–33; cf. Castro, *op. cit.*, pp. 135–41.

5. A. de Capmany y de Monpalau, *Memorias históricas del comercio, marina y artes de la antigua ciudad de Barcelona*, two vols in three (Barcelona, 1961–3), ii, pp. 918–21.

6. A. Duran i Sanpere, *Barcelona i la seva història*, two vols (Barcelona, 1973), i, 362; A. Ponz, *Viage de España*, xiv (Madrid, 1788), p. 14.

7. Duran, *op. cit.*, i, pp. 288–9.

8. Ibid., i, pp. 332–3.

9. *¡Cu-cut!*. 21 January 1909.

10. E. Jardí, *Història de Els Quatre Gats* (Barcelona, 1972).

11. C. and E. Mendoza, *Barcelona modernista* (Barcelona, 1989), p. 138.

12. *Ibid.*, p. 158.

13. O. Bohigas, *Barcelona entre el Pla Cerdà i el barraquisme* (Barcelona, 1963), pp. 105–21.

14. *Diario oficial de la Exposición Internacional de Barcelona*, 22 January 1929.

15. *Catálogo histórico y bibligráfico de la Exposición International de Barcelona*, two vols (Barcelona, 1931–3).

16. *La Vanguardia*, 14 September 1923.

17. *Ibid.*, 9 October 1929.

18. D. Mackay, *Modern Architecture in Barcelona* (London, 1985), p. 61.

19. *Actividad contemporánea*, iii (1933), no. 11.

20. G. Orwell, *Homage to Catalonia* (London, 1938), pp. 3–5.

21. J. Pujol Garcia, *Garbo* (London, 1981), p. 36; R. Fraser, *Blood of Spain* (London, 1988), p. 148.

22. Pujol, *op. cit.*, p. 41.

23. Fraser, *op. cit.*, p. 379.

24. Orwell, *op. cit.*, p. 199.

25. Fraser, *op. cit.*, p. 481.

26. *Ibid.*, p. 446.

27. C. Solé, *Los inmigrantes en la sociedad y la cultura catalanas* (Barcelona, 1982), p. 116; S. Balfour, *Dictatorship, Workers and the City* (Oxford, 1989), p. 193.

28. C. Esteve Fabregat, 'Les relacions interètniques: el cas de Barcelona', *Perspective social*, v (1975), pp. 41–68.

29. Balfour, *op. cit.*, p. 8.

30. *Ibid.*, pp. 214–15.

31. A. de Palecia, *Tratado de la perfección militar*, ed A.M. Fabié (Madrid, 1874), p. 41.

Bibliographical Essay

The purpose of these pages is to provide, in conjunction with the notes, a basic, selective bibliographical guide, and to supplement the notes by mentioning works which have influenced my interpretation or, in some cases, from which I have chosen to dissent at my peril. Works already cited in the notes are not mentioned again here, unless of exceptional importance.

General Histories

F. Carreras Candi, *La cuitat de Barcelona*, two vols, (Barcelona, n.d.), which forms vols iii and v of *Geografia general de Catalunya*, under the general editorship of the author of the other city volumes, has not been surpassed. A facsimile edition was published in Barcelona in 1980. A. Duran i Sanpere and J. Sobrequés i Callicó, *Història de Barcelona*, i (Barcelona, 1975) promised well, but the interesting text was smothered by dingy coffee-table *manqué* production and the project never got beyond vol. i. F. Udina Martorell and J.M. Garrut, *Barcelona: vint segles d'història* (Barcelona, 1963) makes a good introduction. A. Avelino Pi y Arinon, *Barcelona antigua y moderna*, two vols (Barcelona, 1854) is a valuable old civic history, extremely informative on buildings and the 'merits' of the city as perceived in the middle of the last century; industrial pride is well exemplified by these volumes. A. Bofarull, *Barcelona: su pasado, su presente y su porvenir* (Barcelona, 1878) is a competition piece, celebrating Barcelona's industrial future. P. Vila Dinarés and H. Cassassas Simó, *Barcelona i la seva rodalia al llarg dels temps* (Barcelona, 1974) is useful, particularly for the illustrations, although these are surpassed by the lavish presentation of L. Pericot, A, Castillo, J. Arnaud and J. Vicèns, *Barcelona a través de los tiempos* (Barcelona, 1944). A. Pérez-Bastardas and V. Scholz, *El govern de la ciutat de Barcelona, 1249–1986* (Barcelona, 1986) is a more or less random collection of facts, but its subject can be studied directly from the *Manual de novells ardits, vulgament apellat Dietari del antich consell barceloní*, nineteen vols (Barcelona, 1892–1922).

No general history of Spain does justice to Barcelona, although two short works by distinguished historians of Catalonia attempt to include the insights of a Catalan perspective: J. Vicèns Vives, *Aproximación a la historia de España* (Barcelona, 1960) and P. Vilar, *Historia de España* (Barcelona, 1978). The same virtues on a larger scale are exemplified by the austerely objective work of F. Soldevila, *Historia de España*, eight vols (Barcelona, 1961–4.)

Of general histories of Catalonia, that of F. Soldevila, *Història de Catalunya*, three vols (Barcelona, 1934–5), is an outstanding work by any standards, but only goes up to the eighteenth century. P. Vilar, ed., *Història de Catalunya*, seven vols (Barcelona – in progress) promises to be the most useful and comprehensive work of all.

Guides

Among many of ephemeral interest, the nineteenth century produced two guides of lasting merit: P. Piferrer and F. Pi i Margall, *Recuerdos y bellezas de España: Cataluña*, ii (Barcelona, n.d.) and V. Balaguer, *Las calles de Barcelona*, two vols (Barcelona, 1865), which is suitably romantic in tone, with splendid and spirited engravings. Alongside these, F. Carreras y Candi, *La via Layetana* (Barcelona, 1913) should be consulted, because it captures in scholarship and photographic record the medieval streets demolished during the urban 'reform' that cleft the old town with the new thoroughfare, the via Layetana.

Of conventional modern guides, apart from the *Guide Bleu* (N.M. Schveitzer, *Barcelone et la Catalogne*, Paris, 1959) the only one which seems to assume any genuine interest on the reader's part is A. Cirici, *Barcelona paso a paso* (Barcelona, 1975); but M. Fernández *et al.*, *Passat i present de Barcelona (1)* (Collecció Pau Vila, no. 4, Barcelona, 1983) is a brilliant selection of itineraries: apparently intended for schoolteachers to plan perambulations with their pupils, this is a fine work of scholarship which deserves a wider public. C. Soldevila, *Barcelona* (Madrid, 1944) is more of an evocation than a guide.

For any serious explorer in the city, *Catàleg del patrimoni arquitectònic historico-artistic de la ciutat de Barcelona* (Barcelona, 1987) is indispensible, while J. Ainaud, J. Guidol and F.P. Verrié, *Catalogo monumental de España: la ciudad de Barcelona* (Barcelona, 1947) remains useful. J. Fabre and J.M. Huertas, *Carrers de Barcelona: com han evolucionat els seus noms* (Barcelona, 1986) is a photographic essay, of much wider interest than the title implies. J.M. Espinàs, *Vint segles de carrers a Barcelona* (Barcelona, 1980) is a mine of critical reflections. J.E. Hernández *et al.*, *Guía de arquitectura de Barcelona* (Barcelona, 1973) makes a serviceable introduction. J. Fabre, *Barce-*

lona 1888–1988: la construcció d'una cuitat (Barcelona, 1989) is invaluable for the period it covers. J. Fabre *et al.*, *Monuments de Barcelona* (Barcelona, 1984) is a marvellous fund of quirky information on the statues, supplementing the guide to commemorative art in the city compiled in *Cuadernos de arqueología e historia de la cuidad*, viii (1970)-xviii (1980).

In the regrettable absence of a genuine companion to Barcelona, M.R. Bultó Blajot, *Antología de elegios y descripciones de Barcelona* (*Documentos y estudios*, xix) (Barcelona, 1968) collects an interesting if unsystematic array of texts.

Chapter I

I have been selectively influenced by the work of J. Ruiz Doménec, who has stressed the limitations of the early development of Barcelona and its agrarian basis. See especially 'The Urban Origins of Barcelona: Agricultural Revolution or Commercial Development?', *Speculum*, lii (1977), pp. 265–86 and 'La cuidad de Barcelona durante la edad media', *Quaderns d'arqueologia i història de la cuitat*, xviii (1980), 69–77.

The 'Frankishness' of early Catalonia is illuminatingly examined, with a point of view different from the one I have adopted, by G. Feliu Montfort, 'El condad de Barcelona de los siglos IX y X', *Cuadernos de historia económica de Cataluña*, vii (1972), pp. 10–32. See also the contribution by J. Sobrequés i Callicó to R. d'Abadal i de Vinyas, *Catalunya carolíngia*, i (Barcelona, 1986).

The archaeology of the development of late Roman and Visigothic Barcelona has benefited enormously in recent years from the critical scrutiny of J.-O. Granados García, to whom I owe a lot of my scepticism about what might be called the catastrophe theory of the early history of Barcelona. In addition to the works mentioned in the notes, I have been helped by *La transformación de la colonia Barcino* (Barcelona, n.d.), published by the Servei d'Activitats Arqueológiques of the Ajuntament de Barcelona.

P. Wolff, 'Quidam homo nomine Roberto negociatore', *Le Moyen Age*, no 69 (1963), pp. 129–39, argues that the benefactor whose gift led to the foundation of the Pia Almonya must have been a northerner, probably a Fleming, on grounds of the high value of the cloth he left for the canons to employ for the good of his soul. If true, this would considerably modify the picture I have tried to convey. On the development of the city in this period, I have not seen the obviously important unpublished thesis by P.J. Banks, 'The topography of the city of Barcelona and its urban context in eastern Catalonia from the third to the twelfth centuries' (University of Nottingham, Ph.D, 1982), since the librarians of Nottingham University, faced with a request for an inter-library loan, claimed to be unable to identify the work! To the material in print, P. Bonnassie, *La catalogue du milieu du Xe à la fin du XIe siècle*, two vols (Toulouse, 1975–6) is an excellent guide up to the early seventies. On al-Mansur's raid, the extensive bibliography is gathered by M. Rovira i Solà, 'Notes documentals sobre alguns efectes de la presa de Barcelona per al-Mansur', *Acta historica et archaeologica medievalia*, i (1980), pp. 31–54.

On the municipal institutions of 1258, see additionally J.M. Font Rius, 'La universidad de prohombres de Ribera de Barcelona y sus ordenanzas marítimas', *Estudios de derecho mercantil en homenaje al profesor A. Polo* (Madrid, 1981), pp. 199–240, and the same author's pamphlet, 'Jaume I y la municipalitat de Barcelona' (Barcelona, 1977). As my notes to this chapter imply, the study of late medieval government in Barcelona has been dominated by the work of C. Batlle, and particularly by her 'El municipio de Barcelona en el s. XIV', *Cuadernos de arqueología e historia de la ciudad*, iii (1962), *La crisis social y económica de Barcelona a mediados del siglo XV*, two vols (Barcelona, 1973) and *Barcelona a mediadios del s. XV* (Barcelona, 1976). Additionally, on the conflict of the Busca, her 'El sindicato del pueblo de Barcelona en 1454', *VI Congreso de Historia de la Corona de Aragón* (Madrid, 1969), pp. 291–303 is helpful. The most important collection of sources is A.M. Aragó, M. Costa and F. Udina Martorell, eds, *Privilegios reales concedidos a la ciudad de Barcelona* (Barcelona, 1971), which forms vol. xlii of the generally indispensible *Colección de documentos inéditos de la Corona de Aragón*, fifty vols (Barcelona, 1847–1982). Vols xlvi and xlix of the collection, *Dietari de la Deputació del General de Cathalunya*, ed. F. Udina Martorell *et al.*, (Barcelona, 1974–7) are a fascinating, charmingly illustrated contemporary record, compiled month by month and sometimes day by day, of events in the city and principality, at intervals, between 1411 and 1512. The four volumes of the Llibre Vert are available in photocopied form in the library of the Institut Municipal d'Història. As well as by works cited in the notes, my picture of the fourteenth century has been influenced by J.M. Casas Homs, *Llibre del batlle geial de Barcelona Berenguer Morey, 1375–8* (Barcelona, 1976).

A great survey of the minute transactions of daily life, mainly of the XIth and XIIth centuries, is assembled in J. Alturo i Perucho, ed.,

L'arxiu antic de Santa Anna de Barcelona del 942 al 1200, three vols (Barcelona, 1985), ii and iii. For the constitutions of medieval guilds, see *Colección de documentos inéditos del Archivo de la Corona de Aragón*, xl (1876), pp. 171–496.

Chapter II

On the port, see additionally J.F. Cabestany i Fort and J. Sobriqués i Callicó, 'La construcció del port de Barcelona al s. XV', *Cuadernos de historia económica de Cataluña*, vii, (1972), pp. 41–113, and J. Alemany, *El port de Barcelona* (Barcelona, 1984). My pages on Mediterranean expansion derive from my own *Before Columbus* (London, 1987), pp. 11–42, 126–48. On the Jews, the most useful account can be found in a series of articles by J.M. Madurell Marimón in *Sefarad*, xvi (1956), xxi (1961), xxv (1965) and xxvii (1967), in which the Jewish artisanate of Barcelona is studied trade by trade. See also J. Riera i Sans, *Disputa de Barcelona de 1263* (Barcelona, 1985) on the intellectual life of Barcelona's medieval Jews; the commercial activities of the community have not, as far as I know, attracted systematic study.

Further information on the economic effects of the Mediterranean empire can be found in J. Sobriqués i Callicó, 'Contribució económica del municipi de Barcelona a l'empresa de recuperació del regne de Mallorca', *VII Congreso de Historia de la Corona de Aragón*, ii (Valencia, 1973) and M.T. Ferrer i Mallol, 'Les relacions del rei Martí l'Humà amb la cuitat de Barcelona', *V Congreso de historia de la Corona de Aragón* (Barcelona, 1962), iii, pp. 161–70.

On the merchant ethos, the fundamental study is that of A. Sayous, in the revised Catalan version cited in the notes. As well as other cited works, knowledge of the subject has been greatly advanced by C. Carrère, 'La vie privée d'un marchand barcelonaise dans la première moitie du XVe siècle', *Anuario de estudios medievales*, iii (1966). Much further information is dispersed throughout the same author's *Barcelona centre économique à l'époque des difficultés* (Paris, 1967).

On the late medieval building boom, the collection of essays by A. Duran i Sanpere, *Per a l'història de l'art a Barcelona* (Barcelona, 1960) provides commentary on some important sources. On the glass of Santa Maria del Mar, see J. Ainaud *et al.*, *Els vitralls medievals de l'església de Santa Maria del Mar* (Corpus Vitrearum Medii Aevi, Espanya vi) (Barcelona, 1985). See also J.F. Cabestany, 'L'Urbanisme català a la baixa edat mitjana', *Cuadernos de historia económica de Cataluña*, xx (1979); J.M. Madurell i Marimón, 'Los contratos de obras en los protocolos notariales', in *Estudios históricos y documentos de los archivos de protocolos* (Barcelona, 1948); J. Mutgé i Vives, 'Algunes millores urbanístiques a Barcelona durant el regnat d'Alfons el Benigne', *El Pla de Barcelona i seva història* (Barcelona, 1984), pp. 161–72, and S. Claramunt, 'La formació del Raval de la Rambla', *ibid.*, pp. 183–203.

On the rediscovery of the Atlantic, see additionally C. Martínez Shaw, *Cataluña en la carrera de Indias* (Barcelona, 1981).

Chapter III

The dilemma of 'Difficulties or Decline?' is posed by C. Carrère, *Barcelona, centre économique à l'époque des difficultés*, (Paris, 1967). See also the works of C. Batlle, cited under Chapter I above. On the response in Barcelona to the settlement of Casp, see J. Sobrequés i Callicó, 'Agitació política a Barcelona devant l'interegne de 1410–12', *Miscellanea en honor de J.M. Madurell i Marimón*, iii (Barcelona, 1979). On this episode, and the political background of late medieval Catalan history generally, J.N. Hillgarth, *The Spanish Kingdoms*, two vols (Oxford, 1976–8) is the most authoritative work. On the reign of Ferdinand the Catholic see additionally, J.M. Madurell i Marimón, 'Legaciones barceloneses en la corte de los Reyes Católicos', *Hispania*, lxvii (1957), and on that of Charles V, 'Las cortes de 1519 en Barcelona', *Homenaje a J. Reglà Campistol*, i (Valencia, 1975), pp. 173–88. On the Renaissance in Barcelona, the first volume of Duran's *Barcelona i la seva historia* and his *Per a l'història de l'art* contain valuable nuggets. See also R. Casellas, 'Origens del renaixament barceloní', *Anuari del Institut d'estudis Catalans*, i (1907).

Important collections of sources on the civil war of 1462–72 are *Colección de documentos inéditos del Archivo de la Corona de Aragón*, xiv-xv (1858) xvi-xvii (1859), xviii-xix (1859), xx-xxi (1861) xxii-xxiii (1862), xxiv-xxv (1863), xxvi (1864); *Catálogo de la documentación de la cancillería regia de Pedro de Portugal*, two vols (Madrid, 1953–4).

My sketch of Olivares is based on J.H. Elliott, *The Count-Duke of Olivares* (Newhaven and London, 1976) and for the war of 1640–58 and its background I rely heavily on the works of Elliott and Sanabre cited in the notes. These works have not been modified by more recent research, though an interesting perspective, and some bibliographical updating, can be had from H. Kirchner i Granell and M. Jové i Campmajó, 'Capitaires i Rodamons: Barcelona 1600–40', *La historia i els joves historiadors Catalans* (Barcelona, 1986), pp. 265–81. A new edition of the *Dietari* of J. Pujades appeared in four volumes in Barcelona in 1975, edited by J.M. Casas Homs.

The study of Barcelona during the War of the Spanish Succession has been dominated by P. Voltes Bou, especially *Barcelona durante el gobierno del Archiduque Carlos de Austria*, two vols in three (*Documentos y estudios*, xi and xx) (Barcelona, 1963 and 1970). I have been influenced by A. Porta i Bergada, *La victoria catalana de 1705* (Barcelona, 1984), although wary of the work's partisan tone. Military aspects are very thoroughly covered in A.J. Hugill's posthumous *No Peace without Spain* (Oxford, forthcoming). An excellent sketch of Barcelona after the war is provided by J. Nadal and E. Giralt, 'Barcelona en 1717–18: un modelo de sociedad pre-industrial', *Homenaje a D. Ramón Carande* (Madrid, 1963).

On the Llotja, the work by J. Carrera Pujal cited in the notes can now be supplemented by J. Bassegoda i Nonell, *La Casa Llotja de Mar de Barcelona* (Barcelona, 1986), where a study of the building is amplified by useful illustrations. J. Carrera Pujal, *La Barcelona del segle XVIII* (Barcelona, 1951) is useful, albeit rather shallow, for the eighteenth-centruy background. On the effects of Bourbon policy, the arguments of M. Arranz, 'Demanda estatal i activitat econòmics a Catalunya sota els primers Borbons', *Actes del primer congrès d'història moderna de Catalunya* (Barcelona, 1984) are attractive. The economy of the city in the late eighteenth century has been studied closely by R. Grau (not all of whose contributions I have seen), especially in 'Las transformaciones urbanas de Barcelona', *Estudios geográficos*, xxxi (1970) and 'La metamorfosi de la cuitat emmurallada: Barcelona de Felip V a Ildefons Cerdà', *Cuadernos de historia económica de Cataluña*, xx (1979). On social conditions in eighteenth-century Barcelona, the work of P. López is particularly important, especially 'Vivienda y sociedad en la Barcelona del setecientos', *Estudis històrics i documents dels arxius de protocols*, viii (1980), and 'Les transformacions de l'habitat: la casa i la vivienda a Barcelona entre 1693 y el 1859', *Actes del primer congrès d'història moderna de Catalunya* (Barcelona, 1984).

To my account of the impediments to Barcelona's industrialisation, problems with water supply might perhaps be added. These are studied, over a long period, in P. Voltes Bou, *Historia del abastecimiento de agua de Barcelona* (Barcelona, 1967), which is particularly entertaining on the politics of water supply in the nineteenth century, and F. Udina Martorell, *L'aigua a Barcelona* (Barcelona, 1987).

Chapter IV

On Bartolomeu Robert, see E. Jardí, *El doctor Robert i el seu temps* (Barcelona, 1969) and on M. Duran, J. de Camps, *Duran i Bas* (Barcelona, 1961). For introductions to the works on cultural anthropology praised on p. 154, see J. Pitt-Rivers, *The People of the Sierra* (London, 1954), G. Brenan, *South from Granada* (London, 1957) and *The Face of Spain* (London, 1950), William A. Christian Jr, *Person and God in a Spanish Valley* (New York, 1972) and *Local Religion in Sixteenth-Century Spain* (Princeton, 1981), and J. Caro Baroja, *Estudios sobre la vida tradicional española* (Barcelona, 1968).

There are useful pages on Ribot Fontseré and Ferrer Subirana in J. Carrera Pujal, *Historia política de Cataluña en el s. XIX*, iii (Barcelona, 1957), pp. 360–407.

On devotional life in Barcelona, see additionally J. Madurell i Marimón, 'L'antiga devoció popular barcelonina a Sant Magí', *Boletín de la Real Sociedad Arqueológica Tarraconense*, lxvi, pp. 161–8. The most important collection of source material is in the rambling work by R. d'Amat i de Cortada called *Calaix de Sastre*; the relevant portions have been edited as *Costums i tradicions religiosos de Barcelona* by J.M. Martí i Bone, L. Bonet i Armengol and L. Juncosa i Ginesta (Barcelona, 1987).

The continuing debate on Catalanism has been interestingly explored by J.M. Colomer, *Espanyolisme i catalanisme: la idea de nació en el pensament polític català, 1939–79* (Barcelona, 1984). The 'Catalanism' of the Junta of 1808 is put in context by A. Moliner Prada, 'El concepto de patria y nación en la Junta Superior de Cataluña', *La història i els joves historiadors catalans* (Barcelona, 1986), pp. 337–44. The background to Catalanism, as to any subject of Spanish history in the nineteenth and twentieth ceturies, cannot be understood without taking account of R. Carr, *Spain, 1808–1975* (Oxford, 1982). J. Vicèns Vives, *Los catalanes en el siglo XIX* (Barcelona, 1986) had been the starting point for all studies of Catalan history in this period since its first appearance, in a Catalan edition, in 1958. J. Nadal, *El fracaso de la revolución industrial en España* (Barcelona, 1975) includes an influential study of the economic background. On Aribau and the origins of the *Renaixença*, see M. de Montoliu, *Aribau i la Catalunya de seu temps* (Barcelona, 1936). The Jocs Florals were published in

Jocs Florals de Barcelona, fifty-six vols (Barcelona, 1859–1935) For the political background of the *Renaixença*, I have relied fairly heavily on J. Carrera Pujal, *Historia política de Cataluña en el siglo XIX*, vii (Barcelona, 1958).

On the late nineteenth-century press, and the background of city politics generally, P. Voltes Bou, *La política de fin de siglo a través de la prensa barcelonesa de la época* (*Documentos y estudios* xxii) (Barcelona, 1978), is an inestimable guide, though the author has a rather strong penchant for *La Vanguardia*. Being unable to make a systematic study of the sources, I have relied heavily on the Bodleian Library's collection of Barcelonese ephemera of 1881–1909, shelved at 2479116 d. 602.

On the influence of the Icarus image, see J. Ventura Subirats, 'Icaria: vida, teorías y obra de Étienne Cabet, sus seguidores catalanes y experimentos communistas icarianos', *Cuadernos de historia económica de Cataluña*, vii (1972), pp. 140–251. Cemetaries are studied by C. Riera, *Els cementeris de Barcelona* (Barcelona, 1981). On the Stock Exchange see J. Fontana Lázaro and V. Villacampa, *La Bolsa de Barcelona, 1851–1930* (*Documentos y estudios*, viii) (Barcelona, 1971). P. Voltes Bou, 'Effects of the Spanish Government's Economic Policy in Barcelona between 1884 and 1914', *Journal of Economic History*, i (1972), pp. 128–34 and 'Aportación al analisis del proteccionismo catalan de 1880–90', *Cuadernos de historia económica de Cataluña*, i (1969), pp. 93–109 are good on the links between the material circumstances and political activities of the élite. J. Cassassa i Ymbert, *L'Ateneu barcelonès* (Barcelona, 1986) depicts an important part of the intellectual and social milieu.

For 'The City of Bombs', see E. Jardí i Casany, *La cuitat de les bombes: el terrorisme anarquista a Barcelona* (Barcelona, 1964). On the background to the Tragic Week see additionally J. Romero Maura, *La rosa de fuego* (Barcelona, 1975); On the *¡Cu-cut!* incident, the same author's *The Spanish Army and Catalonia* (Beverly Hills, 1976). On the tax and bank strikes of 1899, P. Voltes Bou, 'Las dos huelgas de contribuyentes en la Barcelona de fin del siglo', *Cuadernos de historia económica de Cataluña*, v (1971), pp. 43–66 is an economic historian's study.

Chapter V

D. Mackay's important *Modern Architecture in Barcelona* (London, 1985) is now available in an illustrated Catalan edition. See also, in addition to the other works cited in the notes, the Arts Council exhibition catalogue, *Homage to Barcelona* (London, 1986). On Do-mènech, see O. Bohigas *et al.*, Lluís Domènech i Muntaner (Barcelona, 1973). Gaudí has generated a bafflingly extensive bibliography, with which I can only claim a superficial acquaintance. The opinions I attribute to Gaudí are derived from the highly personal account of his pupil, J. Bergos, *Gaudí* (Barcelona, 1954) and the memorial miscel-lany, *Antoni Gaudí* (Barcelona, 1926). Among the other main books about him, some which can be recommended are G.R. Collins, *Antonio Gaudí* (Barcelona, 1961) for its scholarship and concision: J.Ll. Sert and J.J. Sweeney, *Antoni Gaudí* (Buenos Aires, 1970), which is mainly about the Sagrada Familia, for its brilliance, curiosity value and fine photographs, and I. de Solà-Morales, *Gaudí* (Barcelona, 1983), for its considered judgements. The impact of the Tragic Week is set in context by J. Benet, *Maragall i la Setmana Trajica* (Barcelona, 1963). E. Jardí i Casany, *Puig i Cadafalch* (Barcelona, 1975) gives a rounded portrait of the man. Puig's own works, particularly *L'Arquitectura romànica a Catalunya*, written with A. de Falguera and J. Goday, three vols in four (Barcelona, 1909–18) remain well worth reading for their own sakes. On the denizens of Els Quatre Gats, see additionally J. Pla, *Santiago Rusiñol i el seu temps* (Barcelona, 1961) and R. Planes, *El modernismo a Sitges* (Barcelona, 1969). E. Jardí's readable contributions on Noucentism include *El noucentisme* (Barcelona, 1980) and a lively study of *Eugeni d'Ors* (Barcelona, 1967). *El noucen-tisme* by J. Axlet and others (Barcelona, 1987) includes valuable contributions, especially by J. Murgades, J. Benet and J.M. Cadera. On Primo's policies in Barcelona, I have been helped by P. Voltes Bou, 'Enfoque barcelonés de la política económica del gobierno del general Primo de Rivera', *Cuadernos de historia económica de Cata-luña*, ii (1970), pp. 113–56, to which I owe my quotations from *La Vanguardia*. On Sert, the most important contribution is J. Freix, *Josep Lluís Sert* (Barcelona, 1979). On Macià, see the rather ebullient E. Jardí i Casany, *Francesc Macià: el camí de la llibertat* (Barcelona, 1977). On the period of the Second Republic, see F. Cucurull, *Catalunya, republicana i autònoma* (Barcelona, 1984), J.A. González-Casanova, *Elecciones en Barcelona, 1931–6* (Madrid, 1969). The most comprehensive work on the background of the Civil War is H. Thomas, *The Spanish Civil War* (London, 1987). I owe the phrase 'The City of Prodigies' to the evocative novel by E. Mendoza, *La cuidad de los prodigios* (Madrid, 1986).

The current trend in the study of Barcelona, espoused by sociologists, historians and architectural writers alike, is towards what might be called a micro-sociological view, based on the close scrutiny of individual districts. Exemplary works of this type include M. Tatjer Mir, *La Barceloneta del siglo XVIII al Plan de Ribera* (Barcelona, 1985); J.M. Casasús i Gurí, *Les Corts: un poble perdut, un barri introbable* (Barcelona, 1976), which has, however, a rather polemical tone; and C. Carreras Verdaguer, *Hostafrancs* (Barcelona, 1974). J. Fabre and J.M. Casasús give a conspectus of the physical environments in *Tots els barris de Barcelona* (Barcelona, 1987). J. Carbonell, ed., *La lucha de barrios en Barcelona* (Madrid, 1976) is polemical, but contains interesting material.

A lively introduction to the problem of immigration is F. Candel, *Els altres catalans* (Barcelona, 1964). The topic is treated fictionally in J. Marsé, *Ultimas tardes con Teresa* (Barcelona, 1966).

Index

INDEX